ROUTLEDGE LIBRARY EDITIONS:
ENERGY ECONOMICS

Volume 6

TRANSPORT ENERGY

TRANSPORT ENERGY

Determinants and Policy

JOY DUNKERLEY, IRVING HOCH WITH CAROLINE BOUHDILI

Routledge
Taylor & Francis Group
LONDON AND NEW YORK

First published in 1985 by Resources for the Future

This edition first published in 2018
by Routledge
2 Park Square, Milton Park, Abingdon, Oxon OX14 4RN

and by Routledge
605 Third Avenue, New York, NY 10017

Routledge is an imprint of the Taylor & Francis Group, an informa business

British Library Cataloguing in Publication Data
A catalogue record for this book is available from the British Library

ISBN: 978-1-138-10476-1 (Set)
ISBN: 978-1-315-14526-6 (Set) (ebk)
ISBN: 978-1-138-30861-9 (Volume 6) (hbk)
ISBN: 978-1-315-14351-4 (Volume 6) (ebk)

Publisher's Note
The publisher has gone to great lengths to ensure the quality of this reprint but points out that some imperfections in the original copies may be apparent.

Disclaimer
The publisher has made every effort to trace copyright holders and would welcome correspondence from those they have been unable to trace.

FINAL REPORT

TRANSPORT ENERGY: DETERMINANTS AND POLICY

by

Joy Dunkerley
Irving Hoch

with

Caroline Bouhdili

Resources for the Future
1616 P Street, NW
Washington, D.C. 20036

U.S. Agency for International Development
Office of Energy
Energy Policy Development and Conservation Project

September 1985

Table of Contents

Executive Summary

In many developing countries, transportation is the major market for liquid fuels, accounting for about half of all oil used. Consumption of transport fuels is expected to rise rapidly with economic growth. In transport, unlike the other end-use sectors, possibilities of fuel switching are limited, at least for the time being. A continued rapid expansion in consumption of petroleum products will exacerbate problems of economic management in the oil-importing developing countries. In these circumstances a clearer idea of the relationships determining consumption of transport energy, the likely growth in consumption of transport fuels, and a discussion of the policies which could modify this trend, while still providing the transport services necessary for economic development, is of interest not only for energy management but also for wider macro-economic policy aims.

We begin with a survey of past trends in transport energy consumption. Per capita consumption rose in all countries, though there is wide variation in consumption levels among countries. Road transport is the largest single sector accounting in many countries for 80 percent of total transport fuel consumption. Per capita consumption in road transport has increased rapidly over the past ten years, with higher rates of growth associated with higher income levels. Again there is considerable variation among countries. Gasoline is the main road transport fuel but the share of diesel appears to have been increased in this period. In the other transport sectors (rail, air, internal navigation) per capita consumption fell or remained constant.

In order to investigate these trends systematically a unique energy/transport data base was developed covering some 80 developing and industrial countries and including new data on total and sectorial transport energy consumption, numbers of trucks and buses, GDP, gasoline and diesel prices, demographic and geographic characteristics.

This data base was used to estimate through regression analysis the effect on transport energy consumption and the stock of road vehicles of per capita income, price and other variables. On the basis of the regression analysis it was concluded that for developing countries consumption of transport fuels and the stock of road vehicles rises substantially in excess of income. On the other hand, it was found that per capita consumption of transport fuels falls less than proportionately as price increases. Summary results are given below.

	Developing Countries	
	Income Elasticity	Price Elasticity
Total energy transport	1.2	-.15
Road transport fuels	1.3	-.2
Motor gasoline	1.4	-.4
Automobiles	1.65	-0.65
Trucks	1.1	-0.5

Thus for transport energy as a whole, a 10 percent increase in per capita income brings about approximately a 12 percent increase in consumption of all transport fuels, while a 10 percent increase in prices implies a drop of only 1.5 percent in the consumption of transport fuels. Similarly a 10 percent increase in income is associated with 16.5 percent increase in numbers of cars while a 10 percent increase in price implies a drop of only 6.5 percent in consumption. These income elasticities are higher than the sparse results reported in the literature for the transport sector of developing countries, due largely to the more realistic measurement of real income using purchasing power parity rates of exchange. The price elasticity for total transport energy is exceptionally low as it covers not only gasoline but also diesel which has been widely substituted for gasoline in developing countries as gasoline prices rise.

The results of the regression analysis were supplemented by two case studies of India and Ecuador. These countries offer interesting contrasts. In India consumption of transport fuels is low and has risen quite slowly. In Ecuador consumption is high and has risen rapidly. The role of transport fuel pricing policies is found to be critical in explaining the different consumption levels. However, comparison between countries captures long run impacts of different price levels in contrast to short- and medium-run impacts which are often the focus of policy concern.

With regard to the future, our assumptions about future trends in prices and incomes combined with the high income and low price elasticities given above suggest that the consumption of transport fuels and vehicle ownership will continue to rise rapidly, outstripping in most part the increase in economic activity; and that the expected rise in prices of transport fuels will not be sufficient to moderate this trend significantly. Given the severe foreign exchange constraints faced by most developing countries conservation of oil in the transport sector is likely to be high on the policy agenda.

Our analysis leads to a number of conlcusions relevant to policy. The first is that given low price elasticities, especially for total transport fuel, the magnitude of the price rises resulting from higher crude oil prices alone will not be sufficient to achieve significant savings in transport energy. Higher taxes and increases in other elements of transport costs could induce further savings. Important though pricing policies are, however, low price elasticities suggest that additional actions to moderate the rise in transport energy will be necessary. The most promising areas appear to be increases in the efficiency of the vehicle fleet, attractive alternatives to private passenger transport such as improved bus and small taxi (three wheelers in India) services, reduction in road congestion, and improvements in truck load factors.

Part I

Overview

Transportation is the major market for liquid fuels in most developing countries. A continued rapid expansion in consumption of petroleum products will exacerbate problems of economic management. The purpose of this report is therefore to examine the determinants of transport energy consumption and discuss policies which could modify rising transport energy consumption while still providing the transport services necessary for economic development.

Surveying past trends in transport fuel consumption it appears that per capita consumption rose in all developing countries but more rapidly in the middle and high income countries. There is a wide variation in per capita consumption of transport fuels among developing countries. Per capita energy consumption in road transport, invariably the largest single transport sector, rose sharply. Gasoline is the main road transport fuel though the share of diesel is increasing. In the other transport sectors per capita consumption fell or remained constant.

Chapter 1

Introduction

In many developing countries, transportation is the major market for liquid fuels (see table 1). Although the share of oil supplies accounted for by the transport sector varies from country to country, it is estimated that for developing countries as a group about half of the oil used is consumed in transport.

Consumption of transport fuels is expected to rise rapidly with economic growth, both as cause and effect. Industrialization and agricultural development imply increased freight and passenger transport; further, higher real incomes stimulate demand for leisure related transportation.

In transport, unlike the other end-use sectors, possibilities of fuel switching are limited, at least for the time being. Given the existing stock of transport equipment, virtually all of the increase in consumption of transport fuels for the next fifteen years or so will be in the form of petroleum products.

A continued rapid expansion in consumption of petroleum products will exacerbate problems of economic management in the oil-importing developing countries. For many of these countries the importation of transport fuels alone is equivalent to 20 percent of total export earnings. Rising consumption of transport fuels, by cutting into exportable surpluses, also poses problems for some oil-exporting countries.

In these circumstances a clearer idea of the relationships determining consumption of transport energy, the likely growth in consumption of transport fuels, and an evaluation of the policies which could modify this trend, while still providing the transport services necessary for economic development, is of interest not only for energy management but also for wider macro-economic policy aims.

This report is in five parts. The first contains an overview of trends in transport energy consumption. In the second and third, relationships expressing basic determinants of transport energy are investigated. Although the focus in this report is on the developing countries, a certain number of other country groupings (industrial and centrally planned economies) are included for reference purposes and also to extend the range of policy variables studied. The determinants of transport energy consumption considered in this section include population, income level, prices of transport fuels, the stock of transport vehicles, demographic trends and a number of land use variables. The data set underlying the second and third parts of the report, though extensive, does not cover in depth several economic and policy factors of interest. For this reason, the fourth part of the report consists of more detailed case studies of two countries, India and Ecuador, as examples of different types of developing countries. India is a poor country with a per capita income level of about $260 in 1981. Gasoline prices in India are among the highest in the world. Ecuador, on the other hand, has a per capita income of $1180, and like many oil exporters, has exceptionally low gasoline prices. The greater detail of the case studies permits the consideration of additional policy variables in the analysis of transport fuel consumption.

Table 1. Share of oil consumption going to various sectors of the economy, 1980
(Percent)

	Electricity Generation	Refinery losses	Industry	Transportation	Households	Agriculture
African Countries						
Ivory Coast	9	7	13	62	5	-
Kenya	8	5	28	29	8	8
Malawi	5	-	4	55	4	5
Senegal	5	4	17	22	8	2
Zimbabwe	-	-	11	54	16	13
Asian and South Pacific Countries						
India	7	5	13	36	22	1
Indonesia	5	1	31	30	24	-
Korea	25	1	28	20	1	2
Philippines	21	2	15	19	20	13
Thailand	24	5	15	36	6	8
Latin American Countries						
Argentina	17	4	11	37	11	4
Bolivia	5	3	17	62	15	-
Brazil	3	3	27	49	6	4
Chile	8	6	16	25	10	-
Colombia	5	7	14	55	10	4
Dominican Republic	2	3	21	30	8	1
Ecuador	16	6	10	45	10	5
El Salvador	2	4	22	54	8	3
Guatemala	25	1	27	38	7	-
Mexico	14	9	7	37	8	2
Peru	9	4	25	33	19	3
Venezuela	37	26	1	16	1	-

Note: Percentages do not add up to 100 because total oil consumption used to determine the shares includes energy converted in other conversion industries besides refineries and electric power plants. The total energy requirement also include net transfers, consumption by energy sector, losses in transport and distribution, consumption for non-energy uses and statistical differences.

(-) means zero

Source: Data for countries in Africa and Asia and South Pacific were obtained from *Energy Balances 1977-1980 and Electricity Profiles 1976-1981 for Selected Developing Countries and Areas*, United Nations, New York, October 1983 except for data for Senegal obtained from a paper presented at the conference on Energy Analysis Planning and Policy Development in Reston, Virginia, February/March 1983.

Data for the Latin American countries were obtained from *Energy Balances for Latin America*, OLADE, 1981.

Chapter 2

Trends and Variations in Transport Fuel Consumption

In this chapter we examine trends in transport fuels consumption--in the entire transport sector and in its constituent sectors road, rail, air and waterways, and consumption of the main transport fuels gasoline and diesel. Many of the summary tables appearing in the text have counterpart tables giving detailed country data in the Statistical Appendix. The summary tables throughout the report are based on categories of selected countries grouped according to income per head. The countries appearing in each category are given in Appendix 1A. When the representative countries in each category change from table to table because of data availability notes to that effect are given in each table. The six categories--low income developing, middle income developing, high income developing, high income oil exporters, centrally planned economies, industrial countries--are basically those adopted by the World Bank in their Annual Development Report.[1]

There are considerable contrasts in transport energy consumption among these income categories. From 1971 to 1981 consumption in the low income developing countries rose very gradually, by about 1 percent a year (see Table 2.1 and Appendix table 1). As the Appendix Table shows, this experience was shared by most of the countries in this group. By contrast, the increase in consumption in both middle and high income developing countries was much more rapid, about 3.5 percent annually. Per capita consumption of transport fuels in the high income oil exporting countries rose even more rapidly, by 14 percent annually. In the industrialized countries the overall annual average increase at 1.5 percent was barely higher than in the low income developing countries.

Although the period covered by these data is not long it includes two major events, the increases in the international price of petroleum in 1973/74 and 1979/80. These events appeared to have a distinct impact in the different groupings. In the selected Low Income Developing Countries consumption continued at a relatively stable level throughout the two oil shocks. In the middle and high income developing countries rapid rates of growth came to a halt in both 1974/75 and 1980/81. In the high income oil exporters rapid rates of growth continued throughout the period. In the industrial countries consumption levelled off after 1974 and fell after 1979.

Another set of contrasts lies in the wide variation in consumption of transport fuels among country groupings (see again Table 2.1 and Appendix Table 1). Per capita consumption of transport fuels is almost 40 times higher in the industrial countries as in the low income developing countries. Consumption in the middle and higher income developing countries is also much lower than in the industrial countries though less so in 1981 than ten years earlier. In 1971, for example, per capita consumption in the middle income developing countries stood at 6 percent and high income developing countries at 20 percent of industrial countries levels. By 1981 these shares had increased to 8 percent and 25 percent. But the most striking of all is the case of the high income oil exporters. In 1971 per capita consumption of transport fuels in these selected countries was about one quarter the level of the industrial countries. By 1981 their consumption had risen to 77 percent of industrial countries.

The transportation sector comprises road, rail, air and inland waterways (see Table 2.2). Road transport is, for most countries, the largest single transport sector accounting for about 80 percent of the total. The share of road in some countries such as India, is much lower due to well developed railway systems. Road has always been the predominant form of transport for those countries which do not have well developed rail networks. Developments in oil prices over the last decade have not, as Table 2.3 shows, lead to any decline in roads share of total transport fuels. On the contrary there has been a distinct increase especially for those countries with major railroad networks where traffic has continued to move from rail to road.

Road Transport

Per capita consumption of road transport fuels in the selected low and middle income developing countries increased quite rapidly from 1971 to 1981 (see Table 2.3 and Appendix Table 2.2). In the high income developing and the industrial countries the rate of increase is typically much lower. Within the industrial countries there is an interesting contrast. Consumption in the high consuming countries such as the U.S. and Canada increased very moderately while consumption in the lower consuming countries increased more rapidly, implying perhaps some saturation but only at the very highest levels of consumption and income.

The differences in levels of consumption among countries are as great in road transport as in total transport fuels. In three low income countries (see again Table 2.3 and Appendix Table 2.2)--not in fact the poorest of the low income countries--per capita consumption in road transport is about 20 koe per year. In the U.S. it is 80 times higher at 1600 kilos.

Gasoline is the major road transport fuel accounting for about 70 percent of the total. Data (see Table 2.4 and Appendix Table 2.3) on gasoline consumption is available for a larger number of countries (67 in all) for the 1960 to 1982 period thus enabling us to make a more complete analysis of gasoline use.

There are two things to note from the tables. The first is the wide variation in rates of increase in gasoline consumption over this 22 year period. In the 1960/70 period, that is before the increase in oil prices, the lowest annual rates of growth (2%) were in the low income developing countries. Rates of growth were much higher in the other groups--3.5 percent in the middle income developing countries, 4.4 percent in the high income developing and 5.7 in the high income oil exporters. So far it appears that the rates of increase of gasoline consumption accelerated as average incomes rose. However, at the highest income levels, in the industrial countries, rates of increase fell back to 4 percent. In this latter case the lower rate of consumption was largely due to the U.S. where consumption of gasoline rose by only 2.6 percent a year in this period. In many other industrialized countries consumption per capita doubled from 1960 to 1970, that is an annual average increase of over 7 percent. Thus the picture emerges of a rapid increase in annual consumption as incomes rise tapering off only at the very highest income levels as in Sweden and North America.

This pattern was disturbed during the 1970/82 period when oil prices rose five fold in real terms. In all countries except for the high income oil exporters the rates of increase in consumption after 1970 fell significantly. However, there was little indication of a consistent pattern of growth rates across categories of countries as there was before 1970.

Another noticeable characteristic of gasoline consumption is the wide variation in consumption levels among countries. Per capita consumption in the industrial countries is well over 100 times higher than in the low income developing countries. The extremes are even greater between individual countries. Gasoline consumption in the United States is, for example, over 300 times higher than in India and the People's Republic of China.

The gap between the developing and industrial countries in gasoline consumption levels did not change significantly from 1960 to 1982, but the difference between the industrial countries and the high income oil exporters and east bloc narrowed substantially. In 1960 per capita gasoline consumption in the high income oil exporter countries was about 17 percent of industrial countries. By 1982 this had risen to 61 percent. In the east bloc countries consumption levels rose from 26 to 41 percent over the same period.

Part of the wide disparity in gasoline consumption between the lowest and highest income groups could be due to differences in consumption of diesel, the other major road transport fuel. Data for diesel fuel consumption in road transport are not available for many countries and are in any event subject to some inaccuracy as it is frequently not possible to obtain accurate information on what share of total gas oil/diesel fuel supplies go to the transport sector rather than other sectors. The data in Table 2.5 must therefore be reviewed as approximate, and the conclusions derived from the Table highly tentative.[2] With this reservation, the rise in diesel fuel consumption in transport appears to have been much more rapid than the rise in consumption of gasoline in all groups of countries. This is confirmed by World Bank estimates that the share of diesel in total road transport fuels in the developing countries rose from 20 percent in 1970 to 30 percent in 1981, and in the industrial countries from 13 to 17 percent. While the share of gasoline in road transport has fallen, it still remains the major road transport fuel in both groups of countries.[3]

Air transport

Air transport is for many countries the largest consumer of transport fuels after road though of much lesser importance. There are two things to notice about consumption of transport fuels in air transport. The first (see Table 2.6) is that there is less variation between consumption levels in the different income cataegories for air than for total transport, road transport or gasoline. This is because the amounts consumed in air transport, particularly for the developing countries, are strongly influenced by the existence of an international airport in a given country. This effect is particularly marked in countries with small populations such as Hong Kong, Kuwait, and even Kenya where airport activity in relation to population is exceptionally high.

The second point to notice about consumption in the air transport sector is that unlike the various measures of road transport fuel consumption it did not increase substantially over the last ten years despite the invariably rapid increase in air traffic in all countries. The reason here is the dramatic increase in aircraft size and efficiencies (documented in greater detail in the Indian case study, see page 8.11) which has taken place over this period.

Rail transport

The pattern of energy consumption in rail transport is different from road and air. Relatively few countries have significant rail networks as can be seen in Table 2.7 but among those that do, energy consumption per capita does not vary greatly, and certainly by less than the variation among countries in road transport fuels. For example, in 1971 per capita energy consumption in railways in two low income countries, India and Pakistan, was about one half the consumption in many industrial countries. Consumption of energy in road transport by contrast was only about one percent.

A second feature of consumption in railroads was the general pattern of declining energy consumption over the last 10 years. This trend was particularly marked in the developing countries (see again Table 2.7) where consumption fell on average by one half in major railroad countries such as India, Turkey, Chile, Greece and Portugal. In the industrial countries on the other hand consumption generally did not vary over the ten years. Part of this contrast between developing and industrial countries is due to technological change. In the developing countries (see for greater detail the India case study) diesel and electric locomotives were being substituted for steam locomotives thus achieving major savings in efficiency. This means that the decline in energy consumption in the railway sector in developing countries does not necessarily imply that the size of the sector was shrinking in other respects, as for example in tonnage or passengers carried.

Water transport

Water transport has many similarities to railroad. A few of the developing countries--Turkey, Brazil, Chile--have significant inland waterway or coastal traffic (see Table 2.8). These are all countries with long coastlines or in other cases major port or transhipment facilities. As with railroads, the level of per capita energy consumption in water transport in the developing countries is comparable with the industrial countries.

It is not easy to assess trends in per capita energy in this sector as water transport frequently includes some amounts of transport energy not otherwide specified and in some cases may include ocean bunkers as well as coastal and inland waterways. This factor may account for Hong Kong's exceptionally high per capita consumption level. However, from the data available and other evidence (see again the India case study) it seems likely that consumption in this sector fell over the last 10 years.

* * * * *

In summary, the main developments in transport fuel consumption are:

1. During the last 10 years per capita consumption of transport fuels rose in all categories of countries but more slowly in the richest and the poorest. Reactions to the oil price increases also differed.

2. There is a wide variation in per capita consumption of transport fuels between categories of countries with some closing of the gap between industrial countries and other high income categories.

3. Road transport is the largest single sector accounting in many countries for 80 percent of total transport fuel consumption. Per capita consumption in road transport has increased rapidly over the past ten

years, with higher rates of growth associated with higher income levels except at the very highest levels such as the U.S. Again there is considerable variation among countries. Gasoline is the main road transport fuel though the share of diesel appears to have been increasing in this period.

4. For the other transport sectors: per capita consumption in air transport has not increased due to energy saving technology; per capita energy consumption in both rail and water transport has declined. In these last three sectors there is much less variation in per capita consumption levels between the rich and poor countries than in road transport.

Footnotes

1. See Appendix 1A for text of the robustness of this categoriztion over time and for an alternative categorization.

2. As a check against the data in Table 2.5 data on gasoline consumption was deducted from total energy consumption in road transport on the assumption that all transport fuel consumption consisted of either gasoline or diesel fuel. For the countries listed in Table 2.7, the deduction method yielded similar results to the data in Table 2.7.

3. B.J. Choe, A Model of World Energy Markets and OPEC Pricing, World Bank Staff Working Paper #633, Washington, D.C. 1984.

Table 2.1

Per Capita Transport Energy Consumption
in Selected Countries by Categories of Countries
(koe)

	1971	1973	1974	1979	1980	1981	Annual Avg. Increase
Low Income Dev.[1]	24.1	22.8	23.5	25.1	25.7	26.6	1.0
Middle Income Dev.[2]	58.0	69.5	71.7	88.2	88.1	83.2	3.7
High Income Dev.[3]	177.2	201.4	203.0	247.2	252.3	250.2	3.5
High Income Oil Exp.[4]	215.0	245.8	281.6	589.2	688.8	772.9	13.6
Centrally Planned	n.a.	n.a.	n.a.	n.a.	n.a.	n.a.	
Industrialized[4]	887.5	985.0	958.9	1102.3	943.4	1030.1	1.5

Note: Weighted averages

[1]Includes Bangladesh, Burma, India, Kenya, Pakistan, Zaire, Zambia.

[2]Includes Bolivia, Colombia, Ecuador, Egypt, Indonesia, Iran, Ivory Coast, Jamaica, Korea, Morocco, Nigeria, Peru, Philippines, Thailand, Tunisia, Turkey.

[3]Includes Algeria, Argentina, Brazil, Chile, Gabon, Greece, Hong Kong, Iraq, Malaysia, Mexico, Panama, Portugal, Singapore, Taiwan, Uruguay, Venezuela.

[4]Includes all countries listed in Appendix Table 1.A.1.

Table 2.2

Shares of Subsectors in Total Transport Energy Consumption: Selected Countries, 1981 (%)

	Road	Rail	Air	Water
Low Income Dev.				
India	56	36	7	1
Kenya	35	31	32	2
Pakistan	56	19	24	1
Middle Income Dev.				
Indonesia	92	1	3	4
Rep. of Korea	63	4	13	17
Nigeria	95	2	3	-
Turkey	83	10	3	3
High Income Dev.				
Argentina	88	3	8	1
Brazil	84	3	8	6
Chile	82	2	8	8
Greece	59	2	28	11
Mexico	93	-	6	1
Industrial				
France	87	4	7	1
Italy	90	3	6	2
United Kingdom	79	3	15	3
United States	85	3	12	n.a.
W. Germany	86	4	8	2

Table 2.3

Per Capita Fuel Consumption in
Road Transport Sector by Income Category:
Selected Countries
(kgoe)

	1971	1973	1974	1979	1980	1981	Annual Avg. Increase
Low Income Dev.	10.1	10.2	11.2	14.3	14.8	15.6	4.4
Middle Income Dev.	27.2	35.7	38.3	53.3	54.3	51.3	6.6
High Income Dev.	165.8	189.3	188.5	229.0	236.0	235.5	3.6
High Income Oil Exporters	n.a.	n.a.	n.a.	n.a.	n.a.	n.a.	n.a.
Industrial	711.7	797.9	778.5	913.3	869.1	851.1	1.8

Note: Subsectoral detail is not available for all (58) countries in Table 2.1. The above table covers 37 countries. Insufficient data were available to derive an average for the High Income Oil Exporters.

Table 2.4

Per Capita Motor Gasoline Consumption
(koe)

	1960	1965	1970	1975	1980	1982	Annual average income 1960-72	1970-82
Low Income Dev.	3.2	3.5	3.9	3.2	3.4	3.6	2.0	-0.7
Middle Income Developing	20.0	21.2	28.1	37.9	42.3	40.9	3.5	3.2
High Income Developing	70.6	84.4	108.1	124.9	133.0	135.2	4.4	1.9
High Income Oil Exporters	69.3	97.3	121.1	204.5	397.9	408.9	5.7	10.7
East bloc.	103.5	136.5	182.2	242.4	257.1	275.4	5.8	3.5
Industrial Countries	399.7	476.2	595.7	677.1	694.0	668.9	4.1	1.0

Countries not included are: Bangladesh, China, Malawi, Zambia, Malaysia, Panama, Taiwan, Trinidad & Tobago, Yugoslavia, Czechoslovakia, New Zealand.

Table 2.5

Per Capita Diesel Consumption
in Road Transport
(koe)

	1965	1970	1975	1980	Annual Average Increase
Low Income Dev.					
India	2.9	5.0	n.a.	12.1	10.0
Kenya	6.1	9.6	11.8	5.0	-1.3
Malawi	4.0	7.3	10.3	8.4	5.1
Middle Income Dev.					
Indonesia	10.9	6.2	n.a.	20.3	4.2
Morocco	11.9	17.2	30.6	41.2	8.6
High Income Dev.					
Argentina	87.1	128.3	214.9	124.1	2.4
Hong Kong	23.3	39.7	59.4	57.2	6.2
Industrial					
Belgium	79.0	108.5	121.5	186.6	5.9
Finland	131.9	166.6	193.4	236.0	3.9
France	56.4	91.2	126.2	176.2	7.9
Italy	58.1	84.2	92.0	172.4	7.5
Japan	39.5	93.7	119.5	67.3	3.6
Netherlands	63.5	76.8	110.2	156.0	6.2
Sweden	112.3	140.4	166.3	185.1	3.4
Switzerland	79.8	101.2	100.4	124.8	3.0
United Kingdom	72.7	93.9	98.9	108.4	2.7
United States	54.1	103.4	124.0	211.6	9.5
W. Germany	84.2	108.5	114.1	167.9	4.7

Table 2.6

Per Capita Consumption of Energy in
Air Transport for Selected Countries, 1971-81
(koe)

	1971	1973	1974	1979	1980	1981
Low Income Dev.						
India	1.6	1.6	1.5	1.8	1.7	1.7
Kenya	18.3	23.6	21.7	22.1	22.9	19.1
Pakistan	8.0	3.2	3.3	5.8	8.6	8.4
Middle Income Dev.						
Egypt	2.8	4.6	5.4	4.8	4.0	3.7
Rep. of Korea	16.0	13.7	12.7	18.2	16.0	18.0
Thailand	11.6	19.7	15.5	16.9	17.7	18.7
Turkey	2.8	3.9	4.6	4.5	3.5	3.4
High Income Dev.						
Argentina	16.4	16.6	18.0	24.5	29.7	30.4
Brazil	8.9	10.3	11.4	14.6	14.1	15.0
Hong Kong	119.5	132.8	131.9	160.2	161.4	166.0
Malaysia	11.8	13.0	12.7	10.7	12.2	13.0
Mexico	10.1	12.5	15.5	19.0	19.8	19.0
Singapore	61.1	104.6	121.3	213.4	204.5	191.0
Venezuela	25.1	20.7	31.3	64.8	68.9	40.2
Industrial						
France	31.7	37.3	37.2	48.9	48.1	44.0
Italy	28.0	28.4	26.2	29.4	25.8	26.0
United Kingdom	72.3	81.8	71.6	88.7	89.1	85.4
United States	247.2	249.4	234.8	254.3	251.5	235.5
W. Germany	36.6	40.3	41.8	47.4	48.6	51.6

Table 2.7

Per Capita Consumption of Energy in
Rail Transport, Selected Countries 1971-81
(koe)

	1971	1973	1974	1979	1980	1981
Low Income Dev.						
India	15.3	13.5	13.0	10.1	10.1	9.6
Kenya	14.6	13.5	15.8	13.8	15.2	18.8
Pakistan	1.3	2.3	2.3	2.5	3.1	6.7
Middle Income Dev.						
Korea	5.8	2.9	3.1	6.5	5.9	5.1
Turkey	22.1	21.8	20.0	12.9	9.7	9.9
High Income Dev.						
Argentina	8.4	9.8	10.7	10.7	10.0	9.4
Brazil	5.1	5.0	5.5	5.4	5.5	5.2
Chile	22.5	18.0	16.7	8.3	7.0	5.5
Greece	15.8	16.8	11.1	6.5	5.4	6.4
Mexico	6.8	6.6	7.0	0.9	1.0	1.0
Portugal	13.8	13.3	11.9	8.2	7.1	8.0
Industrial						
France	23.5	25.4	25.2	24.8	23.9	23.3
Italy	12.4	10.9	11.5	12.0	11.2	11.0
United Kingdom	27.1	24.2	22.9	21.3	20.9	20.1
United States	71.1	71.3	70.3	69.0	65.8	64.0
W. Germany	38.9	33.9	31.3	29.3	29.1	28.3

Table 2.8

Per Capita Consumption of Energy in Water Transport, Selected Countries 1971-81 (koe)

	1971	1973	1974	1979	1980	1981
Low Income Dev.						
India	0.5	0.3	0.3	0.4	0.3	0.3
Kenya	0.6	0.5	0.6	1.0	1.2	1.2
Middle Income Dev.						
Indonesia	0.8	0.8	1.2	1.7	2.0	2.0
Korea	6.8	8.2	10.9	28.4	22.4	24.8
Turkey	9.7	15.0	14.6	12.4	13.2	3.4
Brazil	3.3	5.9	8.3	11.7	7.6	10.6
Chile	23.9	22.3	18.6	16.8	16.7	17.7
Mexico	1.5	8.0	0.9	4.4	4.8	5.0
Industrial						
Canada	118.0	134.6	121.9	65.5	75.6	91.2
France	13.9	13.5	14.1	3.2	3.6	3.0
Italy	8.5	8.2	11.7	6.3	6.5	6.6
United Kingdom	18.5	18.8	21.3	23.2	21.5	18.8
W. Germany	15.6	17.7	14.6	17.0	14.3	14.2

Part II

The Determinants of Transport Fuel Consumption

The level of income emerges as a major factor in transport energy consumption. Freight transport increases slightly faster than GDP in developing countries, while passenger traffic rises typically by two to three times the rise in GDP. The influence of energy prices occupies a central role in our analysis. Gasoline and diesel prices vary widely among countries according to tax policies and resource endowments. Gasoline prices in the oil importing developing countries have increased by about 80 percent, but diesel prices have risen more modestly. Car ownership rates have increased dramatically throughout the world, though gasoline consumption per car appears to have fallen. The number of trucks has also increased but more slowly than cars, so that the share of cars in the total vehicle fleet has risen.

Chapter 3

Relationship between Transport Fuel Consumption and Level of Income

In this study we hypothesize that the level of transport fuel consumption, and particularly road transport consumption is determined by levels of income and standard of living, the prices of transport fuels, the size of the transport infrastructure (particularly the road vehicle fleet), demography, and a number of land use characteristics (such as population density and urbanization).

There are clearly many other aspects of economic and social activity that affect consumption of transport fuels. These include changes in distances travelled over time and among countries, the structure of economic activity as it affects the demand for transport services, shifts between different transport modes all with varying energy using characteristics, the vintage and energy using characteristics of transport equipment, load factors, and transport policies which are not captured in the price variables. Furthermore, it can be argued that transport fuel consumption is more appropriately treated as a derived rather than a final demand, estimating first the demand for total transport services and from that deriving the demand for transport fuels. In this way the typically small share of gasoline (say 20 percent) in the total cost of passenger transport can be explicitly taken into account.[1]

In our general analysis, however, we have been constrained by data availability to the use of the principal variables described in the first paragraph. Some of the other aspects are investigated in the more detailed case studies and incorporated albeit in a qualitative manner into our discussion of future transport energy consumption. In this Chapter and in Chapters 4 and 5 we discuss briefly the relationship of the variables used in the regression analysis to transport energy consumption. Full documentation of the variables discussed here, their availability by country and year, and their sources are given in Appendix 1-B.

The level of income

The level of income would be expected to be a major factor in the amount of transport demanded and therefore in consumption of transport fuels. Indeed, this relationship was already built into the summary tables presented in Chapter 2 where categories of countries were defined by income level. From these tables it will be recalled that level of income appeared to have a strong influence on energy consumption. Invariably levels of transport energy consumption were lower in low income countries and higher in the rich countries.

The reasons for this pattern are clear enough. As economic activity expands there is need for more transport of both freight and passengers. At the same time, higher incomes lead to increased demand for leisure related travel. As Table 3.1 shows, freight transport increases faster--about 10 to 20 percent faster--than GDP in developing countries and only slightly less in the industrial countries. In some countries, (see Table 3.2), especially those undergoing structural change, the increase in freight transport is much higher than the rate of increase in GDP. The increase in passenger traffic far exceeds the rise in freight traffic. Thus passenger traffic in the developing countries rises by 2 to 3 times the rise in GDP.

Most of the freight and passenger traffic is carried by rail or road.

Data on road transport is unfortunately hard to obtain but as Appendix Tables 4 and 5 show, the amount of both passenger and freight traffic carried by rail tended to decrease in most countries implying that road transport--the more energy intensive mode--rose much more rapidly than GDP.

These conclusions suggest that level of income has a particularly close relationship with transport energy consumption. We measure income in two ways. First it is measured by per capita Gross National Product, which is available for all of our countries except the centrally planned economies from 1960 to 1981 (see Appendix Table 6). This series is expressed in constant prices, thus providing an indication of "real" output in any one country over time, taking into account the rate of inflation. These data are converted to U.S. dollars using market rates of exchange.

An important part of our analysis concerns the comparison of income levels among countries and for this purpose these data have major defects. Rates of exchange between local currencies and the dollar vary considerably from year to year thus distorting the value of real output in a country when it is expressed in dollar terms. Real output could, for example, remain constant in local currency terms over two years but a 50 percent devaluation of the currency would result in an apparent 33 percent decline in real output expressed in dollar terms. Furthermore, movements in exchange rates are largely determined by the balance of traded commodities and invisibles and do not take into account commodities and services, (such as hairdressers and bread) which are not normally traded but which may and do differ considerably in price among countries. While GNP per head may be a reasonable measure of "real" income in any one country over time therefore, it is not be a good indication of "real" differences in living standards across countries.

To overcome this difficulty we use an alternative series--(RGDP)--in which measures of output expressed in local currencies are converted to a common unit (the US$) using purchasing power rather than market rates of exchange (see Appendix Table 7).[2] Such purchasing power rates of exchange seek to equate prices of comparable goods (or baskets of goods) between the U.S. and other countries. In this way the volatility of market rates of exchange are avoided and the important non-traded aspects of consumption can be included.

A comparison of the two approaches for 1981 is given in Table 3-3 for selected countries and Appendix Table 8 for all countries. Using purchasing power parity rather than market exchange rates can make a considerable difference to levels of GDP per capita relative to the U.S. This is measured by the deviation column which is equal to the RGDP divided by the market GNP. If the deviation is 1.00, there is no difference between the two. If it is greater than 1.00, the RGDP is higher than the market rate GNP and if it is less than 1.00 the RGDP is lower than the market rate.

The deviation index is substantially above 1.00 for the poor and middle-income countries, and within these countries it is particularly high for the poorest countries--over 3, implying that their real per capita GDP is three times higher relative to the US than given by market rates of exchange. In the rich countries, on the other hand, the rates are substantially under 1.00, implying that the use of market rates of exchange over-values their level of real output relative to the U.S.

Combining these results indicates that the range of income between rich and poor countries is considerably compressed when RGDP per capita rather than GNP is used as a measure of real income. For example, from

Table 3-3, in 1981 the GNP per head of selected low income developing countries was on average about 3 percent of U.S. income. If income is measured by RGDP, however, the average rises to almost 8 percent of the U.S. level. This trend holds for all groups of developing countries though to a lesser extent than in the low income developing countries. In the industrial countries, on the other hand, the trend is reversed: GNP per head shows an average level of 13 percent below the U.S. level. In RGDP terms their income per head falls to 25 percent below the U.S. level. If the U.S. is included in the industrial country average then the gap between rich and poor countries is narrowed further--from 4 percent in GNP terms to 11 percent in PPGDP.

This substantial difference in income levels depending on the measure used has important implications for regression analysis. We therefore use both series in our regression analysis to compare the results using different measures, and to compare our results with other studies using market rates of exchange. The measurement of income per head or living standards is a complex matter and no completely satisfactory measure has yet been developed. We feel, however, that RGDP per head which attempts a realistic measure of living standards across countries as well as over time is conceptually and intuitively superior to GNP per head. In the balance of this chapter therefore we use RGDP to describe trends and variations in income levels.

Income and transport energy consumption

It will be recalled from Chapter 2 that consumption of energy in the transport sector for the 58 countries for which data were available rose significantly in the 10 year period from 1971 to 1981. Over the same period per capita income (see Table 3.4) also rose by an annual average of 1 percent in the low income developing countries, 2 percent in the industrial countries, and by 4 and 3 percent, respectively, in the middle and high income developing countries. These rates of increase closely parallel the rates of increase in transport energy consumption over the same period. One way of illustrating this close relationship is to express consumption of transport energy per unit of RGDP (see Table 3.5). This shows very little change in transport energy intensity of these economies over the last ten years despite two oil shocks. In other words, this Table would seem to suggest that income accounted for all changes in energy consumption.

If the different categories of countries are compared, however, considerable differences in energy intensity can be observed with the average energy intensity rising with average income level. The energy intensity of the low income developing countries is for example less than one third of the enegy intensity of the industrial countries. These results suggest that factors other than income have an important role to play in determining energy intensities.[3]

A component part of transport fuel--gasoline consumption--can, due to data availability, be investigated over a longer time period 1960 to 1980. Table 3.6 shows that the rise in income over this longer period also correlates closely with per capita gasoline consumption (in Table 2.4). However, there is a distinct difference between the 1960-1970 period and the subsequent ten years. In 1960-1970 the rise in gasoline consumption was in all groups higher than the rise in income. After 1970, gasoline growth rates were lower than income growth rates. This is again illustrated in Table 3.7 which gives gasoline consumption per unit of RGDP.

In all regions this rises from 1960 to 1970, but in all (except the centrally planned economies) it falls from 1970 to 1980. Again comparison across country regions indicates wide disparities, with the industrial countries consuming 16 times more gasoline per unit of output than the low income countries.

While income is therefore a major determinant of transport energy consumption other factors are also of importance. We examine these other factors in the next two chapters.

Footnotes

1. Chatelin, Bernard M. "The Economic Aspect of Transport and Energy" paper presented at the seminar on the Effects of Energy price Increases in the Transport Sector, Bogota, Colombia (Washington, D.C., 1980), unpublished.

2. For example, Irving B. Kravis, Zoltan Kenessey, Alan Heston and Robert Summers A System of International Comparisons of Gross Product and Purchasing Power (Baltimore, MD) published for the World Bank by The Johns Hopkins University Press, 1975, and Irving B. Kravis, Alan Heston and Robert Summers World Product and Income published for the World Bank by the Johns Hopkins University Press, 1982.

   The data used in this report (see Appendix 1-B) are from "Improved International Comparisons of Real Product and its Composition 1950-1980" by R. Summers and A. Heston in the Review of Income and Wealth, Series 30, #2, June 1984, pp. 207-262. Note that these measure Gross Domestic rather than National Product but for almost all countries there is relatively little difference. Indeed, GDP which measures the goods and services produced within a country's national frontiers (rather than throughout the world) is a more appropriate measure to relate to domestic energy consumption.

3. Part of the increasing energy intensity as average incomes rise across countries is a product of choice of denomination (RGDP). If GNP expressed in $ at market rates of exchange is used the transport energy intensity of the different groups is very similar, indeed there is a tendency for such transport energy intensities to be higher in low income countries than in the industrial countries. This derives from the undervaluation of real product in poor countries produced by conveting to GNP to dollars at market rates.

Table 3.1

Freight Transport and Economic Growth

Country	Time period	Increase in freight transport (avg. annual %)	Increase in real income (avg. annual %)
India	1960-75	5.3	3.6
Rep. of Korea	1976-78	7.6	7.2
Costa Rica	1968-78	7.2	4.2
Colombia	1958-78	8.8	5.5
Argentina	1975-78	3.2	0.0
Brazil	1960-78	10.0	8.7
France	1963-78	3.6	6.4
Japan	1965-78	6.3	7.8
United Kingdom	1968-78	2.0	1.9
United States	1960-78	3.6	3.6
West Germany	1963-78	3.7	3.9

Source: Fred Moavenzadeh and David Geltner, Transportation Energy and Economic Development, Elsevier, Amsterdam, 1984.

Table 3.2

Passenger Transport and Economic Growth

Country Group	Income Elasticity of Demand* Freight	Income Elasticity of Demand* Passenger
Wealthier Nations:		
OECD	0.8	1.0
East Europe	1.3	1.5
Major Oil Exporters	1.5	2.0
Poorer Nations:		
Middle Income	1.2	2.0
Asia Central Planned	1.1	3.0
Low Income	1.1	2.5

*Growth in ton-kilometers and passenger kilometers demand with respect to growth in per capita income.

Source: As for Table 3.1.

Table 3.3

Comparison of Per Capita GNP and RGDP
for Selected Countries, 1981
(1975$)

	Per Capita GNP	US = 100	Per Capita RGDP	US = 100	Deviation RGDP/GNP
Low Income Dev.					
Ghana	284	3.4	715	8.8	2.5
India	153	1.9	516	6.3	3.4
Pakistan	218	2.6	680	8.3	3.1
Zambia	360	4.4	645	7.9	1.8
Unweighted Avg.		3.1		7.8	
Middle Income Dev.					
Colombia	778	9.4	1907	23.3	2.5
Ecuador	812	9.8	1639	20.1	2.0
Korea	110	13.3	2092	25.6	1.9
Morocco	532	6.4	1166	14.3	2.2
Philippines	442	5.3	1018	12.5	2.3
Thailand	469	5.7	1177	14.4	2.5
Unweighted Avg.		8.3		18.4	
High Income Dev.					
Argentina	1569	19.0	2839	34.8	1.8
Brazil	1256	15.2	1981	24.3	1.6
Malaysia	1152	13.9	2274	27.8	2.0
Taiwan	1488	18.0	2594	31.8	1.7
Unweighted Avg.		16.5		38.4	
Industrial					
France	7672	92.7	6625	81.1	0.9
Japan	7134	86.2	5839	71.5	0.8
United Kingdom	4658	56.3	5108	62.5	1.1
W. Germany	9200	111.3	6805	83.3	0.7
Unweighted Avg.		86.6		74.6	
United States	8269	100.0	8168	100.0	1.0

Table 3.4

Per Capita RGDP by Income Category and Annual Rate of Growth for Subset of 58 Countries (1975$)

	1971	1973	1974	1979	1980	1981	1971-81
Low Income Dev.	455	454	449	479	494	508	1.1
Middle Income Dev.	902	1028	1117	1369	1350	1351	4.1
High Income Dev.	1799	2028	2170	2470	2563	2463	3.2
Industrial	5425	5979	5835	6554	6498	6548	1.9

Table 3.5

Transport Energy Consumption Relative to RGDP
for 58 Selected Countries by Income Category
(Koe per 000 1975$)

	1971	1973	1974	1979	1980	1981
Low Income Dev.	52.9	50.3	52.3	52.3	52.1	52.3
Middle Income Dev.	64.5	67.6	64.1	64.5	65.4	61.7
High Income Dev.	99.0	99.0	93.5	100.0	99.0	102.0
Industrial	163.9	163.9	163.9	169.5	144.9	158.7

Table 3.6

Per Capita RGDP*
(1975$)

	1960	1965	1970	1975	1980
Low Income Dev.	421	433	464	479	502
Middle Income Dev.	654	727	865	1149	1341
High Income Dev.	1313	1501	1792	2247	2571
East Bloc.	2157	2582	3200	3710	4031
Industrial	3573	4386	5291	5756	6508

* Countries excluded are Bangladesh, China, Malawi, Zambia, Malaysia, Panama, Taiwan, Trinidad & Tobago, Yugoslavia, Czechoslovakia, New Zealand.

Table 3.7

Motor Gasoline Consumption per RGDP
(koe per 000 1975$)*

	1960	1965	1970	1975	1980
Low Income Dev.	7.60	8.08	8.40	6.68	6.77
Middle Income Dev.	30.58	29.16	32.49	32.98	31.54
High Income Dev.	53.77	56.23	60.32	55.58	53.68
East Bloc.	47.98	52.87	56.94	65.34	68.32
Industrial	111.87	108.57	112.6	117.63	106.64

* Countries excluded are: Bangladesh, China, Malawi, Zambia, Malaysia, Panama, Taiwan, Trinidad & Tobago, Yugoslavia, Czechoslovakia, New Zealand.

Chapter 4

Prices of Transport Fuels

One of the most debated, and debatable, issues in transportation is the influence of the price of transport fuels--gasoline and auto diesel--on consumption. This issue is of major policy importance. If it can be shown that higher fuel prices significantly decrease consumption, than government taxation policy is a potentially effective instrument for securing conservation. If, on the other hand, higher prices appear to have little effect on consumption then conservation in the transport sector will have to be reinforced by other means such as regulation, administrative fiat, physical constraints, or taxes on energy using transport equipment and the like.

As the responsiveness of transport energy consumption to higher transport fuel prices is so critical to policy decisions, a major part of this study will be devoted to estimating the magnitudes of this response. To introduce this analysis the structure and trends in transport fuel prices both among countries and over time within countries are first discussed.

One of the difficulties in assessing the impact of prices on consumption in the transport sector, particularly in developing countries, has been the paucity of regular, consistent and comparable price data. The sole source which satisfies all of these conditions is the Department of Energy's International Energy Annual which gives price data for 25 developing countries and a wide range of industrial countries for 1965 and then each year from 1970 to 1982. Pump prices are given for a gallon of premium and regular gasoline and auto diesel in the capital cities of these countries for 31st July and 31st January of each year, expressed in U.S. cents per gallon at current exchange rates.

A second source of price data is the World Bank Energy Transition in Developing Countries which gives pump prices for 1981 only in U.S. $ per gallon for premium gasoline and diesel for 54 developing countries including 23 covered in the International Energy Annual.[1] A comparison of the two series for those countries included in both shows them to be reasonably consistent.

There are obvious shortcomings with these data. Prices observed at limited time periods and locations may not be typical of prices over the year as a whole throughout the country. The prices given here may be official, controlled prices rather than the prices at which purchases are actually made. Moreover, the conversion of local currencies to dollars at market or official rates of exchange rather than purchasing power parity rates of exchange introduces distortions into comparisons among countries analagous to those described in the section on income levels. While estimates of real Gross National Product per head corrected to take into account differences in purchasing power parity are available for a large number of developing countries, it has proved unfeasible to make a similar adjustment for prices. All that can be said is that the use of market rates of exchange rather than purchasing power rates to compare fuel prices among countries will underestimate the difference in prices between developing and industrial countries.

Some idea of this effect can be derived from price data for member countries of the European Communities contained in their Bulletin of Energy Prices.[2] Here, prices of premium gasoline (and other fuels) are given in both European Currency Units (ECU) and on a purchasing power standard.

Taking prices expressed in ECU before taxes (to avoid the distortion introduced by differential tax rates) there is relatively small variation in prices among community members. The same prices expressed on a purchasing power standard show much greater variation, with prices in the poorer member countries increasing sharply in relation to prices in the richer members. In ECU terms, for example, prices of premium gasoline before taxes in Italy are some 2 percent higher than in Germany. In purchasing power standard terms they are 27 percent higher. Similarly, for Greece whose prices are 10 percent higher than Germany's in ECU but 50 percent high in purchasing power. This reasoning can be extended to the more extreme income ranges encountered in a global study. The cost of a gallon of regular gasoline in the United States in 1975 was 60 cents and in India about two and a half times higher at $1.60, if market exchange rates are used to convert the rupee price to dollars. However, if the purchasing power of the currencies were taken into account the India price would be much higher, say between $3 and $4 a gallon. These considerations imply that price elasticities based on price data converted at market exchange rates will tend to be overestimates.

Despite these deficiencies, the existing body of price data is adequate to throw considerable light on the structure of energy prices among countries and trends over time. Table 4.1 shows prices (at current prices and exchange rates) of premium gasoline and diesel for 70 countries (55 developing, and 14 industrial and Saudi Arabia) in one year, 1981. The first thing to notice is the wide range of prices for both gasoline and diesel, even though they are highly standardized products. For premium gasoline, prices range from just over 30 cents a gallon (in Trinidad and Tobago and Venezuela) to over $5.00 (in S. Korea and Uganda). For diesel, prices range from around 10 cents a gallon (Venezuela and Egypt) to over $3.00 (in Burundi and Uganda).

A second feature of comparative energy prices illustrated in Table 4.1 and again in Tables 4.2 and 4.3 is that countries are not distributed evenly throughout this wide range but tend to be concentrated, or clustered around three distinct levels which in Tables 4.2 and 4.3 are labelled Low, Medium and High. For premium gasoline, for example, Low prices are defined as those under $1.60 a gallon. Although there is a considerable range of prices in this category, this group of countries is quite distinct from the next group of countries (with Medium price levels) whose prices are concentrated in the $2.10 to $2.60 a gallon range. In the third group of countries with High prices, prices are typically near $3.00 and over.

A similar pattern of concentration applies to diesel prices, though at generally lower levels. Thus in the Low price group prices are well under $1 per gallon, Medium prices are concentrated in the $1.20 to $1.70 level, and High prices are well in excess of $2.00. The distinction between medium and high diesel prices is much clearer than between medium and high gasoline prices.

A further observation from Tables 4.2 and 4.3 is that differences in price levels of transport fuels are not closely related to level of income and development. Poor, middle income and rich countries appear in each category for both premium gasoline and diesel. This is illustrated in Table 4.4 which gives the number of countries appearing in each pricing category. Both groups of countries are represented in all price categories, and in both fuels the largest category is the medium price level. However, there are differences between industrial and developing countries. Although the distribution of countries among the 3 price categories appears to be fairly similar for both developing and industrial countries, all of the industrial countries in the high category are in fact near the lower end of that category, and quite close to the upper end of the medium category. In other words, the industrial countries do not have the extremely high gasoline prices experienced by some of the developing countries especially those in Africa.

In diesel automotive fuels, the distribution of the two groups of countries is more distinct; a much higher share of the developing countries fall into the low price category while a much higher share of the industrial countries are in the high price category.

There are two main reasons for these differences in price levels among countries--differences in tax treatment of transport fuels and differences in crude oil prices. A third factor, of importance to a limited number of countries, is exceptionally high transport and distribution costs which are largely responsible for the high prices in landlocked countries such as Malawi and Zambia. For most countries, however, variations in tax policies and crude oil costs are the major source of variation.

Gasoline has traditionally been subject to excise taxes, imposed originally for revenue raising purposes rather than conservation. As a taxable commodity gasoline had several advantages: sales of gasoline until recently rose steadily and rapidly thus ensuring a increasing tax revenue, and, as private motoring was confined in many countries to the relatively well to do, excise taxes on gasoline did not raise politically difficult problems of social equity.[3]

Gasoline taxation is widespread, even in those countries such as the oil exporters where pump prices are quite low. Table 4.5 illustrates tax levels for a number of countries for which data are available. These data should be interpreted with caution as they are subject to a wide margin of error. In principle, they cover both customs and excise taxes. In practice it may not be easy to capture in one figure the multiplicity of taxes imposed, both ad valorem and some specific. While the data in Table 4.5 may not be an entirely reliable indication for any one country in any one year, they are useful in indicating broad diffferences between groups of countries, and, as we shall see later, in trends over time. These data for 1981 indicate a considerable range in tax rates for premium gasoline, from under 20 percent to over 60 percent. Most countries, however, fall into the 30 to 50 percent range. In the majority of countries therefore, whether developing or industrial, taxes accounted for between one third and one half of the pump price of regular gasoline in 1981.

As the pump price varies so greatly taxes expressed as a share of the total can be misleading. The 30 percent tax of a country with $3.00 gasoline ($1.00) is obviously higher than the 70 percent tax of a country with $1.00 gasoline (70 cents). Table 4.5 therefore also gives the amount of tax in cents per gallon. Again this varies widely from under 20 cents Saudi Arabia, the USA, Bolivia, Venezuela) to well over $1.50 (in Portugal and France). As might be expected, the tax per gallon tends to be lower in low price countries.

It is not easy to generalize about the reasons behind different tax rates. History, tradition, fiscal needs, and the structure of revenues have all played a part. In recent years balance of payments problems and security concerns have played a larger role. In 1981 for example virtually all of the countries in the High price category were totally dependent on imports for their oil supplies and therefore more likely to be concerned about both the cost of imports and the vulnerability of their economies to disruption.

Differences in pump prices are also due to differences in pricing policies for crude oil. Countries which import all petroleum supplies have little choice but to pass on the full costs to consumers.[4] Countries which have domestic production, however, can and frequently do price supplies to the domestic market lower than international prices. Thus, for gasoline, all the countries in the low price category are oil producers. Nine out of a total of 15 are net exporters, and 5 are virtually self-sufficient. The United States is the only country in the Low category which imports a significant share of its petroleum supplies. Within the low price category there is a marked tendency for prices to be lower in the producer exporter countries than in the self-sufficient or importing country.

While all (except the US) of the countries in the low category are self-sufficient in petroleum and most are exporters, not all self-sufficient or exporting countries are in the low category. Malaysia, Tunisia, Cameroon and the U.K. for example all have gasoline prices in excess of $2.00 a gallon. The reason for this apparent anomaly is that these countries are recent producers whose supplies came on stream when international prices had already risen and whose domestic pricing policies were rooted in the era of oil import dependency. It was therefore easier for these countries to base domestic pricing of crude on the new higher prices than for those countries where prices of domestic crude had been traditionally set by low domestic production costs.

A rough illustration of differences in domestic pricing policies for petroleum is provided in Table 4.5 where premium gasoline prices before taxes are given for a number of countries. In principle these represent the cost of crude oil plus refinery and distribution margins. As the international cost of imported gasoline in 1981 was about $1 a gallon, the pre-tax price, including distribution, in oil importing countries would be expected to be substantially above that level. This is bourne out by the Table. However, there are several countries (Colombia, Mexico, Peru, Venezuela, Saudi Arabia), all either net exporters or self-sufficient in petroleum, in which pre-tax prices are well below international levels, due to domestic pricing policies. Such policies confer an economic if not necessarily a financial subsidy on consumers.

The total difference in pump prices between Low price gasoline countries, say where gasoline is on average about $1.00 a gallon, and Medium price countries where it is over $2.00 is therefore due to both lower prices before taxes (reflecting lower domestic crude oil prices) and lower tax rates. The relative weight will vary from country to country but from the data in Table 4.5 the $1.40 per gallon difference in prices between the low price countries and the others is about 40 percent due to higher taxes and 60 percent due to higher pre-tax prices.

Variations in tax rates rather than in pre-tax prices are largely responsible for much of the difference in prices between medium and high price countries. Many of the medium price countries and virtually all of the high price countries import all of their petroleum supplies and therefore face very similar crude prices. There are undoubtedly differences in refining and distribution costs among countries but such variations are likely to be much less than variations in tax rates. To take an example from Table 4.5 all of the difference between gasoline prices in India and Pakistan is due to taxes, as is much of the difference in prices between Turkey and Spain.

As with gasoline, variations in pump prices of diesel among countries are also due to both differences in tax rates and before tax policies (see Table 4.6). Tax rates vary from 0 to about 50 percent of pump prices, translating into taxes of between 0 and $1.40 a gallon. There is a particularly marked contrast between the developing and industrial countries. In the developing countries taxes on diesel are on average very much lower (about 17 cents a gallon) than in the industrial countries (an average of 67 cents).

For most of the oil importing countries pre-tax prices are in line with international prices of about $1.00 cif. However, in countries which are self-sufficient or net exporters pre-tax prices are well below the international level--16 cents in Mexico, 9 in Venezuela, and 8 in Saudi Arabia. The case of Brazil is of interest here. Although Brazil in 1981 relied on imports for 80 percent of total petroleum supplies, the pre-tax price of diesel was substantially below international levels, implying a major subsidy to diesel fuel.

A comparison of Table 4.5 and 4.6 indicates that diesel prices are invariably lower than gasoline. This differential is related to the different markets for the two fuels. Traditionally gasoline has been used for private passenger transport, and diesel in mass transit and freight transport. Governments, especially in developing countries, therefore kept tax rates lower on diesel in order to help develop these markets.

The differential between diesel and gasoline prices varies from country to country. A fairly typical range is for gasoline prices to be some 50 to 100 percent higher than diesel but there are examples of gasoline prices being 3 times higher or more. If the gap between the two grows too wide the purpose of the differential will be defeated as the cheaper diesel fuel will be diverted increasingly to private passenger use or other nontransport use. There is evidence that this happened on a significant scale in both Costa Rica and Brazil during the 1970's. Although the change from an internal combustion engine to diesel is not costless, a widening gap between the process of the two fuels will reduce these costs. These considerations limit the freedom of governments to manipulate the prices of transport fuels (see further discussion in Chapter 10).

In Brazil, for example, the price of gasoline rose much more rapidly in 1970's than the price of diesel. In 1970 gasoline was priced at 21 cruzeiros (1981 cruzeiros) per litre or 17 percent higher in price than diesel. By 1980, gasoline prices were 130 percent higher than diesel. This relative cheapening of the price of diesel led to a rapid switch from gasoline to diesel trucks. In 1970 45 percent of new truck registrations were gasoline powered. By 1979 this share fell to 3 percent when diesel vehicles accounted for 45 percent of the commercial vehicle fleet (including buses) compared with 27 percent in 170.[5]

The foregoing analysis of the structure of transport fuels applies to one year, 1981. Over the past 10 years or more, however, there have been major changes in the crude oil market which have affected both trends and the structure of transport fuel prices.

The outstanding development has been the increase in prices of transport fuels since 1973. Before 1973 in most countries real gasoline and diesel prices had declined, reflecting the decline in the real price of crude oil which took place in the 1960's. From 1973, however, this trend was reversed, with significant increases in gasoline prices in almost all countries (see Table 4.7 and Appendix Table 9).

There are notable exceptions, such as prices in two major exporters

Mexico and Saudi Arabia which declined, but in most other cases including other self-sufficient or exporting countries there was a substantial increase. While the increase in gasoline prices from 1973 to 1981 varied from country to country, it was on average much higher (about 85 percent) in developing countries than in the industrial countries where prices increased on average by about 35 percent.

The reason behind this difference in rates of increase lies largely in the tax structure--the higher the tax, the smaller the increase in the final price resulting from higher crude prices. In countries with high taxes, crude represents a relatively small part of the total sales prices so that even a large increase in crude oil prices has quite a limited impact on the final price. This effect is illustrated in Table 4.8 which gives hypothetical examples of the effect of higher crude oil prices on pump prices of gasoline in both industrial and developing countries totally dependent on imports for oil supplies, and therefore paying the international prices. Though hypothetical the assumptions are based on, and are consistent with, the data presented in foregoing tables.

To start with the industrial countries. The average price of a gallon of premium gasoline in 1973 was about $1.10 (in 1975 prices) of which 70 cents was tax and of the remaining 40 cents, 15 cents was the cost of crude oil and 25 cents all other costs such as refining, distribution, etc. By 1981 the real cost of oil had quintupled so that oil inputs into a gallon of gasoline increased from 15 to 65 cents. It is assumed that the 25 cents allowance for refining and distribution costs remains constant in real terms. It is assumed, however, that taxes fell in real terms from 70 cents to 50 cents. (Although taxes per gallon rose in current values from 1973 to 1981 they rose by less than the cost of living leading therefore to a decline in real taxes per gallon.) The net result is an increase in the real price of gasoline from $1.10 to $1.50. Crude oil now accounts for 50 percent of the total cost of a gallon of crude in place of 15 percent in 1973, and taxes have declined from 64 percent to just under 33 percent.

This example should be contrasted with the case of the developing country oil importers. In 1973, prices of gasoline were somewhat lower at about 70 cents than in the industrial countries (see again Table 4.7) due to lower tax rates (44 percent in place of the industrial countries 70 percent). The cost of crude oil and refining and distribution costs is assumed to be the same.

By 1981 the cost of crude oil had increased to 75 cents as in the industrial countries, and refining and distribution costs are assumed to be constant. Unlike the industrial countries it is assumed that taxes remained constant in real terms i.e. they increased at the same rate as the rise in the cost of living. This is bourne out by the fragmentary data available. The 1981 price of a gallon of gasoline in a developing country is then $1.30, some 85 percent higher than in 1973. The gap between prices in the industrial ($1.50) and developing ($1.30) countries has therefore narrowed although again it should be remembered that the use of market rates of exchange in these comparisons will underestimate the size of the gap.

Due to lack of data for the developing countries it has not been possible to trace trends in diesel prices over time as in Table 4.7. However, from the experience of the industrial countries and from analysis similar to that in Table 4.8 it is possible to make some estimates.

Prices of automotive diesel in the oil importing industrial countries of Europe rose by about 80 percent in real terms from 1973 to 1981, that is over twice as fast as gasoline prices. The reason for this sharper rise is that tax rates on diesel are lower than those on gasoline in the industrial countries so that more of the increase in crude prices is passed through to the consumer. It will be recalled in the case of gasoline that prices in the developing countries rose more rapidly than in industrial countries, implying that if diesel were like gasoline the rate of increase in diesel prices in developing countries would be in excess of the 80 percent increase in industrial countries, particularly as tax rates on diesel in developing countes are well below those in industrial countries.

In practice, the rise in diesel prices may have been rather less than the rise in diesel in industrial countries or than in gasoline prices in developing countries due to increased subsidization. The data in Table 4.6 supports this view. In most cases prices before tax are lower than they would be if the full cost of imported oil, refining and distribution were included. It may be therefore that diesel prices rose by some 40-50 percent in the oil importing developing countries and that this relatively slow rate of growth is due to policy decisions to limit the increase in price of what is considered to be a strategic development input.

A final question is how the increase in crude oil prices has affected the relative ranking of countries over time as regards their transport energy prices. Would, in other words, the relative standing of countries in Table 4.2 have been the same in 1973, before the crude oil price rise? This question is of technical interest to this study as if it can be shown that there is a certain robustness in a country's classification it is possible to make inferences about price behavior in periods for which we have no direct data, thereby extending our analysis of the impact of energy prices on consumption over a wider period. The answer to this question can also throw some light on the comparative pricing policies of the individual countries.

An examination of the relative prices of a number of countries in both 1973 and 1981 indicates that there is considerable stability among groups over time. The chances are that a low price country in 1973 was still a low price country in 1981. There is some changing between high and medium among the European countries but this is largely due to the fact that several countries straddle the boundary betwen high and medium. In the developing countries there is a more distinct separation in both years.

The major exceptions to this general stability is the movement of 4 Low price countries (Brazil, Philippines, and Thailand) into the medium category with exceptionally high rates of increase in real prices--tripling or even quadrupling over an eight year period. Increases of these magnitudes imply a major rise in taxation.

In summary, an examination of prices of transport fuels for a larger number of countries in one year and for a lesser number of countries over time shows:

1. Countries, and especially developing countries appear to cluster around three price levels which we have termed low, medium, and high.

2. This categorization which is related to a country's petroleum balance appears to be quite robust over time. The exceptions were changes in an upward direction for a limited number of countries.

3. The domestic petroleum balance also affected trends in gasoline prices over time. Between 1973 and 1981 prices in exporting countries either fell, remained constant or increased rather slowly. In the oil importing developing countries they rose by about 85 percent. This increase was much larger than that in the industrial oil-importers due to differences in tax structure and tax policies.

4. Diesel prices are believed to have increased very modestly in the oil importing developing countries and many are subsidising diesel in one way or another.

Footnotes

1. Most of the prices are for the third quarter of 1981 but several apply to other periods between 1980 and 1982.

2. For example, Bulletin of Energy Prices #1-84 Commission of the European Communities, Brussels 1984.

3. The original rationale for taxing gasoline was that the demand for gasoline was price inelastic such that an increase in price did not lead to a marked fall in consumption thus protecting total revenues. In reality it may have been the high income elasticity which was largely responsible for the steady increase in consumption.

4. Note, however, that within this overall constraint there can be considerable variation in the structure of petroleum product prices. Thus a tax on gasoline can offset a subsidy to kerosene, or diesel.

5. "Un Modelo Econometrico para a demanda de Gasolina pelos Automoveis de Psseio" by Richardo Paes de Barros and Silverio Soares Ferriera and "Sobra a ieselizacao da Frota Brasileira de Caminhoes" by Armando Castelar Pinheiro, both Working Papers of Instituto de Planejamento Economico e Social, Rio de Janeiro 1982 and 1983.

Table 4.1

Prices of Premium Gasoline and
Automotive Diesel in Selected Countries, 1981
(US cents per US gallon)

Country	Premium Gasoline	Automotive Diesel
Developing countries		
Argentina	156	60
Bangladesh	207	74
Bolivia	140	91
Burma	42	30
Brazil	300	146
Burundi	450	305
Cameroon	240	187
Chile	207	170
Colombia	96	81
Dominican Republic	257	115
Ecuador	80	44
Egypt	71	14
El Salvador	256	170
Ethiopia	236	99
Ghana	394	273
Greece	237	112
Guatemala	200	103
Honduras	208	121
India	253	119
Indonesia	133	32
Israel	307	126
Ivory Coast	365	250
Jamaica	217	135
Kenya	274	178
Republic of Korea	582	153
Malawi	317	290
Malaysia	213	83
Mexico	110	16
Morocco	275	146
Nicaragua	272	145
Nigeria	128	120
Pakistan	216	117
Panama	226	133
Paraguay	451	174
Peru	110	58
Philippines	250	148
Portugal	299	134
Rwanda	283	271

Table 4.1 continued

Country	Premium Gasoline	Automotive Diesel
Developing countries		
Senegal	302	186
Sierra Leone	238	132
Singapore	191	123
South Africa	223	222
Spain	284	167
Sri Lanka	200	119
Sudan	230	62
Tanzania	437	183
Thailand	214	133
Trinidad & Tobago	35	29
Turkey	174	110
Uganda	544	327
Uruguay	417	170
Venezuela	31	9
Yugoslavia	286	241
Zambia	432	223
Zimbabwe	312	206
Industrial Countries[1]		
Australia	183	190
Belgium	280	191
Canada	126	121
Denmark	289	175
Finland	288	200
France*	299	215
W. Germany*	243	226
Italy	284	126
Japan	272	172
Netherlands	258	176
Saudi Arabia	24	8
Switzerland	249	234
Sweden	266	134
United Kingdom	265	269
USA	136	104

Source: The Energy Transition in Developing Countries, the World Bank, Washington, D.C., 1983, and International Energy Annual 1980 and 1981, U.S. Department of Energy, Washington, D.C., September 1981 and 1982.

[1] Data for July 1981 except for those countries marked * = January 1981.

Table 4.2

Premium Gasoline: Selected Countries
Ranked by Price Level
(US $ at 1981 prices and exchange rates)

LOW (under $1.60 a gallon)

Developing				Industrial & Saudi Arabia	
Argentina	156	Mexico	110	Canada	126
Bolivia	140	Nigeria	128	USA	136
Burma	42	Peru	110		
Colombia	96	Trinidad & Tobago	35		
Ecuador	80	Venezuela	31		
Egypt	71				
Indonesia	33				
			12		

MEDIUM ($1.61 TO $2.80)

Developing				Industrial	
Bangladesh	207	Singapore	191	Australia	183
Cameroon	240	S. Africa	223	Belgium	280
Chile	207	Thailand	214	Japan	272
Dom. Repub.	257	Turkey	174	Netherlands	258
El Salvador	256	Greece	237	Switzerland	249
Honduras	208	Ethiopia	266	Sweden	266
India	253	Guatemala	200	United Kingdom	265
Jamaica	217	Malaysia	213		7
Kenya	274	Nicaragua	272		
Morocco	275	Sierra Leone	238		
Pakistan	216	Sri Lanka	200		
Panama	226	Sudan	230		
Philippines	250	Yugoslavia	286		
			26		

HIGH (over $2.81)

Developing				Industrial	
Brazil	300	Uruguay	417	Denmark	289
Burundi	450	Zambia	432	Finland	288
Ghana	394	Paraguay	451	France	299
Israel	307	Rwanda	283	Italy	284
Ivory Coast	365	Senegal	302		
Korea, Rep. of	582	Tanzania	437		4
Malawi	317	Uganda	544		
Portugal	299	Zimbabwe	312		
			16		

Table 4.3

Automotive Diesel: Selected Countries
Ranked by Pricel Level
(US $ at 1981 prices and exchange rates)

LOW (Less than $1.00 per US gallon)

Developing				Industrial and Saudi Arabia	
Argentina	60	Indonesia	32	Saudi Arabia	1
Bangladesh	74	Malaysia	83		
Bolivia	91	Mexico	16		
Burma	30	Peru	58		
Colombia	81	Venezuela	9		
Ecuador	44	Trinidad & Tobago	29		
Egypt	14	Sudan	62		
Ethiopia	99				
			15		

MEDIUM ($1.00 TO $2.00)

Developing				Industrial	
Brazil	146	Pakistan	117	Australia	190
Cameroon	187	Panama	133	Belgium	191
Chile	170	Paraguay	174	Canada	121
Dominican Rep.	115	Philippines	148	Denmark	175
El Salvador	170	Portugal	134	Italy	126
Greece	112	Senegal	186	Japan	173
Guatemala	103	Sierra Leone	132	Netherlands	176
Honduras	121	Singapore	123	Sweden	134
India	119	Spain	167	USA	104
Israel	126	Sri Lanka	119		9
Jamaica	135	Thailand	133		
Kenya	178	Turkey	110		
Korea	153	Uruguay	170		
Morocco	146	Tanzania	183		
Nigeria	120				
Nicaragua	145				
			31		

HIGH (over $2.00)

Developing				Industrial	
Burundi	305	Uganda	327	Finland	200
Ghana	273	Yugoslavia	241	France	215
Ivory Coast	250	Zambia	223	W. Germany	226
Malawi	290	Zimbabwe	206	Switzerland	243
S. Africa	275			United Kingdom	269
			9		5

Table 4.4

Distribution of Countries within Gasoline and Diesel Price Categories

(number of countries)

A. Premium Gasoline

	Total	Percent	Developing	Percent	Industrial	Percent
Low	15	21	12	22	3	20
Medium	34	49	26	47	8	53
High	20	30	17	31	4	27
	70	100	55	100	15	100

B. Automotive Diesel

	Total	Percent	Developing	Percent	Industrial	Percent
Low	16	23	15	27	1	7
Medium	40	57	31	57	9	60
High	14	20	9	16	5	33
	70	100	55	100	15	100

Table 4.5

Premium Gasoline Prices and Taxes, 1981
Selected Countries
(US cents per US gallon 1981 prices
and exchange rates)

Country	Pump price Premium gasoline	Taxes	Price before tax	Tax as share of pump price %
Developing				
Bolivia	140	16	124	11
Brazil	252	99	153	39
Colombia	96	72	24	75
Greece	237	95	142	40
India	253	106	147	42
Jamaica	217	79	138	36
Kenya	274	120	154	44
Mexico	110	67	43	61
Pakistan	216	68	148	31
Peru	110	40	70	36
Philippines	250	121	129	48
Portugal	299	185	114	62
Singapore	191	66	125	35
Spain	284	97	187	34
Thailand	214	125	89	58
Turkey	174	8	166	5
Venezuela	31	13	18	42
Industrial				
Belgium	280	146	134	52
Canada	126	34	92	27
Denmark	289	149	140	52
France	299	164	135	55
Finland	288	95	193	33
Germany	243	111	132	47
Japan	272	99	173	36
Netherlands	258	127	131	49
Sweden	266	121	145	45
Switzerland	249	111	138	45
United Kingdom	265	136	129	51
USA	136	13	123	10
Saudi Arabia	24	-	24	-

Table 4.6

Automotive Diesel Prices and Taxes, 1981

Country	Pump price Diesel	Taxes	Price before Tax	Tax as share of pump price %
Developing				
Bolivia	91	10	81	11
Brazil	97	20	77	21
Colombia	81	42	39	52
Dominican Repub.	115	0	115	0
Greece	112	6	106	5
India	119	20	99	17
Jamaica	135	14	121	10
Kenya	178	34	144	19
Mexico	16	0	16	0
Pakistan	117	10	107	9
Peru	58	16	42	28
Philippines	148	22	126	15
Portugal	134	30	104	22
Singapore	121	11	110	9
Spain	167	33	134	20
Thailand	133	28	105	21
Turkey	110	6	104	5
Venezuela	9	0	9	0
Industrial				
Belgium	191	77	114	40
Canada	121	32	89	26
Denmark	175	52	123	30
France	215	95	120	44
Finland	200	57	143	29
Germany	226	105	121	46
Italy	126	22	104	17
Japan	173	45	128	26
Netherlands	176	57	119	32
Sweden	132	22	110	17
Switzerland	234	114	120	49
United Kingdom	269	137	132	51
Saudi Arabia	8	0	8	0

Table 4.7

Trends in Prices of Premium Gasoline in Selected Countries (1965, 1973 and 1982)

(1975 $/gallon)

	1965	1973	1982	Percentage Change 1965-73	1973-82
Low Income Dev.					
Ghana	1.22	0.66	1.90	-46	+188
India	1.16	0.87	1.42	-25	+63
Kenya	0.87	0.72	1.51	-17	+109
Pakistan	0.96	0.62	0.94	-35	+52
Middle Income Dev.					
Bolivia	0.38	0.21	0.38	-45	+81
Colombia	0.24	0.17	0.48	-29	+182
Jamaica	0.67	0.47	1.18	-30	+150
Morocco	0.96	1.09	1.53	+14	+40
Peru	0.31	0.26	0.56	-16	+115
Philippines	0.43	0.22	1.25	-49	+468
Thailand	0.60	0.48	1.04	-20	+116
Turkey	0.70	0.51	1.04	-30	+104
High Income Dev.					
Argentina	0.43	0.73	0.61	+70	-16
Brazil	0.51	0.35	1.57	-31	+349
Chile	0.38	0.70	0.96	+84	+37
Greece	1.10	1.08	1.2	- 2	+11
Israel	0.41	0.76	1.14	+46	+50
Mexico	0.41	0.29	0.27	-29	-7
Portugal	1.20	1.04	1.47	-13	+41
Venezuela	0.14	0.11	0.14	-21	+27
High Income Oil Exporters					
Saudi Arabia	0.29	0.27	0.10	- 7	-67
Industrial					
Canada	0.58	0.70	0.72	+21	+3
France	1.23	1.30	1.24	+ 6	-5
Italy	1.15	1.21	1.47	+ 5	+21
Japan	0.87	1.02	1.37	+19	+34
United Kingdom	0.98	0.95	1.55*	- 3	+63
USA	0.55	0.49	0.70	-11	+43
W. Germany	0.92	1.44	1.13	+57	-22

*1981

Table 4.8

Hypothetical Example of Effect of Higher Crude Oil Prices on Prices of Premium Gasoline

(in 1975 US$)

	1973		1981	
	$	%	$	%
Oil importing developing countries				
Crude oil	.15	21	.75	58
Refining and distribution costs	.25	36	.25	19
Tax	.30	43	.30	23
Pump price	.70	100	1.30	100
Oil importing industrial countries				
Crude Oil	.15	14	.75	50
Refining and distribution costs	.25	23	.25	17
Tax	.70	64	.50	33
Pump price	1.10	100	1.50	100

Chapter 5

The Relationship between Transport Energy Consumption: Vehicle Ownership, Population, Land-use Patterns

Car ownership has risen dramatically throughout the world in the last twenty years or so (see Table 5.1 and Appendix Table 10).[1] The lowest rate of increase was in the low income countries where ownership rates typically doubled. In the other developing areas they rose by much more--in the lower and middle income countries on average four fold, and by more in the centrally planned countries and the high income oil exporters. An interesting feature of the industrial countries, whose overall increase was comparatively low, is the variation in rates of increase of car ownership in the different countries. Those with low ownership rates at the beginning of the period increased much more rapidly than those with high ownership rates, with the result that the difference in car ownership rates among these countries were much reduced by 1982. (In 1960 for example, the U.S.A. with highest car ownership rates had 70 times more cars in relation to population than the lowest, Japan. By 1982 the U.S. had only 2.5 times more cars in relation to population than Japan. The relatively slow growth of the high car ownership countries implies an approach to saturation though this still has some way to go in a number of industrialized countries.)

Table 5.1 also shows the marked difference in car ownership across the broad income categories. Thus in low income countries in 1982 there were on average about 2 cars per 1000 population. This rose to about 12 in the middle income countries, to 70 in the high income developing countries and 400 in the industrial countries.

Car ownership and gasoline consumption

This rapid increase in the car population would be expected to lead to a sharp rise in gasoline consumption. It is interesting to note, however (see Table 5.2 and 5.3), that the rise in car ownership was invariably higher than the rise in gasoline consumption. In other words, gasoline consumption per car fell during the period in all areas (for country details see Appendix Table 11). This decline could be due to three main reasons--apart from the inevitable measurement difficulties--energy using characteristics of the automobile fleet, distance travelled by car, and change in type of vehicles within this category.

Before 1970 there may have been some trend to higher gasoline consumption per car. After 1973, however, technology moved in the opposite, energy saving direction. There is some lag in automotive technology transfer especially in car importing developing countries with restrictive import licensing. Because of limited imports the turnover of the car fleet is slow with the result that the car fleet is typically much older in developing countries. Average gasoline per car is, for example, higher in low and middle income countries than in the industrial countries.

Second, the increase in car population means that each car is probably used less. A dramatic example of this effect is provided by China where gasoline consumption per car is an order of magnitude higher than in any other country. Part of this may be due to deficient data but nonetheless the extent of the difference suggests that the exceptionally small number of cars in that country are heavily used. On the other hand, in other circumstances higher incomes for car owners may lead to increased usage. It is difficult to state a priori which trend would dominate.

Finally, data on total car ownership covers a wide range of vehicle types. In some countries such as the U.S. most of these vehicles will consist of private cars. In other countries such as India (see Chapter 8) motorcycles, with much higher energy efficiencies, represent a large share of the total. Differences in composition of "car" fleet will therefore affect the average energy efficiency of the fleet.

Car ownership and income level

Car ownership rates are used as an explanatory variable in our analysis of gasoline consumption. In addition, because of its importance in checking projections of gasoline consumption the car fleet is also estimated independently. The most important determinants of car ownership are assumed to be income, the costs or "price" of car ownership, demographic, geographical and institutional factors.

There appears to be a strong relationship between car ownership and income level. This relationship is implicit in Table 5.1 which ranks car ownership by income categories of countries. It is also illustrated in Graph 5-1 which plots car ownership rates against income in 1972 and 1978. This graph shows the sharp rise in car ownership over the period despite the rise in gasoline prices and in some cases despite falling or constant income. This apparent anomaly has been attributed to the fact that car ownership is determined by expected rather than actual income, and is therefore unaffected by factors, such as a fall in income in a given year, which is perceived to be transitory.[2]

The costs of car ownership

The cost of car ownership, including amortization of the vehicle and operating costs will affect both car ownership, and car utilization. Indeed, it has been argued[3] that changes in operating costs mainly affect car usage rather than car ownership at least over the short term. We use price of gasoline and cars as proxies for total costs of car operation. Based on current U.S. data these two items could account for about 80 percent of the total costs of car ownership.

Data on estimated car prices are given in Table 5.4. The derivation of these estimates is given in Appendix 1-B. In brief, prices for the U.S. are an average of (deflated) domestic and import prices. Prices for the other countries are based on the price of a representative world car (in this case the U.S. import price minus the cost of pollution equipment) increased by the customs and excise taxes imposed by the selected countries in 1981. Recognizing that official market exchange rates may give a misleading indication of real price differences across countries, a second series of car prices roughly based on purchasing power parities has been derived.

Although this procedure gives some indication of relative car prices in selective countries it does not of course tell the whole story. Many countries, particularly those with foreign exchange constraints--that is most of the developing countries--impose other barriers to entry including prohibition. In such cases, domestic prices will be considerably above prices given here. However, as such countries are likely in any event to have high customs and excise taxes the result of such additional restrictions would be to increase the price of cars in that country and thus reinforce the differences in prices across countries rather than to negate them. In other words, the actual difference between prices across countries may be greater than indicated by the data in Appendix Table 12.

Brazil is likely to be an exception to this rule. Here high duties are imposed to protect the domestic industry whose prices are in fact relatively low.

Furthermore, most countries discriminate in their tax treatment between low and high energy efficiency cars. For simplicity we have based our price estimates on a comparable type of car (small with relatively high energy efficiency). Any change in category of car purchased over time would not therefore be reflected in our price estimates.

Given these considerations, the data on car prices must be interpreted with reservation. However, several general conclusions can be drawn. First, prices of cars approximately doubled from 1960 to 1980, in all categories of countries. Second, car prices are distinctly higher (about 100 percent higher) in developing countries compared with prices in industrial countries. If car prices are adjusted to take into account purchasing power differences, this difference is much greater. Car prices in developing countries are then on average some 4 times higher in developing than in industrial countries. The adjustment of prices to take into account purchasing power parities also indicates some variation in prices between the 3 income categories of developing countries with the highest prices in the low income countries.

Prices of gasoline, the other component of ownership costs incorporated in our analysis were described in Chapter 4. It might be thought that in the interests of policy consistency these two items of car ownership costs would be closely correlated--that low car price countries would also have low gasoline prices and vice versa. However, as the matrix in Table 5.5 shows, there is considerable dispersion of countries among the different categories. Only one of the selected countries, Republic of

Korea, has both high car and gasoline prices (and as we have noticed before both car ownership and gasoline consumption is lower than would be predicted by income alone). At the other end of the scale only 5 countries U.S. and Canada, Saudi Arabia, Libya and Kuwait have both low car and gasoline prices. Here again there are exceptionally high rates of car ownership and gasoline consumption in these countries.

In the other countries levels of gasoline and car prices are not closely correlated. Industrial countries typically have low car prices but high gasoline prices, perhaps a legacy of the revenue raising motives behind gasoline taxation. Many of the developing countries with low gasoline price countries have high car prices suggesting that cars are considered luxury items of consumption. From a policy point of view, therefore, in many countries mixed signals are being provided to the motorist, who may be faced with high car prices and low gasoline prices, or low car prices and high gasoline prices. Of the two, car prices are quantitatively the most important in car ownership and operation, but there is some evidence that out-of-pocket costs such as gasoline purchases may weigh more heavily in motorists' decision making.

Demography

Demographic factors also affect car ownership rates. The effect of total population has already been taken into account in our car ownership indicators which are expressed in number of cars per 1000 population. In addition the share of the population in the 15-64 age group could be important as this is the group from which most licensed drivers are drawn. The share of this group is significantly higher in the industrial and east bloc countries than in the developing countries for the period under review (see Appendix Table 12). This factor is of greater relevance to the industrial countries approaching saturation than to the developing countries where ownership rates are very low. Thus, rates of increase in car ownership do not tend to be systematically higher in those countries with an expanding share of the population in the 15 to 64 age group.

Truck registration

Consumption of transport fuels is also affected by the size of the truck fleet. So far it has been assumed that cars are entirely powered by gasoline and despite some increase in diesel cars in the 1970s, that appears to be a reasonable assumption. However, not all gasoline is used in cars. In some countries gasoline powered trucks predominate. As we have no information on how much of total gasoline is consumed in trucks we have been obliged to treat all gasoline as consumed in cars, and all diesel as if consumed in trucks. While this is a gross over-simplification there is no alternative given present data constraints.

The number of trucks in relation to the population increased sharply in the 1960s and '70s (see Table 5.6 and Appendix Table 13). In the low income countries and the industrial countries it probably doubled (although the increase in the low income countries is due mainly to a large increase in Zambia). In the other countries the number increased about three fold, that is in line with economic activity in the respective regions. The amount of freight carried may have increased even further as there appears to have been a move to larger trucks.

Composition of the vehicle fleet

The composition of the vehicle fleet (including both cars, and trucks and buses) has changed considerably. In all income categories (see Table 5.7) the share of cars in the total fleet has increased. The share of cars in the total fleet is lower (under 20 percent) in the low income countries and rises through the income categories. In the industrial countries the share rises to over 80 percent. This illustrates again the growth of private passenger transport as living standards improve.

Transport fuel consumption and land use

A final cluster of factors which we consider is land-use. While comprehensive data on distance travelled are not available, land use patterns can give some indication of these distances and even of modal efficiencies. Size of country can be important. Very large countries such as China, India, Brazil, the USSR, Canada, the USA (see Appendix Table 14) are likely to be more travel intensive measured by passenger and freight kilometers than small countries such as Japan and the Netherlands.[4]

Population density (see Appendix Table 15) also influences traffic patterns. Densely populated countries lend themselves more readily to public transportation which is less energy intensive than private transport systems. For the industrial countries, population densities do appear to explain part of the variations in energy use. Among the industrial countries for example Japan has the highest population density, by far the largest share of public transport, and the lowest transport energy consumption. However, even average population density is not infallible. Some countries, such as Sweden, have low average population densities but because the population is concentrated in a relatively small region, public transport systems are well developed, and transport energy consumption is relatively low.

These generalizations apply more to the industrial than to the developing countries. In the developing countries low population densities may mean that large parts of the population are not served by any mechanized transport system and therefore transport energy consumption is low. It is true that many developing countries with high population densities also consume very little energy but there may be a circularity in this argument. Countries with high population densities may consume little transport fuel primarily because of low incomes caused by high population/land ratios.

Perhaps of greater relevance to developing countries are urbanization rates (percent of total population in urban areas, see Appendix Table 16) which indicate the share of the population using commercial energy services on a regular basis and benefitting from the higher salaries which enable transport to be purchased. Of total energy consumed in developing countries over 50 percent is consumed in intra-urban traffic. An increase in urban population can therefore have an important impact on transport energy consumption. A further refinement of these data is the percent of the urban population in the largest city, typically the capital, which is much higher in the developing countries (see Appendix Table 17). In the developing countries this higher share will tend to lead to higher rather than lower transport energy consumption--the increased access to travel opportunities by the population outweighing the systems efficiencies made possible by dense land-use patterns.

A final factor affecting the consumption of transport fuels is the extent and quality of the road network. While the provision of adequate roads is a necessary rather than sufficient condition for transport development, it appears that the two are closely correlated. Rather patchy data available suggests that there was a widespread increase in road networks from the 1960s to the 1980s but much of the expansion took place in the industrial countries. The notable exceptions in developing countries are Brazil, Thailand, Turkey--all countries in which the increase in transport fuel consumption was particularly rapid.

In summary, the dramatic rise in car ownership which has taken place since 1960 has been closely related to the increase in gasoline consumption. Car ownership rates are, in turn, related to income, costs of car ownership (such as car and gasoline prices) and demographic factors. The number of trucks also increased but more slowly than cars, so that the share of cars in the total vehicle fleet has risen. The share of cars in the vehicle fleet is low in low income countries and high in high income countries. Land use characteristics such as size of country, population density and urbanization also influence transport fuel consumption through in rather different ways in low and high income countries.

Footnotes

1. "Cars" here also includes automobiles, motor bicycles, scooters.

2. See Long Term Outlook for the World Automobile Industry, OECD, Paris 1983, p. 16.

3. Ibid, pp. 16-17.

4. The U.S. for example in 1972 had 2000 passenger miles per $thousand GDP while Japan had just over 1000. In the same year the U.S. had over 4 times more freight tons per unit GDP. See Joel Darmstadter, Joy Dunkerley, Jack Alterman, How Industrial Societies Use Energy, Resources for the Future, Johns Hopkins University Press, Baltimore, MD, 1977.

Table 5.1

Car Ownership
(# cars per 1000 people)

	1960	1965	1970	1975	1980
Low Income Dev.[1]	0.85	1.1	1.4	1.6	1.7
Middle Income Dev.	2.58	3.52	5.19	7.41	11.99
High Income Dev.	14.44	20.79	31.27	49.72	69.54
High Income Oil Exp.	10.91	20.56	33.59	55.11	123.35
Eastern Bloc.	4.88	7.72	13.62	29.31	53.17
Industrialized	154.1	203.3	261.2	323.5	385.2

[1] excluding China.

Table 5.1 continued

Car Ownership
(annual rate of growth %)

	1960-1970	1970-1982	1960-1982
Low Income Dev.	5.24	2.93	3.98
Middle Income Dev.	7.24	7.22	7.24
High Income Dev.	8.03	6.88	7.41
High Income Oil Exp.	11.9	13.89	11.67
Eastern Bloc.	10.8	12.01	11.48
Industrial	5.42	3.29	4.26

Table 5.2

Car Ownership and Gasoline Consumption 1960 to 1982

	Annual rate of increase in car Ownership		Annual rate of increase in Per capita Gasoline consumption		Annual rate (un-weighted) of in-crease in gas con-sumption per car	
	(60-70)	(70-82)	(60-70)	(80-82)	(60-70)	(70-82)
Low Income Dev.	5.24	2.93	0.2	-0.66	-4.1	-1.1
Middle Income Dev.	7.24	7.22	3.46	3.18	-3.67	-3.5
High Income Dev.	8.03	6.88	4.35	1.88	-5.87	-2.54
High Income Oil Exp.	11.9	13.89	5.66	10.67	-4.90	-1.79
East Bloc.	10.8	12.01	5.82	3.50	-3.5	-9.39
Industrial	5.42	3.29	4.07	0.97	-7.8	-1.87

Countries not included are Bangladesh, China, Malawi, Zambia, Burma, Malaysia, Panama, Taiwan, Trinidad & Tobago, Yugoslavia and Czechoslovakia.

Table 5.3

Consumption of Gas per Car
(koe per car)
(unweighted average, using subset of 75 countries)*

	1960	1970	1982
Low Income Dev.	4288	2819	2467
Middle Income Dev.	8870	6106	3957
High Income Dev.	6284	3431	2519
High Income Oil Exp.	6192	3747	3018
East Bloc.	15006	10901	3339
Industrial	3684	1635	1303

*Countries that were excluded are: Bangladesh, China, Malawi, Zambia, Burma, Malaysia, Panama, Taiwan, Trinidad & Tobago, Yugoslavia, Czechoslovakia.

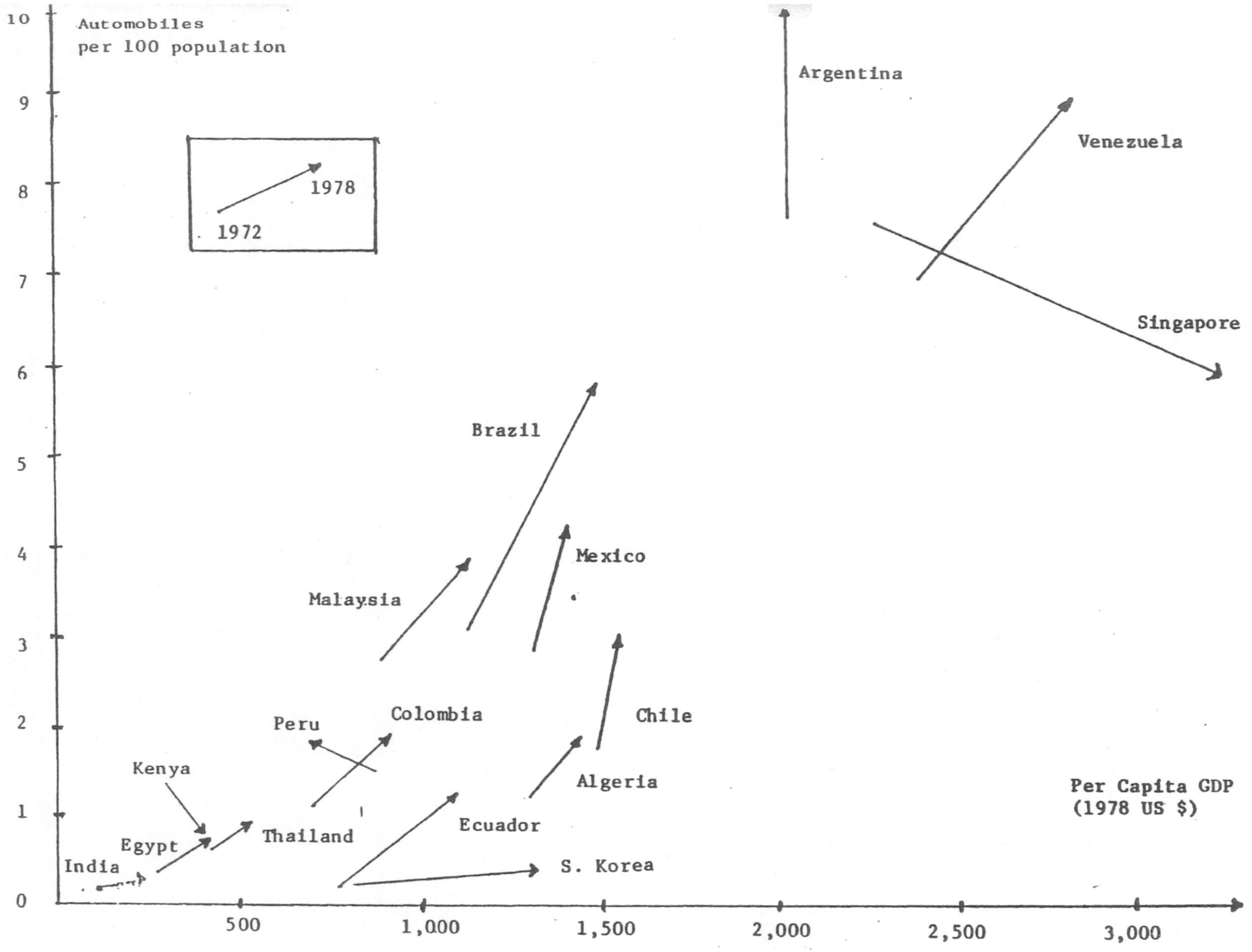

Graph 5.1: Automobiles per 100 Population and Gross Domestic Product, 1972 to 1978, Selected Developing Countries

Table 5.4

Estimated Prices of Cars 1960 and 1980
for Selected Countries at Market and
Purchase Power Exchange Rates
(1975$)

	1960		1980	
	Market exchange rates	Purchasing Power exchange rates	Market exchange rates	Purchasing power exchange rates
Low Income Dev.	6	20	12	37
Middle Income Dev.	6	13	11	22
High Income Dev.	5	8	10	n.a.
Industrial	3	3	8	7

Table 5.5

Selected Countries Categorized by Price of Cars and Gasoline

		Gasoline Prices		
		Low	Medium	High
Car Prices	Low	Kuwait Libya S. Arabia Canada USA	Cameron Netherlands Sweden UK Germany	Malawi Denmark France Italy Brazil
	Medium	Bolivia Colombia Nigeria Peru Argentina Mexico	Kenya Dom. Republic Jamaica Morocco Chile Malaysia Australia Switzerland	Ghana Israel Finland
	High	Ecuador Egypt Indonesia	Bangladesh India Pakistan Philippines	Rep. of Korea

Table 5.6

Per Capita Truck Registrations
1960 to 1982
(# of trucks per 000 people)

	1960	1965	1970	1975	1980	1982
Low Income Dev.	0.45	0.55	0.75	0.97	1.30	1.54
Middle Income Dev.	1.93	2.38	2.95	3.80	6.43	7.35
High Income Dev.	8.53	10.51	13.76	17.45	22.19	23.77
East Bloc.	14.55	14.70	18.82	20.61	27.16	30.61
Industrial	34.92	44.77	57.93	73.72	90.63	98.51

Annual Rates of Increase in
Per Capita Truck Registration

	1960 - 1970	1970 - 1982	1960 - 1982
Low Income Developing	5.24	6.18	5.69
Middle Income Developing	4.33	7.90	6.20
High Income Developing	4.90	4.66	4.72
East Bloc.	2.61	4.13	3.40
Industrial	5.19	4.52	4.78

Table 5.7

Share of Cars and Trucks in
Total Vehicle Fleet

	1960				1982			
	Cars	Trucks	Total	% Cars	Cars	Trucks	Total	% Cars
Low Income Dev.	543	578	1121	48.4	2060	3214	5274	39.1
Middle Income Dev.	918	688	1606	57.2	7643	4683	12326	62.0
High Income Dev.	3630	2143	5773	62.9	30389	10387	40776	74.5
Industrial	89682	20326	110008	81.5	270025	69053	339078	79.6

Part III

Regression Analysis Explaining Transport Energy Variables

In this third part of the report, we apply regression analysis to explain transport energy use. Part III includes Chapter 6, which focuses on how income and price affect transport energy use, and Chapter 7, which considers how an extended set of variables affects that use. That extended set includes measures of density of road network, demographic characteristics and relative change in income ranking over time.

Regression analysis is a by-now standard statistical curve-fitting technique in which a dependent variable is explained by one or more putative explanatory or independent variables; that is, we operate under the hypothesis that changes in the explanatory variables bring about corresponding changes, either positive or negative, in the dependent variable. We then express and test that hypothesis by fitting a curve to a scatter of points exhibiting observed readings on the variables of interest.

For those not well versed in the regression techniques, some explanatory remarks appearing in the next section should be of help in reading the material of chapters 6 and 7. Those familiar with the technique will want to skim or skip that next section.

Regression in a Nutshell

The simplest curve employed in regression analysis is the straight line, expressed by the equation: $y = a+bx$, where y is the dependent variable, x a single independent variable, with a the intercept and b the slope of the line; a is also referred to as "the constant term" and b "the coefficient" of x. When x equals zero, y equals a; a change in x of one unit brings with it a corresponding change in y of b units. When values of a and b are given, the equation can be plotted graphically, as in the following example:

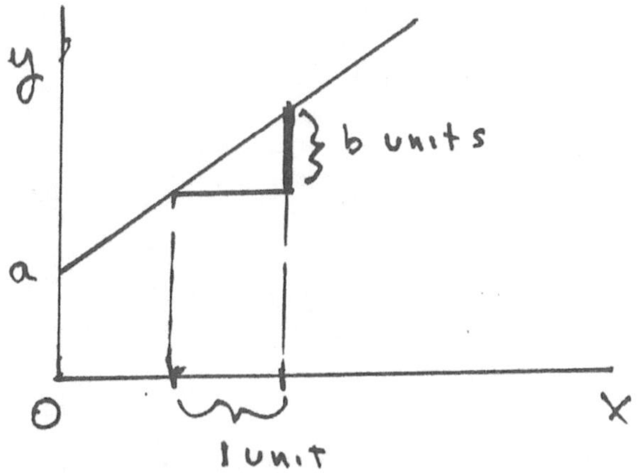

A variant of the linear (or straight line) form is inherent in the equation: $Y=AX^b$. When we take logarithms (logs for short) of both sides of the equation, we obtain the linear in logs equation:

$$\log Y = \log A + b \log X$$

Letting lower case letters stand for logs, that is, letting log Y = y, log A = a and log X = x, the linear-in-logs equation becomes

$$y = a + bx$$

which is seen to be the same form as the linear equation presented initially.

In practice, the investigator begins with a sample of observations, consisting of a set of paired readings on x and y, assuming one independent variable and the linear form; he observes x_1 and y_1, where the subscript 1 indicates that x_1 and y_1 were observed on the first reading; and x_2 and y_2, which were observed on the second reading; and x_3 and y_3; and so on. when plotted on a graph, a scatter of points results. For example, say $x_1=5$,

$y_1=3$; $x_2=4$, $y_2=4$; $x_3=1$, $y_3=1$; and $x_4=3$, $y_4=2$. Those four points yield the following scatter diagram:

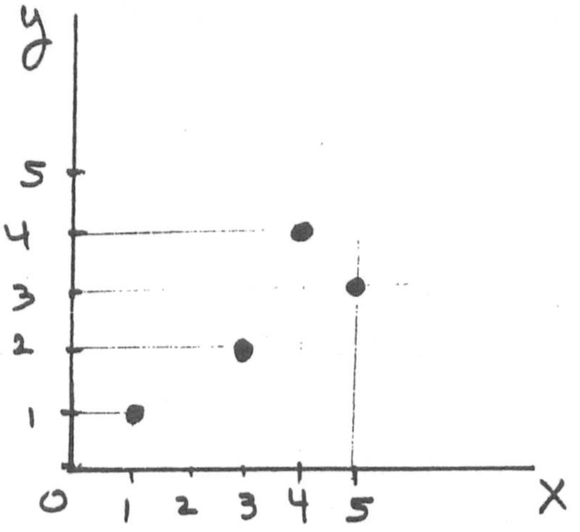

Similarly, in our study, y may be per capita gasoline consumption and x per capita income, and measures of those variables are observed for each year 1960 through 1982 for a set of countries. When those observations are plotted on a graph, a scatter of points results. Regression analysis then, in effect, passes a line through those points to satisfy certain mathematical criteria; the particular line selected to pass through the scatter is the best selection in terms of the criteria. Thus, say we observe the scatter of points shown in the left hand diagram; the application of regression analysis yields the line shown in the right hand diagram, which can be taken as the best representation of the hypothesized (linear) relation between y and x.

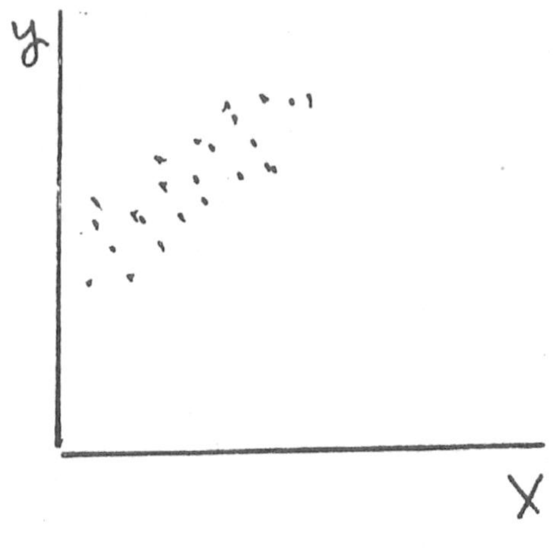

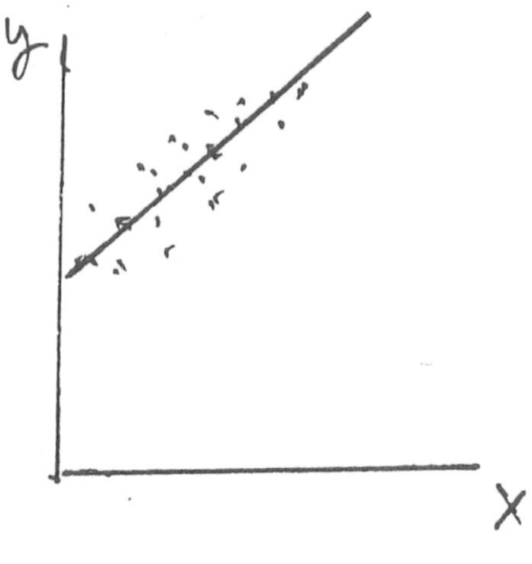

The distance from any point to the line (as shown in the next diagram), is called the "deviation." In its simplest form, the mathematical criteria for regression leads to minimizing the sum of the squared deviations from the fitted line.

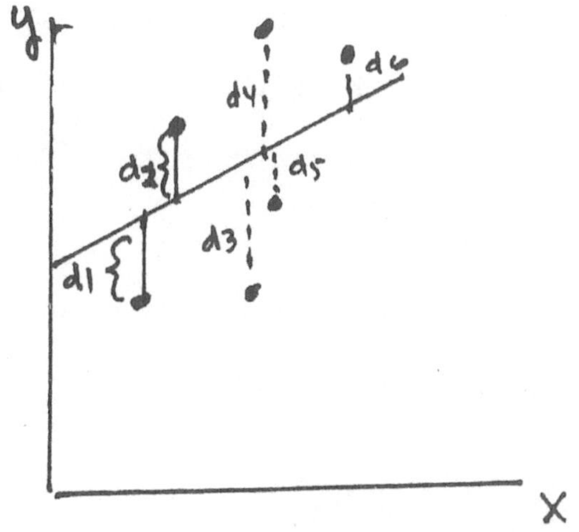

Thus, in the example above, six points are shown, with deviations d_1, d_2, d_3, d_4, d_5 and d_6. A different line would give a different set of deviations. The deviations are squared and summed, that is, we obtain $d_1^2 + d_2^2 + d_3^2 + d_5^2 + d_6^2$. The regression procedure picks that line which minimizes this sum; hence, the name "least squares" which is applied to regression analysis in its simplest form.

The equation of the fitted line is often written as: $\hat{y} = \hat{a} + \hat{b}x$.

The "hats" or carats over the y, a and b indicate that a line has been fitted to the observed data on y and x, which were the source of the scattered points. The $\hat{y}$ falls on the fitted line; that is, for any given x, the corresponding reading for y that emerges from the equation $\hat{a} + \hat{b}x$ will necessarily fall on the line, and will be designated $\hat{y}$.

More than one variable can be used to explain the variation in a dependent variable, with hypothesized equations including the following:

$$y = a + bx + cz;$$

$$y = a + bx + cx^2 + dx^3;$$

$$y = a + b_1x_1 + b_2x_2 = b_3x_3 + \ldots + bmXm$$

In the last equation, there are m explanatory variables, where m can be any number; the three dots indicate that b_4x_4, b_5x_5, b_6x_6, etc., have been omitted for the sake of brevity. Note that the second equation in this group is nonlinear in x; that is, y can be related to x by other than a straight line.

If we wanted to work with the linear-in-log form of equation, we would employ m explanatory variables in this fashion; our original equation would be:

$$Y = AX_1^{b_1} X_2^{b_2} X_3^{b_3} \ldots X_m^{b_m}$$

In the logs, this equation would become:

$y = a + b_1x_1 + b_2x_2 + b_3x_3 + \ldots + b_mx_m$ where lower case again indicates logs.

The fitted regression equation would be:

$$\hat{y} = \hat{a} = \hat{b}_1x_1 + \hat{b}_2x_2 + \hat{b}_3x_3 + \ldots + \hat{b}_mx_m.$$

The linear-in-log form has several advantages over alternative equations. First, fewer variables are needed to account for a non-linear relationship. Thus, for the equation $Y = AX^b$, the arithmetic form of the relationship (prior to taking logs) will look like the following, depending on the value of b:

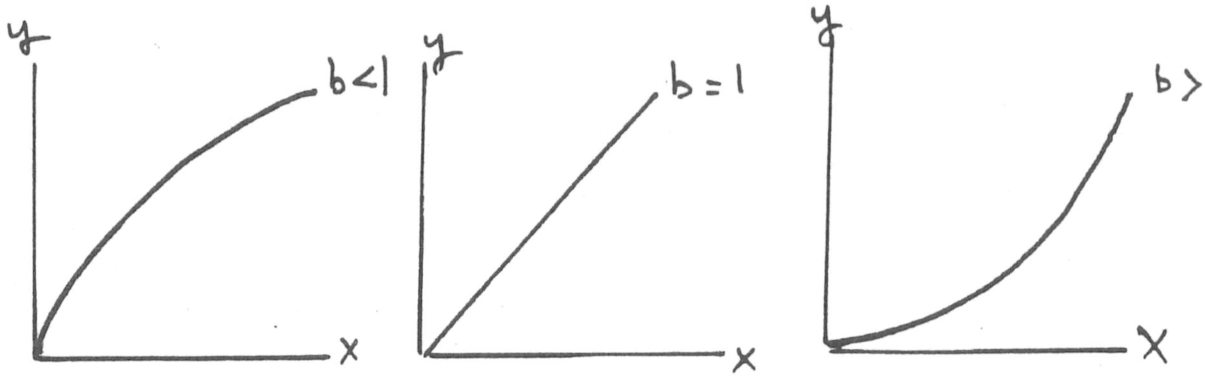

Second, the b are direct measures of economic "elasticities," that is, readings of the percentage change in y for a given percentage in x, if we have one independent variable. If we have a number of independent variables, then a given estimated coefficient is the estimated elasticity of Y with respect to the associated explanatory variable; thus $\hat{b}_5$ is the estimated elasticity expressing the effect of a percentage change in X_5 on Y, in percentage terms.

How good a job is performed by the fitted regression curve is given by several measures. A measure of the amount of variation in y that is attributable to x is given by R^2, the "coefficient of mutual determination." If there is only one explanatory variable, R^2 equals the square of the correlation coefficient measuring the association of x and y. R^2 can range from 0, indicating no explanation of variation, to 1.0, indicating a complete explanation. The extreme cases are illustrated by the following graphic examples:

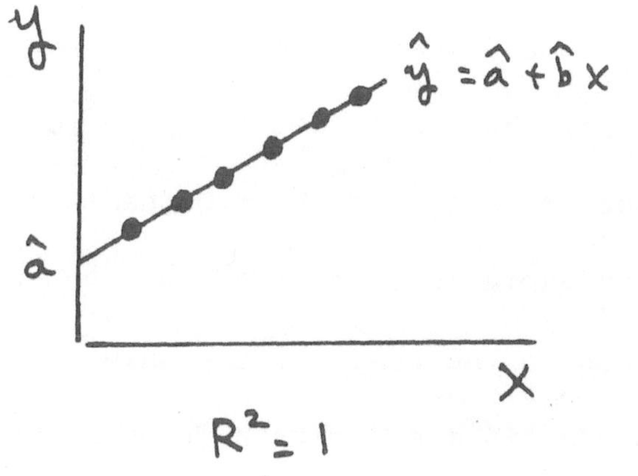

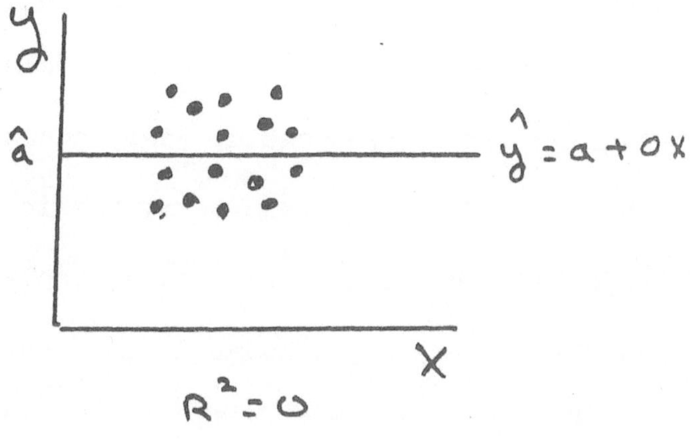

When R^2 equals its maximum value of 1.0, all of the observed points lie on the fitted line; by relating y to x, we explain all the variation that occurs in y. When R^2 equals its minimum of zero, the fitted line has assigned a value of zero to the coefficient of x; the presumed explanatory variable turns out to explain none of the variation in y.

To generalize, when working with a number of explanatory variables, the maximum R^2 of 1.0 means that the set of explanatory variables, in conjunction, have explained all of the variation in y; the minimum R^2 of 0 means that the set of explanatory variables have explained none of the variation.

In practice, the "adjusted" coefficient, $\bar{R}^2$, rather than R^2, is used. $\bar{R}^2$ typically is a bit smaller than R^2, accounting mathematically for a small loss of precision that occurs in curve fitting. The same interpretations hold: the higher the value of $\bar{R}^2$ that is obtained, the better the explanation afforded by the regression equations, with a value of 1.0 the maximum possible. Low values of $\bar{R}^2$, approaching zero, mean that the putative explanatory variables in fact are of lilttle help in explaining y.

The t-ratio is a measure or "statistic" that is obtained as one of the regression results, with a particular t ratio obtained for each coefficient in the regression equation, including a; that is, we are given a t-ratio for a, another for b_1, another for b_2, and so on. The t ratio is used to test the hypothesis that the true value of a coefficient is equal to zero, that is, the corresponding independent variable has no effect on y, or in the case of the constant term, the intercept is zero. If the hypothesis is rejected, then the corresponding explanatory variable is said to be "statistically significant." The test occurs on the basis of the value of the t-ratio. If that ratio, in absolute terms, is greater than or equal to a given "critical value," we reject the hypothesis of a zero coefficient. If not, we accept the hypothesis.

The decision making here is fairly complex, and runs this way. For a very large sample, if the t ratio is greater than or equal to 1.96, or less than or equal to -1.96, we conclude that there is only one chance in 20 that the true value of the coefficient is zero. Given those odds, we are willing to run the associated risk and reject the zero hypothesis. We operate here at the "5 percent significance level" (the source of the one chance in 20 statement). If we are less cautious and are willing to reject the zero hypothesis when there is one chance in 10 that it is really true, then we use the values of 1.645, or -1.645, as our test criterion. A t ratio equal to or above 1.645 or equal to or below -1.645 is interpreted as meaning that b is really not zero, and that the associated explanatory variable is statistically significant. Here we operate at the 10 percent level of significance.

The 1.96 and 1.645 values hold for very large samples (strictly speaking, for samples of infinite size). However, for samples of over 120 observations, those values are good approximations. To be precise, the critical values for the t-ratio depend on sample size and number of explanatory variables including the constant term. The sample size minus the number of explanatory variables equals "degrees of freedom." The following list shows the "critical value" of the t ratio used in testing hypotheses for various degrees of freedom and for the 5 percent and 10 percent significance level. The value is interpreted as a plus and minus reading, for example +1.96 and -1.96.

	Critical Value	
Degrees of freedom	5% level	10% level
Infinite	1.96	1.645
120	1.98	1.658
60	2.00	1.671
30	2.04	1.697

Strictly speaking, for samples of intermediate sizes, the proper t ratio for testing is obtained by interpolation. For samples of over 120 degrees of freedom, however, the easiest course is to use the values for the infinite sample.

Applications in This Study

In chapters 6 and 7, we report on the regression equations employing hypothesized linear-in-log relationships. In a series of initial regression analyses, results were obtained for both linear and linear-in-log forms of hypothesized relationships, and the linear-in-log forms always yielded better results, as measured by $\bar{R}^2$ and t ratios. hence, the linear-in-log form was chosen as the best vehicle for all of our analyses.

In both chapters, dependent variables employed cover a number of transport energy and associated transport consumption variables. The transport energy variables included per capita levels of motor gasoline use, all transportation fuels, transportation fuels by mode (road, rail, air and water) and diesel fuels used in transport (total and specific mode). The associated transport consumption variables included per capita measures of rail passenger use, rail freight use, automobile registrations and truck registrations. Finally, the level of motor gasoline per registered automobile was also used as a dependent variable. In Chapter 6 we discuss results obtained when each of those variables, in turn, was related to per capita income and a relevant price. In Chapter 7, those explanatory variables were augmented by a number of variables including density of the road network; three measures of population distribution: population density, percent of population in urban areas, and percent of the urban population in the largest city; year, to measure time trend; percent of the population of medium age (15-65); and rank change in per capita income from 1960 to 1980, a measure of relative growth in income. In some equations, per capita use of an alternative mode was also included, to examine competitive relationships.

As noted in the earlier sections, sample coverage included 77 countries with 54 categorized as developing countries. The latter were further categorized into low, medium, and high income groupings. In the regression work of Chapters 6 and 7, that income categorization was based on average RGDP ranking over the three periods 1960, 1970 and 1980, since the concern was with accounting for behavior during the period under study. An alternative categorization, used in the remainder of this report, was based on RGDP ranking in 1980. That approach appeared best for purposes of prediction, with a year close to the present used as base period. Differences between the two sets of groupings were relatively minor. Thus, Indonesia and Cameroon were included, and Zambia and Ghana excluded from the low income category employed in the regression analyses. The respective coverage of the two groupings is indicated by this list:

1960-80 Grouping	1980 Grouping: Low income	Medium income	High income
Low income	8 countries in common	Indonesia Cameroon	None
Medium income	Zambia Ghana	13 countries in common	Dominican Republic
High income	None	Iran Colombia Peru Turkey	24 countries in common

Additional detail on country coverage appears in appendix I, as do details on sources of data, variable definitions and measurement.

A difficulty with our data is worth dwelling on. Because many of the data series were obtained from a variety of sources, and because some of those series, in turn, involved incomplete coverage, many of our variables differ considerably in country and year coverage. The regression equations omit all readings on a given year and country when an observation on one variable is not available. This posed several problems. First, when the extended set of explanatory variables was employed, the number of observations available dropped considerably. Thus, for the developing country regressions using only per capita income and price as explanatory variables, 346 observations were available when using motor gasoline as the dependent variable, and 880 observations when using automobile registrations; sample sizes dropped to 150 and 265 observations, respectively, for the full set of explanatory variables. In some cases the sample size fell so low that results had to be treated as unreliable. Second, it became difficult to compare cases, because sample coverage was ever changing. This difficulty applied to comparisons of different equations using the same dependent variable and alternative sets of independent variables, and to comparisons across equations, using different dependent variables. Third, because many different sources were employed, differences in definition and coverage of the same variables inevitably occurred. There were considerable efforts to establish consistency, and these are also documented in appendix I.

A related difficulty in coverage occurred because of limited information on transport prices. Under the heading of fuel prices, use was made of motor gasoline and diesel fuel prices, but the limited nature of coverage for the latter implied the necessity of placing primary reliance on the former. We thus treated gasoline price as a proxy for transport fuel prices, generally. We also employed estimated new automobile price as our measure of the relevant price for both automobile and truck registrations.

Despite these difficulties, our regression equations generally performed well, in terms of explained variances, t ratios, and--most importantly--general reasonableness and consistency of results. There were occasional anomalies and questionable results, ascribable to "sampling variability," which may be a kind way of recognizing occasionally flawed data. But the overall patterns revealed seemed plausible and encouraging.

The tables reporting detailed results of the regression work appear at the conclusions of Chapters 6 and 7, respectively. Results in those cases are carried out to three decimal places. In the body of the chapters, it seemed best to present the results in terms of one decimal place; any loss of accuracy seemed more than made up by ease of communication.

Chapter 6

Regression Analyses Focusing on Income and Price Measures

Overview

Income per capita and price are major determinants of expenditures by the individual consumer. This chapter focuses on those variables in explaining transport energy use and levels of related transport activities. Three sources of statistical information are drawn upon in that explanation. The first is a set of regression results obtained by relating a transport energy or related variable to per capita income and price, only. Those results appear in this chapter. The second is the set of expanded regression equations presented in chapter 7, which also include results for income and price; many of those results are utilized here, while the discussion of results for the other explanatory variables is deferred to chapter 7. Finally, the third set of results is obtained from a literature review, presented for comparative purposes at the conclusion of this chapter.

A major goal of our work was to estimate income and price elasticities to use in projecting future consumption by developing countries. This was done by comparing a number of results and deriving a best estimate on the basis of those comparisons. Motor gasoline, all fuel use in transport, automobile registrations and truck registrations were viewed as the most important of our dependent variables, both in terms of their central importance in transportation, and in terms of reliability of estimates, given the data that were available. The "ultimate" income and price elasticity estimates derived for those dependent variables, for all developing countries as a group, were as follows:

	Income elasticity	Price elasticity
Motor gasoline	1.4	-0.4
All transport fuel	1.2	-0.15
Automobile registrations	1.65	-0.6
Truck registrations	1.1	-0.5

Put intuitively, a one percent increase in per capita income is estimated to cause somewhat more than a one percent increase in consumption in all these cases, with the greatest effect occurring for automobile registrations (a 1.65 percent increase) followed by that for motor gasoline (a 1.4 percent increase). Other evidence shows a fall in motor gasoline use per car as income increases in developing countries, so these results appear consistent. The lower income elasticity for trucks than for cars seems consistent with a general shift from trucks to cars that appears to occur as income increases. That shift, plus relatively slower growth in consumption of fuel for other transport modes as income increases, helps explain the lower elasticity for all fuel use than that for motor gasoline.

A price increase leads to decreased consumption in all these cases, with a one percent increase in price leading to approximately a half-percent decrease in consumption in all cases except all transport fuel, where the decline is only about two-tenths of a percent. The latter result may reflect some intermodal substitution that occurs with fuel price changes. Some of our results suggest that a shift from road to rail transport occurs as price increases, so that all fuel use consequently declines less than motor fuel use does. Since our evidence is not conclusive, we present this inference as an appealing hypothesis.

For the groups of developing countries categorized by income level, the corresponding elasticity estimates were:

	Income elasticity			Price elasticity		
	Low income	Medium income	High income	Low income	Medium income	High income
Motor gasoline	1.2	1.4	1.5	-0.5	-0.4	-0.3
All transport fuel	0.85	1.3	1.1	0	-0.2	-0.1
Auto registrations	1.7	1.5	1.6	-0.6	-0.6	-0.6
Truck registrations	1.2	1.1	1.0	-0.6	-0.4	-0.5

The divergence in income elasticity pattern between motor gasoline and auto registrations may be explainable by differences in gasoline use per car, with lower income developing countries apparently using their cars more intensively than higher income developing countries.

In general, however, though some differences in income and price elasticities occur between the groups, those differences do not seem profound.

The source of these estimates and additional information and hypotheses based on the regression equations will now be considered in some detail.

Regressions Relating Transport Variables to Price and Income Only

Relating each of our dependent variables only to price and income has both benefits and costs. The benefits emerge in part because of data limitations. When we expanded the number of explanatory variables appearing in our regression equations, we shrank our effective sample size, thus limiting the number of regressions that could be performed. This occurred because many of the independent variables spanned an individual set of countries and years, with incomplete overlap in coverage. Combined with limited coverage for some of the dependent variables, this often resulted in a sample size too small for reliable results. Further, in working with a large set of explanatory variables, it is often useful to winnow that set down to a subset of variables that are statistically significant, but this can be a costly, time-consuming process, imposing a constraint on such efforts. A problem that often arises when nonsignificant variables are not eliminated is distorted estimates because of correlations among the independent variables.

On the cost side, the use of only two explanatory variables runs the risk of biased results if other putative explanatory variables are correlated with income or price. That risk seemed worth taking, however, on the presumption that such correlation would be relatively low, limiting the bias. In practice, this presumption generally appeared to be borne out for the developing countries, because the introduction of the other explanatory variables did not greatly affect our income and price elasticity estimates in those cases that were common to each approach.

Tables exhibiting our regression results using only per capita income and price are presented at the conclusion of this section and appear in this sequence of dependent variable coverage: motor gasoline, tables 6.1 through 6.7; motor gasoline per automobile, table 6.8; automobile registration, truck registration, rail passenger use and rail freight use, tables 6.9 through 6.13; and all fuel use and diesel fuel use in transportation, by mode, tables 6.14 through 6.21. All of the tables are organized in the same fashion. Each table exhibits coefficient estimates, number of observations, t ratios and explained variance ($\bar{R}^2$) for each equation estimated. The coefficient estimate and t ratio headings each c ver results for the constant term, income and price.

We will discuss each of the sets of regression results, in turn.

Motor Gasoline

Tables 6.1 through 6.7 exhibit regression results for motor gasoline consumption. Both because of its importance as a major component of transport energy use, and because of a relatively large number of observations covering that use, more detailed results were obtained for motor gasoline than for the other forms of consumption.

In the tables on motor gasoline consumption, as in all the tables of this chapter, income elasticities are shown for income measured both by GNP per capita and by RGDP per capita, both deflated to 1975 dollars. In our predictions, we place primary reliance on RGDP, since that measure purports to account for price level differences between countries. However, because much previous work has been based on the use of GNP, it seemed helpful to include results for that measure as well.

Since the RGDP measure accounts for price level differences between countries, it typically reduces real income disparities between countries, relative to money or nominal income. (This is because poorer countries typically have lower price levels for domestic production than richer.) Consequently, we expected a general tendency for estimated income elasticities to be higher for the RGDP measure than for the GNP measure, and this in fact turned out to be the case, as exemplified in table 6.1. For both the world sample, with observations covering all the countries in our sample, and for the developing country group as a whole, the RGDP income elasticity was around 1.6; in contrast, the GNP income elasticity was 1.1 for the world sample and 1.2 for the developing countries. The likely explanation for the difference in results appears in the following diagram. Here we have a hypothetical situation of two countries, one a low income country, designated as L, and the other a high income country, designated as H. When we measure L's per capita income by GNP and plot it against consumption, we observe the point L_1; when instead, we use RGDP, we increase L's measured per capita income, leaving consumption unchanged, to yield point L_2. The per capita income of H is unchanged in both cases, which in fact is typical for high income countries such as the United States. Lines connecting the observed points show the RGDP line having greater slope than the GNP line, with the slope being the direct indicator of income elasticity. Curve fitting by regression equation yields analogous results.

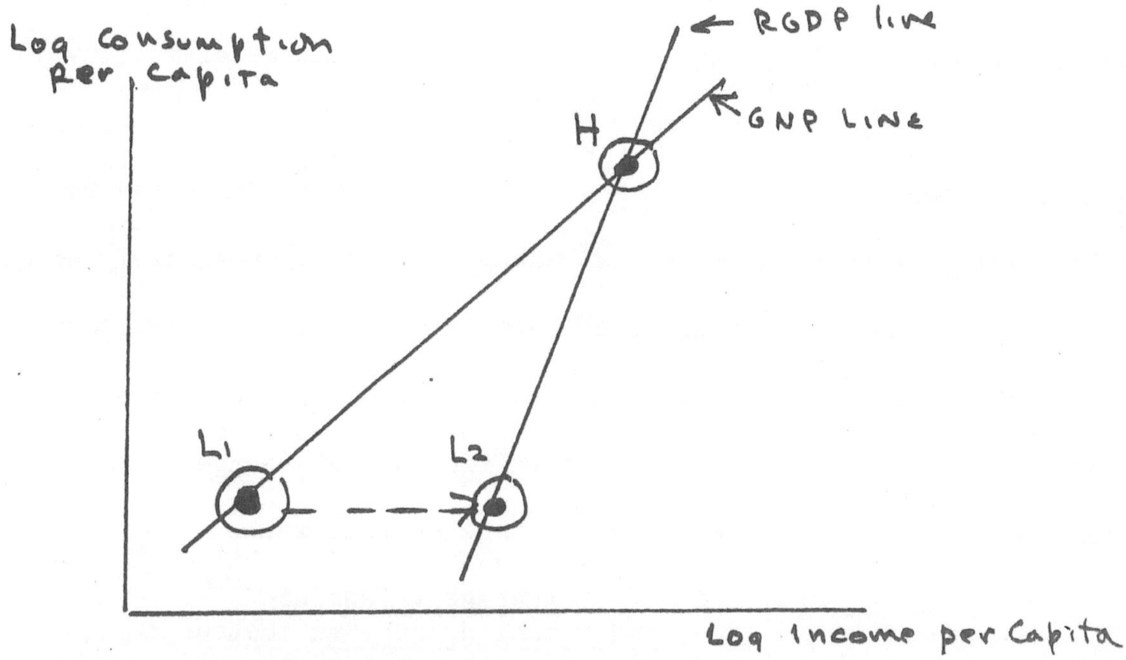

An increase in measured slope need not always occur. Consider a situation of two poor countries, A and B, with observed consumption related to GNP designated as A_1 and B_1, respectively. If replacing GNP by RGDP has a greater impact on B than on A, we will observe points A_2 and B_2. Lines connecting the respective pairs of points yield a higher slope for the GNP than for the RGDP measure. See diagram on next page.

Just this situation apparently occurred for the low income developing countries, which exhibit a lower income elasticity for RGDP (around 0.7)

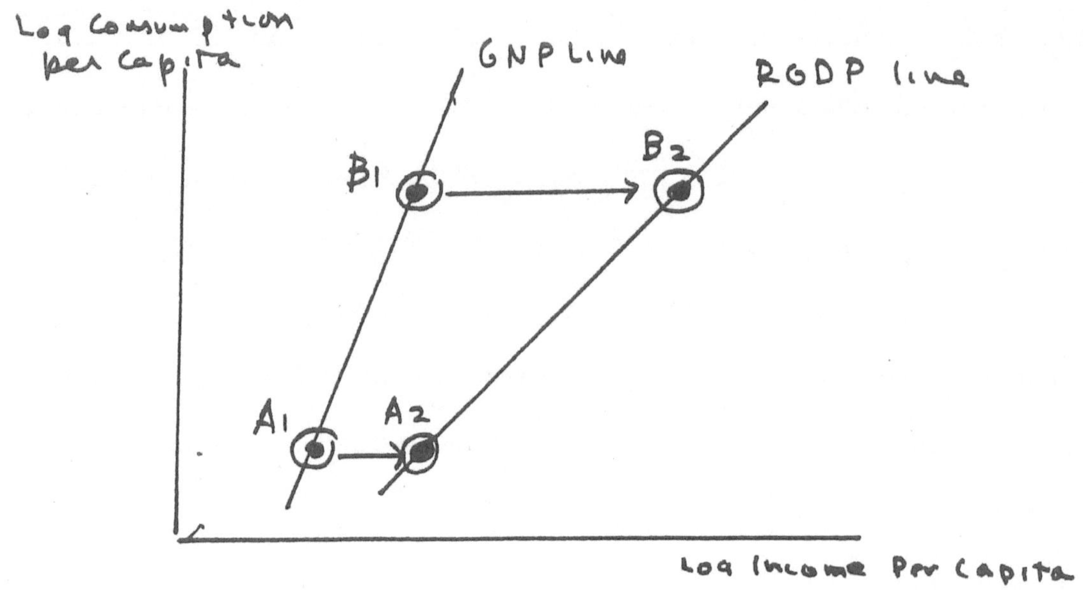

than for GNP (around 1.5), in table 6.1 In all other cases in that table, the RGDP income elasticity was well above the GNP income elasticity.

Table 6.2 exhibits gasoline regression results by continent, and here too, RGDP income elasticities were above corresponding GNP measures, save for the case of Africa where the two estimates were approximately equal. Tables 6.3 through 6.7 list gasoline regression results for individual country and though there is considerable variation between GNP and RGDP estimates, by country, when the country figures are averaged, the two estimates become quite close. The data are as follows:

	Average values of individual country estimates of income elasticity		
	RGDP	GNP	Number of cases
Africa	0.643	0.665	5
Asia	1.058	1.036	9
Europe (Free Mkt.)	1.505	1.474	13
North & Central America	1.108	1.062	6
South America	1.226	1.321	9
Oceania	1.068	1.078	1
All cases	1.187	1.189	43

These results fit the original explanation. Replacing an individual country's GNP by its RGDP measure in effect multiplies all observations through by the same constant. In the logs, this amounts to adding the log of that constant to all observations; but in regression analysis, that kind of change does not change coefficient estimates.

The RGDP results typically show income elasticities above 1.0; this is the case for all of the continent samples covered in table 6.2, as well as for the samples in table 6.1, with the exception of the low income developing country sample. That result also emerged for the individual country averages shown above. It also seems apparent, intuitively, when motor gasoline consumption is plotted against per capita RGDP. An example of that graphic pattern appears as figure 6.1, exhibiting 1970 arithmetic values for the developing countries. Similar patterns hold for 1960 and 1980 plots of the variables of interest.

It is sometimes hypothesized that individual country elasticities can be viewed as corresponding to short-run measures, while combined country elasticities can be viewed as corresponding to longer run measures, since a much greater range of income and prices typically is covered when we combine data on a number of countries. Extending the range corresponds to accounting for a much longer adjustment period.

There seems some evidence of this effect in combining groups of countries, as well. The pattern of a higher elasticity for an augmented grouping occurs in table 6.1; the developing countries as a group have an RGDP income elasticity of 1.6, in contrast to the respective values of 0.7, 1.0, and 1.2 for the RGDP income elasticities of the low, medium and high income subgroups. The effect also seems discernable in the patterns exhibited in figure 6.1.

Figure 6.1

GAS ON RGDP PER CAPITA IN 1970

PLOT OF PCCMGAS*RGDPCAP SYMBOL IS VALUE OF Z

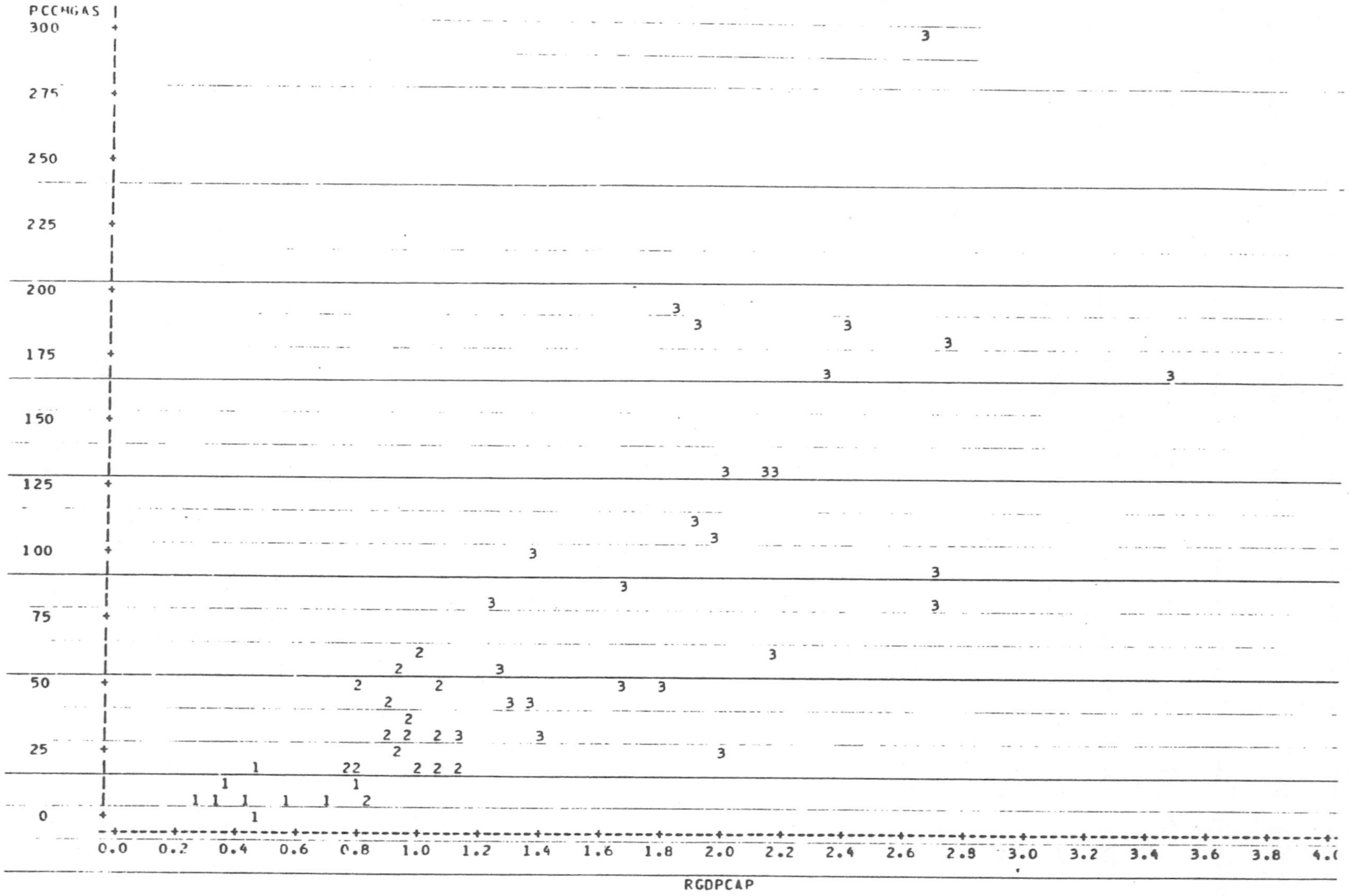

NOTE: 3 OBS HAD MISSING VALUES

LOW INCOME DEVELOPING, Z = 1
MEDIUM INCOME DEVELOPING, Z = 2
HIGH INCOME DEVELOPING, Z = 3

The effect seems marked in the case of price elasticity estimates for motor gasoline. Individual country averages, applying the data of tables 6.3 through 6.7, are as follows:

Average Values of Individual Country Estimates of Price Elasticities

	RGDP equations	GNP equations	Number of cases
Africa	.086	-.042	5
Asia	.063	-.043	9
Europe (Free Mkt)	-.025	-.052	13
North and Central America	-.114	-.179	6
South America	-.206	-.139	9
Oceania	.084	-.008	1
All cases	-.081	-.084	43

The overall average price elasticity of -.08 obtained in both the RGDP and the GNP equations contrasts with an estimated elasticity of -0.5 for the developing countries as a group, shown in table 6.1.

The influence of price on consumption is implicit in figures 6.2, 6.3 and 6.4 which plot motor gasoline consumption per capita on RGDP per capita for Gabon, India and the United States, respectively. The data covers 1960 through 1982, categorized within five year periods through 1979, and then for the period 1980-1982. In all three cases, the plots show a downward shift in consumption as a function of income for 1975-82 relative to the earlier years, no doubt reflecting the influence of higher prices in inhibiting consumption.

Of course, the plots for Gabon and India are indicative of the problems of data variability and reliability faced in analyses of this sort. The data plot for the United States, in contrast, is relatively well-behaved. Similar difficulties are evident in the individual country

Figure 6.2

GAS ON RGDP PER CAPITA FOR GABON

PLOT OF PCCMGAS*RGDPCAP   SYMBOL IS VALUE OF Z

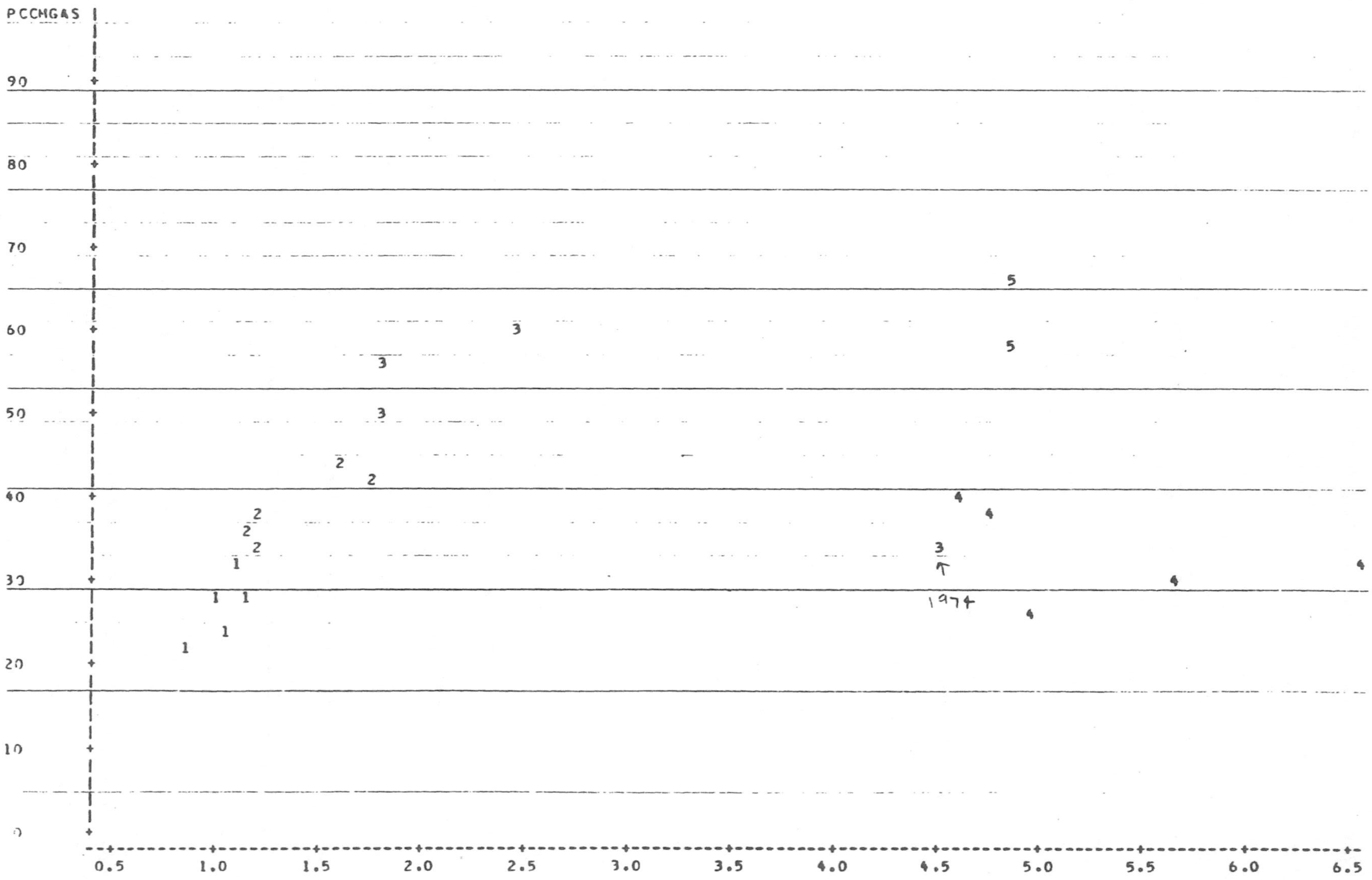

RGDPCAP

NOTE: 1 OBS HAD MISSING VALUES   1 OBS HIDDEN

FOR 1960-1964 : Z=1   1975-1979 : Z=4
1965-1969 : Z=2   1980-1982 : Z=5
1970-1974 : Z=3

Figure 6.3

GAS ON RGDP PER CAPITA FOR INDIA

PLOT OF PCCMGAS*RGDPCAP SYMBOL IS VALUE OF Z

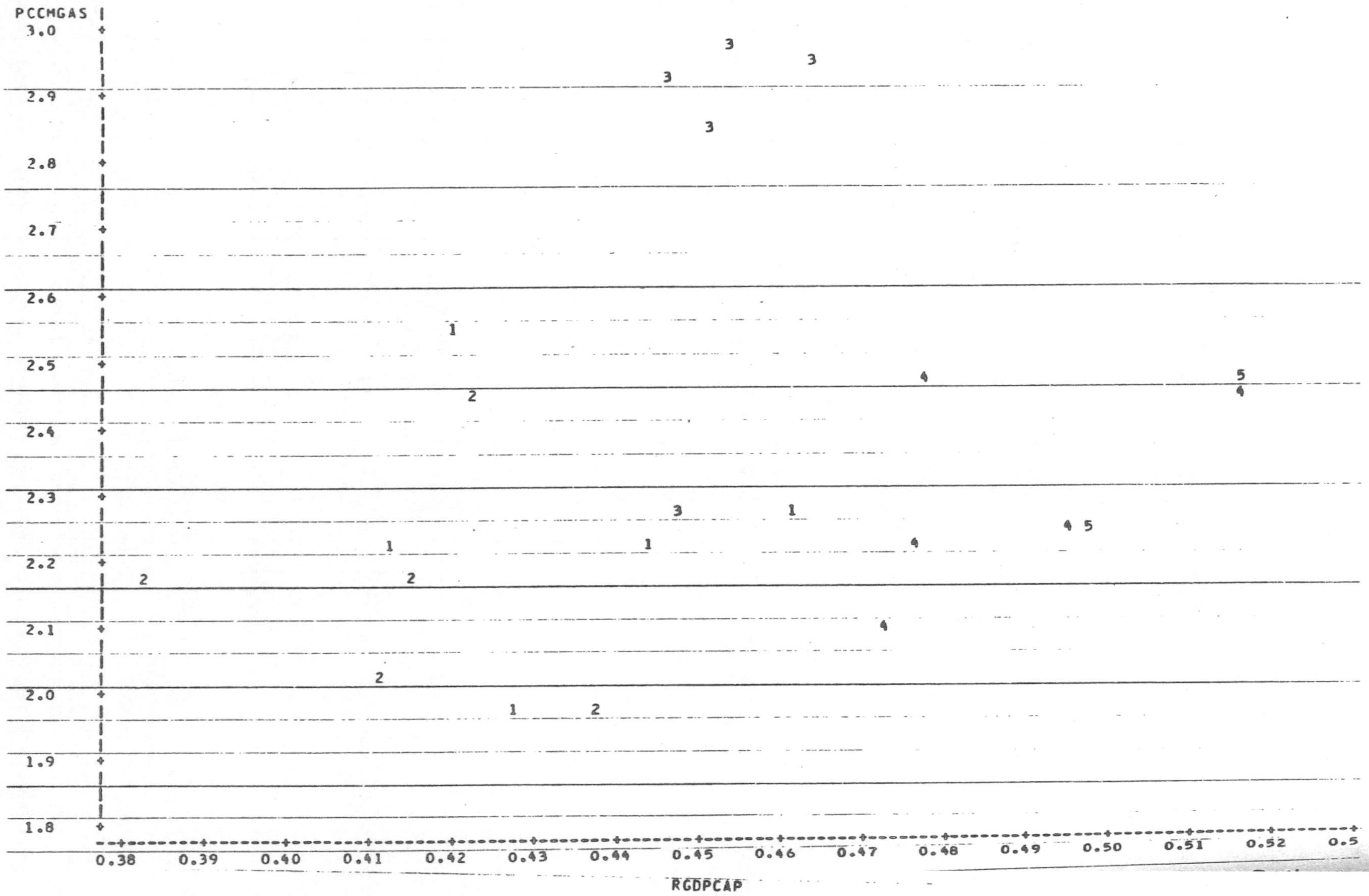

NOTE: 1 OBS HAD MISSING VALUES 1 OBS HIDDEN

FOR 1960-1964 : Z = 1
1965-1969 : Z = 2
1970-1974 : Z = 3
1975-1979 : Z = 4
1980-1982 : Z = 5

Figure 6.4

GAS ON RGDP PER CAPITA FOR U.S.

PLOT OF PCCMGAS*RGDPCAP   SYMBOL IS VALUE OF Z

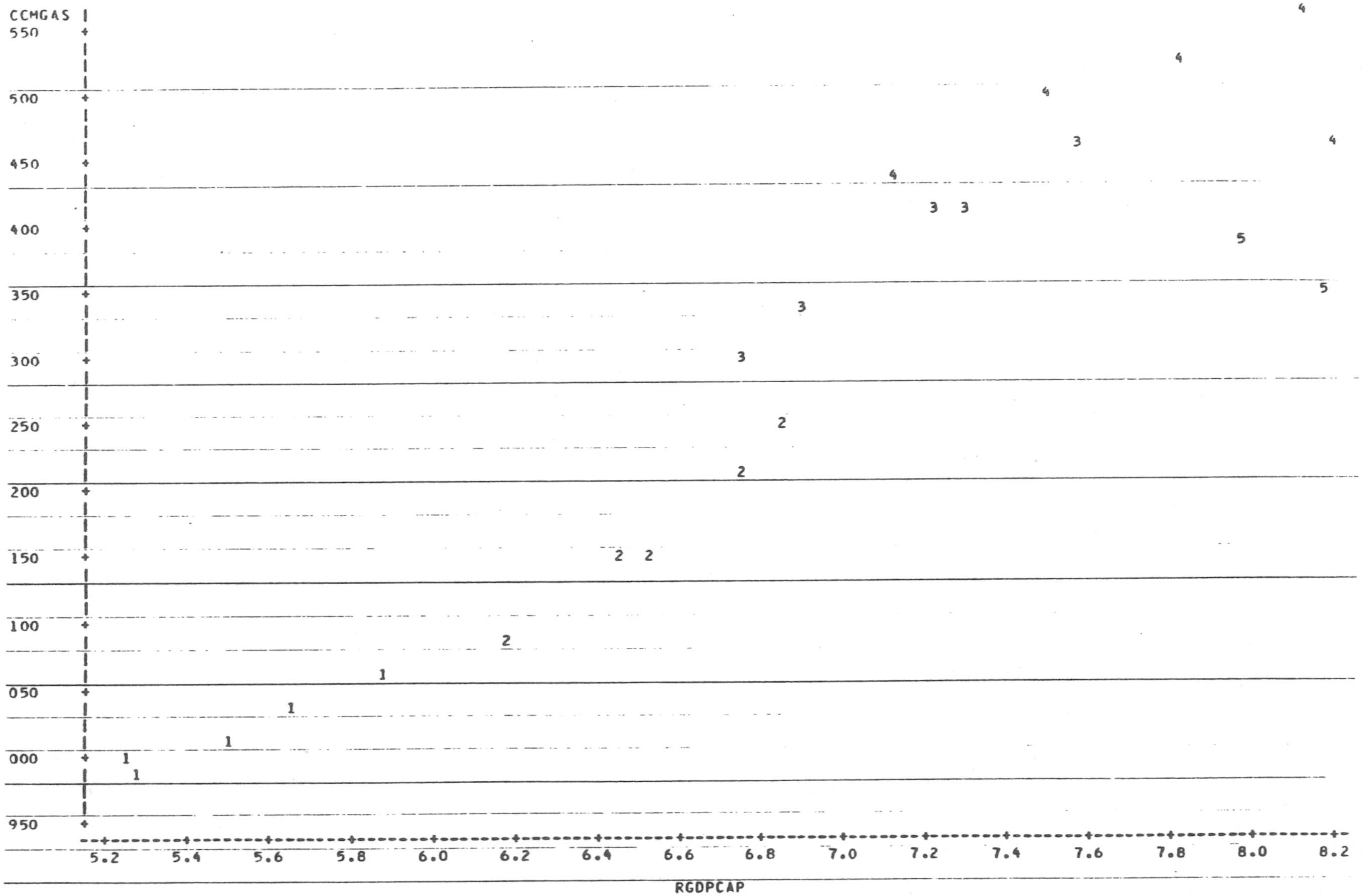

IOTE: 1 OBS HAD MISSING VALUES

For 1960-1964 : Z=1
1965-1969 : Z=2
1970-1974 : Z=3
1975-1979 : Z=4
1980-1982 : Z=5

results of tables 6.3 through 6.7, pointing to the difficulty in attaching much reliability to results obtained from small samples.

To develop the "ultimate" price and income elasticity estimates for use in making projections, key motor gasoline elasticity estimates were assembled from the tables in which they appeared, with this display of information resulting:

Country coverage	RGDP income elasticity	Price elasticity	Table source
World	1.6	-0.6	6.1
World	1.8	-0.4	7.1
Industrial countries	2.4	-0.7	6.1
Industrial countries	0.3	-0.1	7.1
All developing	1.6	-0.5	6.1
All developing	1.5	-0.4	7.1
All developing	1.4	-0.4	7.14
Low income developing	0.7	-0.7	6.1
Medium income developing	1.0	-0.6	6.1
High income developing	1.2	-0.4	6.1

The industrial countries' elasticity estimates changed markedly with the introduction of other explanatory variables (table 7.1 versus table 6.1). In contrast, the estimates for the developing countries were quite stable, changing little between table 6.1 (income and price only), table 7.1 (expanded set of explanatories), and table 7.14 (significant variables only).

The results shown above were integrated into a final set of estimates; in particular, estimated elasticities for the low, medium and high income groups were made consistent with the overall elasticity for the developing countries, while the variation between them was retained. The outcomes were as follows:

	Income elasticity	Price elasticity
All developing countries	1.4	-0.4
Low income developing	1.2	-0.5
Medium income developing	1.4	-0.4
High income developing	1.5	-0.3

Gasoline per Autombile

Table 6.8 presents regression equations that relate gasoline per car to per capita income and price. Both the developing countries as a group and the industrial countries have a strong, negative price elasticity, with coefficients around -0.7 in both cases, and high t ratios. Results in chapter 7 are consistent with these estimates, running at about -0.6 in both cases (see tables 7.2 and 7.14). Hence, a price increase of one percent leads to a gasoline per car decrease of about two-thirds of one percent, presumably reflecting fewer trips, shorter trips and increased fuel efficiency.

The subcategories of the developing countries all show essentially the same price response, with some minor variations in magnitude, perhaps involving sampling variability.

In contrast to the consistency of pattern for the price response, there are marked differences in the effect of income, with a positive RGDP income elasticity of 0.6 obtained for the industrial countries and a negative elasticity of -0.2 for the developing countries.

Parallel results appear in chapter 7, with minor changes in magnitude; there the industrial countries′ elasticity is 0.4 while that of the developing countries is -0.3.

A plausible hypothesis explaining these results is that in poor countries each car is utilized more than in rich countries, so that as income increases, utilization per car declines. There comes a point, however, where the pattern reverses, and increased income implies more and longer trips per car.

Automobile and Truck Registrations

Table 6.9 includes regression results for all countries (the world sample) covering automobile and truck registrations per capita, while tables 6.10 and 6.11 list results by country groups for those respective vehicle categories. The price variable used in all those cases was the price of new cars, since data on truck prices were not readily available. However, it seemed reasonable that car prices would be a good proxy for truck prices. The car price variable had two variants, labeled Price of Cars I and II, respectively. For all countries other than the United States, the first price measure consisted of the price of new imported cars in the U.S. augmented by a scale factor accounting for tariffs and taxes on new cars in each country for which data could be assembled. Those data held for the late 1970s but were assumed applicable to all years in the sample. The second price measure consisted of the first measure multiplied by the ratio of RGDP to GNP in each country; this second measure was employed in conjunction with RGDP, since it appeared consistency would be improved by putting car imports and adjusted income on the same basis. Finally, the U.S. car price was the weighted average price of imports and domestic car sales.

Obviously, the price measure was relatively crude since differences in shipping costs between countries were not included, domestic car production occurs in several countries and likely implies lower prices than we employed for those countries, and tariff rates and taxes change over time. Clearly, improvements in the automobile price measure would be called for in future work. Nevertheless, results obtained for the major country categories seemed quite reasonable. Key results and final estimates were as follows:

Country coverage	Auto registrations: RGDP income elasticity	Auto registrations: Price of cars II elasticity	Truck registrations: RGDP income elasticity	Truck registrations: Price of cars II elasticity	Table source
World	1.8	-0.3	1.3	-0.2	6.9
World	1.6	-0.6	0.8	-0.1	7.4
Developing countries	1.7	-0.4	1.4	-0.4	6.10, 6.11
Developing countries	1.6	-0.7	0.9	-0.6	7.4
Developing countries	1.7	-0.6	1.0	-0.6	7.14
Final estimates Developing countries	1.65	-0.6	1.1	-0.5	

The final estimates represented an integration of the key results to yield the most reasonable set of estimates.

The regressions of chapter 7 included the price of gasoline as well as the price of cars, and here, somewhat surprisingly, a small positive effect was registered. The gasoline price elasticity for automobiles was 0.2 and for trucks it was 0.3. It is possible that because higher gasoline prices have brought in their wake increased fuel efficiency that the upshot is that auto purchases become more attractive, but this interpretation is purely speculative.

For the developing country income subcategories, the income elasticity estimates obtained seemed generally reasonable, but some of the price elasticities were positive, perhaps reflecting omitted variables or flawed data. Hence, primary reliance was placed on the price elasticity estimate for the group as a whole in forming the individual group estimates. The final decisions were as follows:

	Automobiles		Trucks	
	Income elasticity	Price elasticity	Income elasticity	Price elasticity
Low income	1.7	-0.6	1.2	-0.6
Medium income	1.5	-0.6	1.1	-0.4
High income	1.6	-0.6	1.0	-0.5

Rail Passengers and Rail Freight

Table 6.9 includes regression results for all countries (the world sample) covering rail passenger and freight levels per capita, while tables 6.12 and 6.13 list results by country group for those respective categories of transportation consumption. Results obtained exhibit some marked differences in pattern between the two uses and between country groupings, as shown by the following assemblage of key results:

	Rail Passengers		Rail Freight		Table source
Country coverage	RGDP income elasticity	Gasoline price	RGDP income elasticity	Gasoline price	
World	0.6	1.2	1.2	0.8	6.9
World	0.1	0.6	1.4	1.1	7.7,7.8
Developing	0.1	1.0	0.7	1.1	6.12,6.13
Developing	1.1	1.0	1.8	1.8	7.7,7.8
Developing	1.2	0.9	1.7	1.6	7.14
Industrial	-0.9	1.4	2.6	-1.5	6.12,6.13
Industrial	-0.7	1.2	2.6	-0.6	7.7,7.8

In developing the price elasticities, the price of motor gasoline was employed as a surrogate for the relevant rail transport price; this was done to maximize sample size, since a much smaller sample would be available if diesel fuel prices were used.

Price elasticities were positive for rail passenger use in both developing and industrial countries. They were also positive for freight use in developing countries but were negative for that use in industrial countries. A hypothesis explaining these results is that there has been modal substitution of transport use in response to higher prices, at least for some categories of use; that is, some passenger and freight traffic has moved from road to rail, accounting for the positive elasticities that are obtained.

Income elasticities are positive for the developing countries in both passenger and freight use; they are also positive for freight use in the industrial countries, but are negative for passenger use in the industrial countries. This occurred for the regressions using the expanded set of explanatory variables, as well as for the regressions using only income and price; the expanded set included "year" to account for time trend, so the result appears to involve more than the downward trend in rail use; or at least, to help explain that trend. It appears that rail passenger use is a species of inferior good, with use decreasing as per capita income increases. No doubt this reflects the shift from rail to automobile that occurs as income increases. However, that shift is not yet manifest in the developing countries, on the basis of our regression results.

All Fuel Use and Diesel Fuel Use by Transport Mode

We now consider the per capita consumption of all fuel used in transportation, and all fuel used in each transport mode: road, rail, air and water. Elasticities for those categories covering all countries (the world sample) appear as table 6.14. In parallel fashion, regression results for the consumption of diesel fuel, using the same modal classification, appear for the world sample in table 6.15; that is, the table shows elasticities for all diesel fuel use in transportation and in each of the relevant modes for diesel: road, rail and water. Tables 6.16 through 6.20 present elasticities for finer breakdowns of all transport fuel use. Tables 6.16 and 6.17 respectively list results by mode for the developing and the industrial countries. Table 6.18, 6.19 and 6.20 respectively list elasticities by country group for all transport fuel, all fuel use in road transport and all fuel use in rail transport. The country groups include the developing country subgroups categorized by income level.

Finally, table 6.21 lists elasticities for diesel use by transport mode for the developing countries. Small sample size made parallel results for industrial country use unreliable, so those estimates were not developed.

The assembly of key results for all fuel use in transportation, that is, for the aggregate of all modes, follows; in that assemblage, some of the cases first used motor gasoline price and then used diesel price as proxies for all transport fuel prices. Results were quite similar for those variants, indicated by gas and dsl, respectively.

Country coverage	RGDP income elasticity	Price elasticity	Table source
World-gas	1.3	-.2	6.14
World-dsl	1.3	-.2	6.14
World-gas	1.3	-.1	7.9
Developing-gas	1.3	-.1	6.16
Developing-dsl	1.0	-.2	6.16
Developing-gas	1.2	-.1	7.9
Developing-gas	1.2	-.1	7.15
Industrial-gas	1.8	-.6	6.17
Industrial-dsl	2.0	-.5	6.17
Industrial-gas	1.3	-.6	7.9
Developing country final estimates	1.2	-.15	

Within the major groupings, results seem basically consistent between the different equations (and tables) that are their sources. The final estimates then emerged naturally by giving essentially equal weights to the alternative results obtained for the developing countries.

It is noteworthy that both income and price elasticies for the industrial countries are well above those for the developing countries (in absolute terms). Perhaps that is a concomitant of development. The greater price elasticity, (-.6 versus -.15) may indicate greater flexibility of response to price changes. Alternatively, as we saw earlier in the results for rail passengers and rail freight, and as we shall see below for rail fuel use, the low price elasticity for developing countries may be explainable by increased rail use as transport prices rise. A greater income elasticity for industrial countries than for developing countries also occurred in motor gasoline use (table 6.1). We may speculate that this is either a cause or an effect of development.

From table 6.18, the estimated elasticities for the developing country subgroups were:

	Income elasticity	Price elasticity
Low income	0.7	0.2
Medium income	1.8	-0.3
High income	1.1	-0.1

These were modified to yield greater consistency between groups and to establish consistency with the overall elasticity estimates, with the following values obtained as a result:

	Income elasticity	Price elasticity
Low income	0.85	0
Medium income	1.3	-0.2
High income	1.1	-0.1

Turning to all fuel use per capita by individual transport modes, the following key results were obtained for road and rail use; motor gasoline and diesel prices are again indicated by gas and dsl:

Country coverage	Road Use: RGDP income elasticity	Road Use: Price elasticity	Rail Use: RGDP income elasticity	Rail Use: Price elasticity	Table source
World-gas	1.5	-0.3	0.9	0	6.14
World-gas	1.5	-0.3	0.6	0.9	6.14
World-gas	1.4	-0.2	0.5	-0.1	7.10,7.11
Developing-gas	1.5	-0.2	0.4	0.7	6.16
Developing-dsl	1.5	-0.2	0.1	1.4	6.16
Developing-gas	1.2	-0.2	-0.1	0.6	7.10,7.11
Developing-gas	1.3	-0.2	-0.1	0.6	7.15
Industrial-gas	1.9	-0.6	1.8	-0.9	6.17
Industrial-dsl	2.0	-0.5	2.8	-0.4	6.17
Industrial-gas	1.3	-0.6	1.5	-0.8	7.11

The results for road use seem stable, internally consistent and also consistent with the results for motor gasoline and all transport fuels. Our final estimates for those categories were as follows for the developing countries:

	Income elasticity	Price elasticity
Motor gasoline	1.4	-0.4
All transport fuels	1.2	-0.15

The "final" road use elasticities for the developing countries can be estimated as 1.3 for income elasticity and -0.2 for price elasticity, with both falling between the corresponding results for motor gasoline and all fuel use. The road use elasticities are presumably below the motor gasoline values because of lower truck elasticities (compare the truck and auto results, above). And they are above the all fuel elasticities because the latter include other modes with lower elasticities. A prime example is rail use, with documentation in the data shown above. For the developing countries, income elasticity is low and price elasticity is positive, which should drive down the corresponding all transport fuel elasticities.

The positive price elasticity for rail use is consistent with the earlier results for both rail passenger and rail freight use in developing countries, as shown above. The income elasticities in those earlier cases were higher than the results obtained here, though perhaps the correspondence between fuel use and level of service is not one to one. The positive price elasticies again might be hypothesized to reflect some shifting from road to rail use in developing countries as a response to higher prices.

The final set of results for all fuel use per capita by mode cover air and water use, with these estimates, again using both gasoline and diesel prices:

	Air Use		Water Use		Table source
Country coverage	RGDP income elasticity	Price elasticity	RGDP income elasticity	Price elasticity	
World-gas	1.2	-0.1	1.5	-0.5	6.14
World-dsl	1.2	0	1.3	-0.2	6.14
World-gas	1.8	-0.1	-0.2	-0.1	7.12,7.13
Developing-gas	1.0	0.1	1.4	-0.1	6.16
Developing-dsl	1.1	0	1.5	0.3	6.16
Developing-gas	1.0	-0.5	-1.1	0.3	7.12,7.13
Developing-gas	1.1	-0.3	-0.9	0.2	7.15
Industrial-gas	2.0	-0.6	0	-1.5	6.17
Industrial-dsl	2.1	-0.3	0.2	-1.2	6.17
Industrial-gas	2.0	-0.9	-0.3	-1.1	7.12,7.13

In air transport, the income elasticity is stable within groups, and once again, the industrial country elasticity is well above that of the developing countries. The price elasticity for the latter group is essentially zero when only price and income are used, but becomes negative when other explanatory variables are included. If we treat 1.1 and -0.3 as our best estimates of income and price elasticity, respectively, the former is a bit below and the latter a bit above (in absolute terms) the corresponding values for all fuel use.

The results for water transportation are quite variable, probably reflecting small sample size and changes in sample coverage between equations. For the developing countries it seems clear that price elasticity is close to zero, but positive; this too may reflect some substitution of water for road transport, given higher prices. The income elasticity estimates are inconsistent between cases. Accounting for explanatory variables other than income and price causes the income elasticity to change from around 1.5 to around-1.0. That inconsistency suggests that an estimate of zero might be the safest choice. The industrial countries appear to have an income elasticity that is close to zero, while their price elasticity has a value around -1.2. In any event, these estimates must be treated with caution because data for water transport use were limited.

The final set of equations to be summarized here cover diesel use by transport mode. For the sake of brevity, we report on results relating diesel use to RGDP and diesel price, the latter seeming the most appropriate price in this case. Estimated elasticities for the world and the developing countries were as follows, from tables 6.15 and 6.21:

	World		Developing Countries	
Transport mode	RGDP income elasticity	Price elasticity	RGDP income elasticity	Price elasticity
All	1.1	-0.1	1.2	0
Road	1.2	-0.2	1.5	-0.2
Rail	0.8	-0.1	0.4	0.2
Water	1.1	0	1.3	0.1

Results seem basically consistent with those derived for all fuel use in transport.

Final Set of Estimates Over All Cases

If we now assemble and reorder final estimates derived for the developing countries, the following emerges:

	Income elasticity	Price elasticity
Automobiles	1.65	-0.65
Motor gasoline	1.4	-0.4
Trucks	1.1	-0.5
Fuel in road use	1.3	-0.2
Gasoline per auto	-0.3	-0.6
All fuel use	1.2	-0.15
Fuel for air use	1.1	-0.3
Fuel for water use	0	0.2
Fuel in rail use	0.2	0.8
Rail passengers	1.0	1.0
Rail freight	1.5	1.5

There seems a general consistency to the pattern. In particular, future work might be directed to developing information to test the hypothesis of a switch to rail and perhaps water use from road use, given higher prices. There are some obvious policy questions that emerge. If the substitution did in fact occur, was it economically rational? That is, was it justified on the basis of fuel economy and costs or did it occur because of government subsidies to railroads? Did the fuel economies involve other costs that exceeded the savings in fuel? A major problem in considering policy recommendations is the danger of suboptimization, implied by the last question. Fuel saving is an important goal, but it is not a goal to be considered in isolation. It is to be hoped that policy aimed at fuel saving also brings with it economic improvement, generally.

A Brief Review of the Literature on Income and Price Elasticities

To complete our discussion of income and price elasticities of demand, we consider corresponding demand estimates to be found in the literature. Our review will be brief, not only for economy of exposition, but because estimates of developing country demand elasticities are quite sparse, verging on being conspicuous by their absence. In contrast, many estimates are available for the U.S. and other industrial countries, but they are almost exclusively of gasoline use.

Reister estimates income elasticities for all energy demand by developing countries and his results are noteworthy because he compares a 1980 elasticity estimate for RGDP to a corresponding estimate for GDP (essentially the same as GNP). His results parallel ours, with the GDP estimate well below the RGDP estimate. His income elasticity estimates are:

	Income Elasticity	
	RGDP	GDP
1960	1.76	--
1970	1.74	--
1980	1.71	1.22

--: not listed

His results also indicate a slight downward trend in income elasticity over time.

Moavenzadah and Geltner present several estimates of short run and long run price elasticities for commercial energy demand in transport, comparing the U.S., Europe and Developing Countries. Averaging the figures they exhibit, the results are as follows.

	Price Elasticity	
	Short-run	Long-run
U.S.	-0.2	-0.8
Europe	-0.2	-1.0
Developing Countries	-0.3	-0.6

Their long-run elasticities appear to be somewhat above our elasticities, which we interpreted as long-run, but the respective categories are not easily comparable. Their long-run estimates do show developing country values below those of the industrial countries, paralleling what we found.

Choe presents gasoline price and income elasticities for the developing countries which are quite similar to those developed here. His estimates are compared to ours as follows:

Developing Country Estimates

	Income Elasticity	Price Elasticity Short-run	Price Elasticity Long-run
Choe	1.17	-0.12	-0.44
This study	1.4	--	-0.4

Ang projects considerably greater growth in per capita transport energy consumption in developing than in industrial countries, which can also be inferred from our results, which show lower price elasticities and somewhat higher income elasticities for the developing than for the industrial countries.

Not all comparisons yield results as congenial as these. For example, Kravis, Heston and Summers present world estimates that seem generally above the corresponding values found here. Thus we have these comparisons:

World Estimates

	Income Elasticity		Price Elasticity	
	Kravis Heston Summers	This Study	Kravis Heston Summers	This Study
Gasoline	1.6	1.8	-1.5	-0.4
Automobiles	2.1	1.6	-1.2	-0.6
Rail Transport	1.3	--	-0.6	--
Rail Passengers	--	0.1	--	0.6
Rail Fuel	--	0.5	--	-0.1

Wheaton presents world gasoline estimates that can be contrasted with those of Kravis, Heston and Summers; his income elasticity is somewhat elastic (above 1.0) and his price elasticity is somewhat inelastic (below 1.0); specifically, his estimates are 1.26 for income elasticity and -0.7 for price elasticity.

Kouris reviews the literature on gasoline demand elasticities for the industrial countries. For the U.S., he summarizes price elasticity estimates as being around -0.7 for the 1960s and early 1970s, but discerns a more elastic figure of around -1.0 currently.

Kouris also presents results of a series of studies on Western European country gasoline consumption which can be summarized as follows:

Western European Estimates

	Income Elasticity	Price Elasticity Short-run	Price Elasticity Long-run
Cato	0.34	-0.15	-0.69
IEA/OECD	0.85	-0.19	--
Pindyck	0.07	-0.11	-1.40

Dahl presents results for a large number of gasoline consumption studies, primarily covering the U.S., Europe and Japan. Those results were groped and averaged, with these outcomes:

Dahl review	Income	Price	Length of run	Number of studies
U.S.	0.41	-.14	Short run	12
U.S.	1.13	-.44	Long run	12
U.S.	0.36	-.39	Run not specified	15
Europe & Japan	0.57	-.22	Short run	5
Europe & Japan	1.22	-.66	Long run	5
Europe & Japan	0.85	-.61	Run not specified	15

Our industrial country results had gasoline income elasticity at 1.3, and price elasticity at -0.6, which seem more-or-less consistent with the industrial country results shown above, which admittedly are not too consistent among themselves.

The overall impression left by these comparisons is that our income elasticity estimates may be a bit above and our price elasticity estimates a bit below the central tendencies to be found in the other sets of results, but there nevertheless does seem a general consistency of pattern.

References

B. W. Ang, Modelling World Energy Demand for Transport, Energy Research Group, Dept. of Physics, University of Cambridge, Cambridge, England, Aug. 25, 1983.

D. B. Cato, "Energy Demand in the OECD Countries." Washington, D.C.: U.S. Department of Energy, Model Documentation Report, DOE/EIA-0296, March, 1981.

Boum-Jong Choe, A Model of World Energy Markets and OPEC Pricing, Washington, D.C., World Bank Staff Working Paper No. 633, 1984, 169 pp.

Carol A. Dahl, "Gasoline Demand Survey," Department of Economics, Louisiana State University, Baton Rouge, La., February 1984, xerox, 45 pp.

IEA/OECD, World Energy Outlook, Paris, France, 1982.

George Kouris, "Energy Demand Elasticities in Industrialized Countries: A Survey," The Energy Journal, July 1983, 73-94.

Irving B. Kravis, Alan Heston, and Robert Summers, World Product and Income, Baltimore: Johns Hopkins University Press, 1982.

Fred Moavenzadeh and David Geltner, "Transportation Energy and Economic Development," Energy Research 5: Transportation Energy and Economic Development, Amsterdam: Elsevier, 1984, p. 190.

R. S. Pindyck, "The Structure of World Energy Demand," Cambridge, Mass: MIT Energy Laboratory, Sept. 1978.

David B. Reister, "The Relationship Between Energy Demand and Gross National Product in Developing Countries," Oak Ridge, Tenn.: Institute for Energy Analysis, Oak Ridge Associated Universities, Feb. 19, 1985, xerox, 12 pp.

William C. Wheaton, "The Long-Run Structure of Transportation and Gasoline Demand" The Bell Journal of Economics, Autumn 1982.

Table 6.1

Regression Results for
Log per Capita Consumption of Motor Gasoline:
Developing vs. Industrialized Countries,
Using Income and Price Measures as Explanatory Variables

Country group	Coefficients			N	t Ratios			
	Constant	Log Per Cap Income	Log Price Motor Gas	No Obs.	Constant	Log Per Cap Income	Log Price Motor Gas	$\bar{R}^2$
World								
RGDP	3.212	1.604	-0.546	(535)	119.24	73.83	-19.62	.911
GNP	4.084	1.066	-0.642	(535)	192.38	69.90	-21.67	.901
All Developing Countries								
RGDP	3.243	1.565	-0.508	(346)	107.15	42.41	-15.05	.855
GNP	4.227	1.209	-0.550	(346)	159.86	48.22	-18.15	.883
Low Income Dev. Countries								
RGDP	2.350	0.653	-0.691	(60)	8.11	1.74	-3.31	.149
GNP	4.566	1.540	-0.691	(60)	15.72	9.49	-5.26	.653
Medium Income Dev. Countries								
RGDP	3.289	1.032	-0.625	(98)	90.66	7.71	-15.56	.737
GNP	3.884	0.672	-0.621	(98)	47.85	6.82	-14.81	.713
High Income Dev. Countries								
RGDP	3.649	1.178	-0.362	(188)	47.97	14.39	-10.77	.590
GNP	4.400	0.827	-0.400	(188)	129.97	14.55	-11.76	.595
Industrial countries								
RGDP	1.908	2.380	-0.713	(189)	11.99	25.66	-13.76	.839
GNP	3.908	1.127	-0.970	(189)	24.85	13.29	-12.41	.626

Regression Results for Log Per Capita
Consumption of Motor Gasoline: Continents,
Using Income and Price Measures as Explanatory Variables

Country group	Coefficients: Constant	Coefficients: Log Per Cap Income	Coefficients: Log Price Motor Gas	N No Obs.	t Ratios: Constant	t Ratios: Log Per Cap Income	t Ratios: Log Price Motor Gas	$\overline{R}^2$
World								
RGDP	3.212	1.604	-0.546	(535)	119.24	73.83	-19.62	.911
GNP	4.084	1.066	-0.642	(535)	192.38	69.90	-21.67	.901
GNP*	4.096	1.030	-0.518	(547)	174.48	62.37	-17.07	.877
Africa								
RGDP	3.378	1.115	-0.391	(61)	54.67	9.82	-2.16	.617
GNP	4.213	1.140	-0.503	(61)	57.49	14.08	-3.57	.769
Asia								
RGDP	2.899	1.660	-0.864	(114)	61.54	33.12	-9.53	.908
GNP	3.837	1.120	-0.716	(114)	78.37	32.66	-7.94	.905
GNP*	3.793	0.995	-0.280	(126)	67.91	29.89	-4.08	.882
Europe Free Market								
RDGP	2.604	1.843	-0.061	(164)	36.19	40.23	-1.18	.910
GNP	3.901	0.932	0.172	(164)	79.63	34.08	2.87	.878
No. and Cent. America								
RGDP	3.774	1.728	0.038	(73)	82.92	50.61	0.60	.974
GNP	4.721	1.213	-0.132	(73)	195.85	77.89	-3.28	.989
South America								
RGDP	3.666	1.157	-0.380	(111)	79.76	23.56	-16.60	.864
GNP	4.486	0.815	-0.359	(111)	160.65	23.36	-15.68	.862

*Includes Saudi Arabia.

Regression Results for
Log per Capita Consumption of Motor Gasoline: Africa,
Using Income and Price Measures as Explanatory Variables

	Coefficients				t Ratios			
Country group	Constant	Log Per Cap Income	Log Price Motor Gas	N No Obs.	Constant	Log Per Cap Income	Log Price Motor Gas	$\bar{R}^2$
Africa								
RGDP	3.378	1.115	-0.391	(61)	54.67	9.82	-2.16	.617
GNP	4.213	1.140	-0.503	(61)	57.49	14.08	-3.57	.769
Ghana								
RGDP	3.110	0.053	0.042	(13)	64.63	0.15	0.31	-.187
GNP	2.897	-0.190	-0.007	(13)	7.68	-0.56	-0.07	-.154
Kenya								
RGDP	4.273	1.753	0.420	(12)	9.96	3.22	2.94	.607
GNP	5.104	1.604	-0.058	(12)	13.24	5.75	-0.46	.818
Morocco								
RGDP	3.103	-0.001	-0.142	(13)	92.73	-0.002	-0.85	.077
GNP	3.261	0.199	-0.214	(13)	11.10	0.54	-1.38	.103
So. Africa								
RGDP	4.320	0.718	0.031	(12)	22.49	3.05	0.59	.480
GNP	4.646	0.930	-0.013	(12)	61.44	3.47	-0.23	.548
Tunisia								
RGDP	2.905	0.693	0.078	(11)	82.25	7.13	0.71	.873
GNP	3.421	0.780	0.081	(11)	66.36	9.36	0.95	.922

Out: 101 Algeria
102 Cameroon
103 Egypt
104 Gabon
106 Ivory Coast
108 Libya
109 Malawi
111 Nigeria
114 Zaire
115 Zambia

Table 6.4

Regression Results for
Log per Capita Consumption of Motor Gasoline: Asia,
Using Income and Price Measures as Explanatory Variables

	Coefficients				t Ratios			
Country group	Constant	Log Per Cap Income	Log Price Motor Gas	N No Obs.	Constant	Log Per Cap Income	Log Price Motor Gas	$\bar{R}^2$
Asia								
RGDP	2.899	1.660	-0.864	(114)	61.54	33.12	-9.53	.908
GNP	3.837	1.120	-0.716	(114)	78.37	32.66	-7.94	.905
GNP*	3.793	0.995	-0.280	(126)	67.91	29.89	-4.08	.882
Burma								
RGDP	3.219	1.160	0.039	(11)	3.89	1.61	0.52	.061
GNP	4.099	0.954	0.040	(11)	4.18	2.26	0.62	.241
India								
RGDP	1.002	0.018	-0.361	(13)	3.86	0.05	-5.17	.712
GNP	1.086	0.048	-0.364	(13)	1.89	0.17	-5.26	.712
Indonesia								
RGDP	3.293	0.824	0.201	(12)	40.10	10.23	1.36	.954
GNP	4.830	1.407	0.189	(12)	31.62	10.03	1.25	.952
Israel								
RGDP	3.629	1.207	-0.028	(13)	12.55	5.69	-0.51	.852
GNP	4.000	1.184	-0.015	(13)	18.04	5.75	-0.29	.855
Japan								
RGDP	3.275	1.237	0.058	(13)	32.96	18.88	1.37	.982
GNP	3.327	1.135	-0.057	(13)	31.90	17.50	-1.15	.979
Pakistan								
RGDP	2.187	0.734	0.350	(12)	3.54	0.60	0.93	-.017
GNP	2.204	0.227	0.388	(12)	1.70	0.30	1.01	-.047
Philippines								
RGDP	3.598	0.573	-0.309	(13)	119.74	1.57	-5.47	.826
GNP	3.984	0.462	-0.304	(13)	15.12	1.54	-5.55	.825
Thailand								
RGDP	3.471	1.446	-0.148	(13)	55.13	5.01	-0.89	.780
GNP	4.801	1.399	-0.155	(13)	20.00	5.03	-0.91	.781
Turkey								
RGDP	2.331	2.322	-0.372	(13)	11.52	7.46	-2.19	.827
GNP	3.885	2.507	-0.108	(13)	71.91	9.39	-0.86	.885

*Includes Saudi Arabia.

Out: 201 Bangladesh, 203 China, 204 Hong Kong, 207 Iran, 208 Iraq, 211 Jordan, 212 Kenya, 213 Kuwait, 214 Malaysia, 218 Singapore, 219 Syria, 220 Taiwan

Table 6.5

Regression Results for
Log per Capita Consumption of Motor Gasoline: Europe-Free Market,
Using Income and Price Measures as Explanatory Variables

(Out: Cyprus)

	Coefficients				t Ratios			
Country group	Constant	Log Per Cap Income	Log Price Motor Gas	N No Obs.	Constant	Log Per Cap Income	Log Price Motor Gas	$\bar{R}^2$
Europe-Free Mkt								
RGDP	2.604	1.843	-0.061	(164)	36.19	40.23	-1.18	.910
GNP	3.901	0.932	0.172	(164)	79.63	34.08	2.87	.878
Belgium								
RGDP	3.007	1.580	-0.153	(13)	10.14	8.46	-1.64	.919
GNP	2.623	1.557	-0.258	(13)	6.45	7.11	-2.12	.891
Denmark								
RGDP	5.584	0.135	0.040	(11)	16.85	0.71	0.56	.037
GNP	5.711	0.054	0.056	(11)	16.62	0.32	0.72	-.012
Finland								
RGDP	2.721	1.827	-0.185	(13)	9.58	9.99	-2.14	.915
GNP	2.947	1.572	-0.163	(13)	10.27	9.10	-1.76	.899
France								
RGDP	3.495	1.296	-0.126	(12)	28.96	17.43	-2.61	.976
GNP	3.203	1.382	-0.210	(12)	20.28	15.15	-3.55	.969
W. Germany								
RGDP	2.339	1.952	-0.004	(12)	6.91	9.81	-0.04	.955
GNP	1.731	1.997	-0.080	(12)	4.31	9.77	-0.74	.955
Greece								
RGDP	2.292	2.072	-0.126	(13)	21.47	20.73	-1.83	.982
GNP	2.928	1.973	-0.074	(13)	49.87	27.16	-1.45	.990
Italy								
RGDP	3.230	1.602	-0.302	(13)	12.15	7.49	-2.58	.848
GNP	3.577	1.514	-0.414	(13)	15.85	7.30	-3.17	.841
Netherlands								
RGDP	2.976	1.593	0.100	(13)	5.53	4.70	0.71	.857
GNP	2.111	1.830	-0.068	(13)	3.41	5.49	-0.46	.885
Portugal								
RGDP	3.218	1.191	-0.066	(13)	15.90	4.91	-0.34	.713
GNP	3.796	1.299	0.002	(13)	51.82	6.88	0.01	.829
Spain								
RGDP	1.432	2.466	0.154	(13)	4.50	10.09	1.29	.943
GNP	2.109	2.373	0.142	(13)	7.88	9.47	1.12	.936
Sweden								
RGDP	5.345	0.339	0.313	(12)	6.85	0.78	1.95	.529
GNP	5.163	0.379	0.287	(12)	5.24	0.80	1.57	.531
Switzerland								
RGDP	2.450	1.952	0.055	(13)	7.22	10.33	1.42	.945
GNP	1.888	1.733	0.130	(13)	3.29	7.08	2.64	.894
UK								
RGDP	3.305	1.566	-0.020	(13)	11.46	8.28	-0.33	.893
GNP	3.519	1.494	-0.023	(13)	13.52	8.35	-0.38	.894

Table 6.6

Regression Results for
Log per Capita Consumption of Motor Gasoline: North and Central America,
Using Income and Price Measures as Explanatory Variables

	Coefficients				t Ratios			
Country group	Constant	Log Per Cap Income	Log Price Motor Gas	N No Obs.	Constant	Log Per Cap Income	Log Price Motor Gas	$\bar{R}^2$
N. & Cent. America								
RGDP	3.774	1.728	0.038	(73)	82.92	50.61	0.60	0.974
GNP	4.721	1.213	-0.132	(73)	195.85	77.89	-3.28	0.989
N. & Cent. America excluding US & Canada								
RGDP	3.800	1.679	0.051	(47)	40.72	9.59	0.64	0.690
GNP	4.754	1.420	-0.104	(47)	160.96	17.60	-2.24	0.881
Canada								
RGDP	5.352	0.855	-0.092	(13)	40.75	14.07	-1.06	0.943
GNP	5.269	0.911	-0.078	(13)	41.22	15.07	-0.95	0.950
Dominican Rep.								
RGDP	3.668	1.127	-0.270	(12)	35.17	3.52	-3.04	0.501
GNP	4.488	1.076	-0.307	(12)	30.78	3.26	-2.99	0.455
Jamaica								
RGDP	4.353	1.094	-0.037	(13)	16.76	2.05	-0.26	0.357
GNP	4.848	0.456	-0.164	(13)	74.52	0.94	-1.13	0.161
Mexico								
RGDP	3.945	1.253	-0.087	(11)	36.54	10.65	-1.90	0.918
GNP	4.798	1.470	-0.036	(11)	116.34	12.06	-0.91	0.935
Panama								
RGDP	4.070	1.199	0.045	(11)	17.11	3.62	0.43	0.563
GNP	4.824	1.393	-0.016	(11)	111.06	4.90	-0.18	0.712
U.S.								
RGDP	4.842	1.118	-0.294	(13)	11.61	5.84	-2.83	0.729
GNP	4.916	1.064	-0.366	(13)	13.71	6.60	-3.66	0.777

Out:
501 Barbados
503 Costa Rica
505 Honduras
509 Trinidad and Tobago

Table 6.7

Regression Results for
Log per Capita Consumption of Motor Gasoline: South America and Oceania,
Using Income and Price Measures as Explanatory Variables

South America

Country group	Coefficients: Constant	Coefficients: Log Per Cap Income	Coefficients: Log Price Motor Gas	N No Obs.	t Ratios: Constant	t Ratios: Log Per Cap Income	t Ratios: Log Price Motor Gas	$\bar{R}^2$
South America								
RGDP	3.666	1.157	-0.380	(111)	79.76	23.56	-16.60	.864
GNP	4.486	0.815	-0.359	(111)	160.65	23.36	-15.68	.862
Argentina								
RGDP	4.505	0.659	-0.053	(13)	8.54	1.41	-0.63	.006
GNP	5.011	0.439	-0.028	(13)	18.32	0.86	-0.32	-.108
Bolivia								
RGDP	4.242	2.448	0.054	(13)	39.67	9.47	0.66	.883
GNP	7.097	2.842	0.611	(13)	20.29	9.06	0.71	.874
Brazil								
RGDP	3.993	0.835	-0.251	(12)	29.38	3.56	-2.58	.493
GNP	4.375	0.840	-0.242	(12)	99.44	3.54	-2.53	.490
Chile								
RGDP	3.727	1.167	-0.251	(13)	21.12	5.24	-5.49	.801
GNP	4.369	1.083	-0.298	(13)	53.97	3.72	-4.92	.688
Colombia								
RGDP	4.281	0.892	-0.001	(13)	82.90	13.48	-0.05	.944
GNP	5.092	0.921	-0.002	(13)	131.51	12.18	-0.09	.933
Ecuador								
RGDP	3.883	1.234	-0.259	(9)	9.55	2.31	-0.85	.914
GNP	4.128	0.937	-0.482	(9)	4.18	1.14	-1.19	.866
Peru								
RGDP	3.419	1.463	-0.236	(13)	9.34	2.48	-2.55	.389
GNP	5.520	2.187	-0.113	(13)	31.88	7.28	-2.51	.844
Uruguay								
RGDP	3.489	1.064	-0.440	(12)	5.65	1.71	-3.30	.600
GNP	4.299	0.841	-0.432	(12)	35.66	2.05	-3.89	.639
Venezuela								
RGDP	3.550	1.271	-0.414	(13)	20.52	12.70	-5.54	.954
GNP	4.010	1.798	-0.262	(13)	33.88	17.57	-4.54	.975
Oceania								
Australia								
RGDP	4.748	1.068	0.084	(11)	13.17	5.45	1.11	.850
GNP	4.597	1.078	-0.008	(11)	15.48	7.12	-0.11	.903

Table 6.8

Regression Results for Log Motor Gasoline Per Automobile, by Country Groups, Using Income and Price Measures as Explanatory Variables

Country groups	Coefficients			N	t ratios			
	Constant	Log per capita income	Log price motor gas	No. Obs.	Constant	Log per capita income	Log price motor gas	$\bar{R}^2$
World								
RGDP	7.896	-0.295	-0.731	(563)	311.63	-14.41	-28.34	.699
GNP	7.740	-0.202	-0.715	(547)	405.76	-15.06	-28.96	.713
All developing countries								
RGDP	7.928	-0.226	-0.680	(372)	275.83	-6.60	-21.43	.573
GNP	7.796	-0.161	-0.684	(346)	270.57	-5.90	-20.72	.576
Low income dev.								
RGDP	7.396	-0.673	-0.693	(60)	62.16	-4.37	-8.08	.623
GNP	7.535	-0.200	-0.753	(60)	35.84	-1.70	-7.91	.524
Medium income dev.								
RGDP	7.963	-0.091	-0.956	(98)	143.09	-0.44	-15.51	.717
GNP	7.781	-0.235	-0.946	(98)	66.13	-1.64	-15.55	.724
High income dev.								
RGDP	8.247	-0.541	-0.503	(214)	102.96	-6.34	-13.98	.570
GNP	7.901	-0.355	-0.495	(188)	200.26	-5.36	-12.50	.560
Industrial countries								
RGDP	6.322	0.591	-0.746	(191)	56.65	9.09	-20.75	.753
GNP	6.751	0.316	-0.822	(189)	90.18	7.83	-22.09	.739

Table 6.9

Regression Results
for Log Per Capita Purchase of Automobiles, Trucks,
Rail Passenger Use and Rail Freight Use,
Using Income and Price Measures as Explanatory Variables

(World Sample)

Type of Consumption	Coefficients			N	t ratios			$\bar{R}^2$
	Constant	Log per capita income	Log price	No. Obs.	Constant	Log per capita income	Log price	
Automobile Registrations Per Capita								
RGDP, Price Cars I	-1.940	1.946	-0.329	(1232)	-4.42	80.89	-6.67	.857
RGDP, Price Cars I	-2.255	1.954	-0.293	(1181)	-4.98	79.48	-5.75	.858
RGDP, Price Cars II	-1.908	1.811	-0.307	(1181)	-5.97	59.53	-9.25	.864
GNP, Price Cars I	-6.369	1.306	0.277	(1242)	-13.27	74.94	5.09	.837
Truck Registrations Per Capita								
RGDP, Price Cars I	-3.708	1.378	-0.196	(1232)	-9.27	62.86	-4.36	.783
RGDP, Price Cars I	-4.115	1.388	-0.149	(1181)	-10.08	62.63	-3.25	.788
RGDP, Price Cars II	-3.764	1.304	-0.175	(1181)	-12.91	47.01	-5.77	.792
GNP, Price Cars I	-6.728	0.947	0.223	(1242)	-16.48	63.93	4.81	.788
Rail Passenger Kilometers Traveled, Per Capita								
RGDP, P Gasoline	-1.988	0.593	1.221	(419)	-26.86	10.12	16.82	.563
GNP, P Gasoline	-1.676	0.394	1.264	(413)	-29.76	10.12	17.14	.577
Rail Freight, Ton Kilometers, Per Capita								
RGDP, P Gasoline	-2.435	1.213	0.842	(438)	-22.27	14.03	7.90	.446
GNP, P Gasoline	-1.749	0.743	0.941	(433)	-20.86	12.74	8.53	.433

Table 6.10

Regression Results for Log Per Capita Purchase of Automobiles by Country Groups, Using Income and Price Measures as Explanatory Variables

Country groups	Coefficients: Constant	Coefficients: Log per capita income	Coefficients: Log price	N No. Obs.	t ratios: Constant	t ratios: Log per capita income	t ratios: Log price	$\bar{R}^2$
World								
RGDP, Price Cars I	-1.940	1.946	-0.329	(1232)	-4.42	80.89	-6.67	.857
RGDP, Price Cars I	-2.255	1.954	-0.293	(1181)	-4.98	79.48	-5.75	.858
RGDP, Price Cars II	-1.908	1.811	-0.307	(1181)	-5.97	59.53	-9.25	.864
GNP, Price Cars I	-6.369	1.306	0.277	(1242)	-13.27	74.94	5.09	.837
All Developing Countries								
RGDP, Price Cars I	-1.530	1.810	-0.375	(880)	-2.57	45.28	-5.62	.702
RGDP, Price Cars I	-1.833	1.816	-0.341	(831)	-2.95	43.30	-4.90	.695
RGDP, Price Cars II	-1.105	1.694	-0.390	(831)	-2.57	39.56	-8.77	.713
GNP, Price Cars I	-4.953	1.333	0.121	(831)	-8.24	45.63	1.78	.717
Low Income Developing								
RGDP, Price Cars I	1.358	1.514	-0.710	(154)	0.80	7.29	-3.90	.262
RGDP, Price Cars I	1.500	1.541	-0.725	(152)	0.88	7.36	-3.97	.268
RGDP, Price Cars II	5.656	1.620	-1.057	(152)	6.69	11.13	-13.01	.621
GNP, Price Cars I	-0.967	1.743	-0.231	(152)	-1.20	25.15	-2.61	.810
Medium Income Devel.								
RGDP, Price Cars I	-11.688	0.778	0.706	(242)	-8.45	4.31	4.61	.255
RGDP, Price Cars I	-11.754	0.747	0.714	(237)	-8.44	4.09	4.64	.251
RGDP, Price Cars II	-11.877	0.838	0.665	(237)	-9.75	5.03	5.40	.273
GNP, Price Cars I	-13.398	0.292	0.922	(237)	-9.72	2.09	6.29	.212
High Income Developing								
RGDP, Price Cars I	-3.122	1.445	-0.152	(484)	-4.47	18.33	-1.89	.423
RGDP, Price Cars I	-4.416	1.355	0.003	(442)	-5.92	15.97	0.04	.398
RGDP, Price Cars II	-4.459	1.354	0.008	(442)	-8.31	16.57	0.13	.398
GNP, Price Cars I	-7.040	0.842	0.380	(442)	-9.04	12.11	4.31	.286
Industrial								
RGDP, Price Cars I	-4.935	2.332	-0.040	(352)	-9.55	30.91	-0.62	.765
RGDP, Price Cars I	-4.978	2.336	-0.035	(350)	-9.60	30.92	-0.55	.766
RGDP, Price Cars II	-6.548	2.284	0.160	(350)	-15.10	33.27	3.07	.772
GNP, Price Cars I	-6.519	1.215	0.333	(350)	-8.75	16.41	3.66	.506

Table 6.11

Regression Results for Log Per Capita Purchase of Trucks by Country Groups, Using Income and Price Measures as Explanatory Variables

Country groups	Coefficients: Constant	Coefficients: Log per capita income	Coefficients: Log price	N No. Obs.	t ratios: Constant	t ratios: Log per capita income	t ratios: Log price	$\bar{R}^2$
World								
RGDP, Price Cars I	-3.708	1.378	-0.196	(1232)	-9.27	62.86	-4.36	.783
RGDP, Price Cars I	-4.115	1.388	-0.149	(1181)	-10.08	62.63	-3.25	.788
RGDP, Price Cars II	-3.764	1.304	-0.175	(1181)	-12.91	47.01	-5.77	.792
GNP, Price Cars I	-6.728	0.947	0.223	(1242)	-16.48	63.93	4.81	.788
All Developing Countries								
RGDP, Price Cars I	-2.907	1.506	-0.285	(880)	-5.83	45.03	-5.10	.699
RGDP, Price Cars I	-3.384	1.538	-0.230	(831)	-6.68	44.92	-4.05	.709
RGDP, Price Cars II	-1.975	1.428	-0.358	(831)	-5.72	41.54	-10.04	.736
GNP, Price Cars I	-6.087	1.157	0.169	(831)	-13.35	52.21	3.30	.767
Low Income Developing								
RGDP, Price Cars I	4.882	1.755	-1.118	(154)	2.84	8.35	-6.07	.347
RGDP, Price Cars I	5.118	1.801	-1.142	(152)	2.99	8.56	-6.22	.361
RGDP, Price Cars II	7.903	1.809	-1.299	(152)	10.88	14.48	-18.64	.759
GNP, Price Cars I	2.053	1.909	-0.571	(152)	3.05	33.02	-7.71	.885
Medium Income Devel.								
RGDP, Price Cars I	-9.859	1.292	0.467	(242)	-7.61	7.64	3.26	.351
RGDP, Price Cars I	-9.781	1.328	0.457	(237)	-7.52	7.78	3.18	.360
RGDP, Price Cars II	-7.633	1.507	0.201	(237)	-6.51	9.41	1.69	.340
GNP, Price Cars I	-10.441	1.000	0.623	(237)	-8.34	7.85	4.68	.362
High Income Devel.								
RGDP, Price Cars I	-3.960	1.306	-0.146	(484)	-7.69	22.47	-2.45	.524
RGDP, Price Cars I	-5.670	1.203	0.061	(442)	-11.70	21.82	1.08	.561
RGDP, Price Cars II	-4.873	1.234	-0.030	(442)	-13.97	23.24	-0.79	.561
GNP, Price Cars I	-7.908	0.831	0.384	(442)	-15.72	18.51	6.73	.487
Industrial								
RGDP, Price Cars I	-3.783	1.221	-0.169	(352)	-4.77	10.53	-1.69	.252
RGDP, Price Cars I	-3.773	1.220	-0.170	(350)	-4.73	10.49	-1.69	.251
RGDP, Price Cars II	-7.440	1.073	0.291	(350)	-11.17	10.18	3.64	.273
GNP, Price Cars I	-5.077	0.342	0.139	(350)	-5.73	3.88	1.28	.055

Table 6.12

Regression Results for Log Per Capita Rail Passenger Rail, Freight in Ton Kilometers, by Country Group, Using Income and Price Measures as Explanatory Variables

Country groups	Coefficients			N	t ratios			
	Constant	Log per capita income	Log price	No. Obs.	Constant	Log per capita income	Log price	$\bar{R}^2$
World								
RGDP	-1.988	0.593	1.221	(419)	-26.86	10.12	16.82	.563
GNP	-1.676	0.394	1.264	(413)	-29.76	10.12	17.14	.577
All Developing Countries								
RGDP	-2.116	0.097	0.997	(274)	-28.40	1.15	12.83	.378
GNP	-2.083	0.015	1.019	(263)	-28.84	0.23	12.75	.382
Low Income Dev.								
RGDP	-2.243	-0.546	1.361	(46)	-8.46	-1.60	7.26	.531
GNP	-3.761	-1.006	1.210	(46)	-8.53	-4.42	7.83	.658
Medium Income Dev.								
RGDP	-2.799	0.416	0.510	(71)	-22.01	0.90	3.87	.191
GNP	-3.086	-0.454	0.583	(71)	-11.69	-1.39	4.45	.204
High Income Dev.								
RGDP	-1.682	-0.171	1.197	(157)	-7.15	-0.70	11.31	.461
GNP	-1.763	-0.225	1.254	(146)	-14.99	-1.21	11.05	.473
Industrial Countries								
RGDP	0.879	-0.903	1.412	(145)	2.15	-3.74	9.48	.437
GNP	-0.648	0.009	1.514	(144)	-2.35	0.06	9.62	.390

Table 6.13

Regression Results for Log Per Capita Rail Freight Ton Kilometers, by Country Group, Using Income and Price Measures as Explanatory Variables

Country groups	Coefficients			N	t ratios			$\bar{R}^2$
	Constant	Log per capita income	Log price	No. Obs.	Constant	Log per capita income	Log price	
World								
RGDP	-2.435	1.213	0.842	(438)	-22.27	14.03	7.90	.446
GNP	-1.749	0.743	0.941	(433)	-20.86	12.74	8.53	.433
All Developing Countries								
RGDP	-2.254	0.662	1.082	(283)	-19.20	4.90	8.84	.270
GNP	-1.887	0.399	1.122	(272)	-16.98	3.88	8.87	.265
Low Income Dev.								
RGDP	-2.281	0.163	2.527	(44)	-5.36	0.30	7.92	.601
GNP	-3.565	-0.613	2.463	(44)	-4.30	-1.43	7.94	.619
Medium Income Dev.								
RGDP	-2.853	1.955	1.005	(71)	-11.37	2.15	3.87	.247
GNP	-2.174	0.683	1.072	(71)	-4.04	1.02	4.01	.208
High Income Dev.								
RGDP	-0.320	-1.368	1.192	(168)	-1.02	-4.15	8.46	.303
GNP	-1.141	-1.113	1.320	(157)	-7.55	-4.49	8.84	.333
Industrial Countries								
RGDP	-4.302	2.554	-1.539	(155)	-10.85	10.88	-11.35	.650
GNP	-2.231	1.228	-1.816	(153)	-7.87	7.95	-11.86	.556

Table 6.14

Regression Results for Log Per Capita
Consumption of All Fuel, for the World, by Mode,
Using Income and Price Measures as Explanatory Variables

	Coefficients				t ratios			
Transport mode	Constant	Log per capita income	Log price	N No. Obs.	Constant	Log per capita income	Log price	$\bar{R}^2$
All Transport								
RGDP; P Gasoline	4.257	1.304	-0.198	(422)	189.09	73.49	-9.03	.930
GNP; P Diesel	4.974	0.867	-0.278	(422)	263.79	64.60	-11.08	.911
RGDP; P Diesel	4.165	1.345	-0.179	(128)	79.81	38.42	-4.26	.925
GNP; P Diesel	4.902	0.894	-0.301	(128)	115.71	35.05	-6.39	.911
Road Transport								
RGDP; P Gasoline	3.762	1.466	-0.326	(313)	131.04	70.35	-11.14	.941
GNP; P Gasoline	4.546	0.969	-0.421	(313)	178.21	57.46	-11.79	.914
RGDP; P Diesel	3.605	1.543	-0.292	(105)	64.02	42.34	-6.88	.946
GNP; P Diesel	4.416	1.028	-0.442	(105)	91.12	36.62	-8.84	.929
Rail Transport								
RGDP; P Gasoline	1.587	0.906	0.019	(284)	17.39	13.85	0.16	.417
GNP; P Gasoline	2.054	0.615	-0.051	(284)	30.62	13.94	-0.41	.420
RGDP; P Diesel	2.051	0.619	0.877	(92)	11.38	5.50	5.19	.512
GNP; P Diesel	2.365	0.418	0.794	(92)	17.30	5.37	4.48	.506
Air Transport								
RGDP; P Gasoline	2.056	1.208	-0.073	(316)	28.30	22.86	-0.98	.627
GNP; P Gasoline	2.687	0.822	-0.156	(316)	51.75	23.82	-2.15	.646
RGDP; P Diesel	1.977	1.242	0.014	(107)	13.14	12.71	0.12	.624
GNP; P Diesel	2.615	0.848	-0.118	(107)	23.97	13.31	-1.04	.645
Water Transport								
RGDP; P Gasoline	0.681	1.478	-0.503	(246)	5.78	16.88	-3.09	.544
GNP; P Gasoline	1.440	0.979	-0.571	(246)	16.29	16.12	-3.39	.521
RGDP; P Diesel	0.807	1.259	-0.161	(84)	3.04	7.40	-0.68	.431
GNP; P Diesel	1.470	0.825	-0.291	(84)	7.19	6.83	-1.13	.395

Table 6.15

Regression Results for Log Per Capita
Consumption of Diesel Fuel, for the World, by Mode,
Using Income and Price Measures as Explanatory Variables

Transport mode	Coefficients: Constant	Coefficients: Log per capita income	Coefficients: Log price	N No. Obs.	t ratios: Constant	t ratios: Log per capita income	t ratios: Log price	$\bar{R}^2$
All Transport								
RGDP; P Gasoline	3.391	1.053	0.020	(97)	65.06	24.75	0.47	.865
GNP; P Gasoline	4.019	0.706	-0.027	(97)	91.42	19.84	-0.43	.805
RGDP; P Diesel	3.335	1.089	-0.069	(57)	44.24	20.15	-1.26	.882
GNP; P Diesel	3.948	0.745	-0.147	(57)	59.46	16.69	-2.23	.837
Road Transport								
RGDP; P Gasoline	3.125	1.051	-0.021	(258)	63.47	29.95	-0.33	.783
GNP: P Gasoline	3.680	0.677	-0.070	(258)	88.32	25.45	-0.98	.723
RGDP; P Diesel	2.884	1.244	-0.238	(82)	23.82	16.40	-1.78	.792
GNP; P Diesel	3.535	0.823	-0.395	(82)	35.62	14.39	-2.57	.747
Rail Transport								
RGDP; P Gasoline	1.423	0.690	-0.864	(71)	9.36	6.65	-3.77	.449
GNP; P Gasoline	1.778	0.526	-0.925	(71)	16.82	7.73	-4.30	.516
RGDP; P Diesel	1.112	0.776	-0.103	(39)	5.07	5.29	-0.32	.438
GNP; P Diesel	1.444	0.608	-0.365	(39)	9.22	5.96	-1.13	.497
Water Transport								
RGDP; P Gasoline	0.826	1.281	-0.738	(62)	4.29	7.57	-1.82	.491
GNP; P Gasoline	1.523	0.922	-0.833	(62)	10.17	8.16	-2.12	.529
RGDP; P Diesel	0.902	1.142	-0.029	(37)	2.71	4.62	-0.07	.475
GNP; P Diesel	1.441	0.859	-0.251	(37)	6.07	4.86	-0.59	.495

Table 6.16

Regression Results for Log Per Capita
Consumption of All Fuel, Developing Countries, by Mode,
Using Income and Price Measures as Explanatory Variables

	Coefficients				t ratios			
Transport mode	Constant	Log per capita income	Log price	N No. Obs.	Constant	Log per capita income	Log price	$\bar{R}^2$
All Transport								
RGDP; P Gasoline	4.299	1.295	-0.122	(263)	180.43	44.98	-4.85	.886
GNP; P Gasoline	5.125	1.013	-0.158	(263)	253.50	52.52	-7.25	.914
RGDP; P Diesel	4.221	1.296	-0.126	(74)	75.98	22.92	-2.52	.882
GNP; P Diesel	5.060	1.012	-0.173	(74)	117.98	29.06	-4.28	.923
Road Transport								
RGDP; P Gasoline	3.801	1.497	-0.217	(154)	118.72	39.94	-5.69	.918
GNP; P Gasoline	4.712	1.157	-0.222	(154)	176.94	46.22	-6.66	.937
RGDP; P Diesel	3.653	1.524	-0.243	(51)	57.35	23.23	-4.28	.927
GNP; P Diesel	4.579	1.158	-0.307	(51)	92.98	30.48	-7.03	.956
Rail Transport								
RGDP; P Gasoline	1.700	0.433	0.708	(125)	14.33	3.15	3.43	.157
GNP; P Gasoline	1.961	0.343	0.700	(125)	17.91	3.25	3.40	.161
RGDP; P Diesel	2.465	0.069	1.404	(38)	13.48	0.42	7.12	.571
GNP; P Diesel	2.503	0.041	1.400	(38)	15.00	0.33	7.03	.571
Air Transport								
RGDP; P Gasoline	2.110	1.009	0.050	(157)	23.30	9.58	0.47	.366
GNP; P Gasoline	2.745	0.835	0.058	(157)	34.07	10.88	0.57	.428
RGDP; P Diesel	2.022	1.059	0.015	(53)	10.15	5.22	0.08	.335
GNP; P Diesel	2.703	0.881	-0.010	(53)	14.89	6.14	-0.06	.414
Water Transport								
RGDP; P Gasoline	0.704	1.401	-0.105	(105)	5.85	9.95	-0.52	.484
GNP; P Gasoline	1.539	1.164	-0.123	(105)	14.53	10.96	-0.64	.533
RGDP; P Diesel	1.073	1.467	0.332	(35)	4.09	6.20	1.23	.536
GNP; P Diesel	1.904	1.211	0.165	(35)	8.61	6.90	0.64	.589

Table 6.17

Regression Results for Log per Capita Consumption of All Fuel, for Industrial Countries, by Mode, Using Income and Price Measures as Explanatory Variables

Transport mode	Coefficients			N	t ratios			
	Constant	Log per capita income	Log price	No. Obs.	Constant	Log per capita income	Log price	$\bar{R}^2$
All Transport								
RGDP; P Gasoline	3.414	1.813	-0.588	(159)	22.27	20.85	-13.96	.849
GNP; P Gasoline	5.269	0.710	-0.854	(159)	39.61	10.13	-14.07	.655
RGDP; P Diesel	2.978	2.012	-0.479	(54)	8.64	10.46	-4.87	.748
GNP; P Diesel	5.053	0.791	-0.776	(54)	16.88	5.12	-5.54	.478
Road Transport								
RGDP; P Gasoline	2.993	1.916	-0.568	(159)	16.33	18.43	-11.28	.805
GNP; P Gasoline	4.973	0.740	-0.849	(159)	33.11	9.33	-12.39	.602
RGDP; P Diesel	2.698	2.048	-0.483	(54)	7.68	10.45	-4.83	.747
GNP; P Diesel	4.776	0.824	-0.787	(54)	15.86	5.30	-5.59	.488
Rail Transport								
RGDP; P Gasoline	0.268	1.797	-0.857	(159)	1.12	13.22	-13.01	.757
GNP; P Gasoline	2.003	0.759	-1.120	(159)	12.25	8.79	-14.99	.655
RGDP; P Diesel	-1.707	2.770	-0.374	(54)	-3.30	9.60	-2.54	.676
GNP; P Diesel	1.137	1.097	-0.784	(54)	2.65	4.96	-3.90	.387
Air Transport								
RGDP; P Gasoline	0.845	1.984	-0.625	(159)	2.33	9.64	-6.27	.538
GNP; P Gasoline	2.700	0.870	-0.915	(159)	11.88	7.26	-8.82	.449
RGDP; P Diesel	0.418	2.138	-0.301	(54)	0.62	5.65	-1.55	.436
GNP; P Diesel	2.620	0.843	-0.616	(54)	5.60	3.49	-2.81	.230
Water Transport								
RGDP; P Gasoline	3.520	-0.032	-1.499	(141)	4.17	-0.07	-5.64	.177
GNP; P Gasoline	4.101	-0.347	-1.470	(141)	8.98	-1.43	-5.59	.189
RGDP; P Diesel	2.686	0.190	-1.242	(49)	1.60	0.20	-2.62	.093
GNP; P Diesel	3.792	-0.409	-1.147	(49)	4.11	-0.85	-2.37	.106

Table 6.18

Regression Results for Per Capita Consumption of All Transport Fuel, by Country Groups, Using Income and Price Measures as Explanatory Variables

Country groups	Coefficients			N	t ratios			
	Constant	Log per capita income	Log price motor gas	No. Obs.	Constant	Log per capita income	Log price motor gas	$\bar{R}^2$
World								
RGDP	4.256	1.301	-0.189	(448)	193.90	75.09	-8.99	.928
GNP	4.979	0.845	-0.208	(432)	247.88	60.58	-8.44	.928
All developing countries								
RGDP	4.298	1.287	-0.116	(287)	187.46	47.77	-4.85	.890
GNP	5.126	1.013	-0.158	(263)	253.50	52.57	-7.25	.914
Low income dev.								
RGDP	3.934	0.699	0.249	(53)	23.60	3.18	2.31	.254
GNP	5.168	1.008	0.230	(53)	36.60	12.58	4.03	.784
Medium income dev.								
RGDP	4.140	1.807	-0.279	(67)	117.15	14.43	-8.77	.785
GNP	5.146	1.116	-0.268	(67)	61.16	9.78	-6.46	.633
High income dev.								
RGDP	4.490	1.093	-0.081	(167)	65.16	14.78	-3.01	.567
GNP	5.204	0.800	-0.131	(143)	192.99	16.51	-5.03	.657
Industrial								
RGDP	3.398	1.823	-0.581	(161)	22.37	21.16	-14.05	.848
GNP	5.269	0.710	-0.854	(159)	39.61	10.13	-14.07	.655

Table 6.19

Regression Results for Per Capita Consumption of Road Transport Fuel, by country Groups, Using Income and Price Measures as Explantory Variables

Country groups	Coefficients			N	t ratios			$\bar{R}^2$
	Constant	Log per capita income	Log price motor gas	No. Obs.	Constant	Log per capita income	Log price motor gas	
World								
RGDP	3.762	1.466	-0.326	(313)	131.04	70.35	-11.14	.941
GNP	4.546	0.969	-0.421	(313)	178.21	57.46	-11.79	.914
All developing countries								
RGDP	3.801	1.497	-0.217	(154)	118.72	39.94	-5.69	.918
GNP	4.712	1.157	-0.222	(154)	176.94	46.22	-6.66	.937
Low income dev.								
RGDP	3.243	0.657	-0.395	(42)	15.22	2.09	-3.07	.279
GNP	4.787	1.205	-0.176	(42)	23.75	9.92	-2.32	.772
Medium income dev.								
RGDP	3.452	2.260	-0.309	(19)	33.24	5.31	-1.11	.807
GNP	5.148	1.908	-0.426	(19)	27.85	7.05	-1.87	.870
High income dev.								
RGDP	4.024	1.160	-0.148	(117)	27.54	7.72	-2.78	.361
GNP	4.877	0.812	-0.234	(93)	98.14	9.47	-6.27	.578
Industrial								
RGDP	2.993	1.916	-0.568	(159)	16.33	18.43	-11.28	.805
GNP	4.973	0.740	-0.849	(159)	33.11	9.33	-12.39	.602

Table 6.20

Regression Results for Per Capita Consumption of Rail Transport Fuel, by Country Groups, Using Income and Price Measures as Explanatory Variables

Country groups	Coefficients			N	t ratios			
	Constant	Log per capita income	Log price motor gas	No. Obs.	Constant	Log per capita income	Log price motor gas	$\bar{R}^2$
World								
RGDP	1.587	0.906	0.019	(284)	17.39	13.85	0.16	.417
GNP	2.054	0.615	-0.051	(284)	30.62	13.94	-0.41	.420
All developing countries								
RGDP	1.700	0.433	0.708	(125)	14.33	3.15	3.43	.157
GNP	1.961	0.343	0.700	(125)	17.91	3.25	3.40	.161
Low income dev.								
RGDP	-0.352	-2.839	3.066	(42)	-0.64	-3.51	9.24	.742
GNP	1.289	-0.134	3.311	(42)	1.22	-0.21	8.31	.661
Medium income dev.								
RGDP	--[a]	--	--	--	--	--	--	--
GNP	--	--	--	--	--	--	--	--
High income dev.								
RGDP	2.845	-0.799	0.314	(84)	9.93	-2.64	2.01	.069
GNP	2.363	-0.526	0.153	(82)	18.83	-2.15	0.96	.032
Industrial								
RGDP	0.268	1.797	-0.857	(159)	2.33	9.64	-6.27	.538
GNP	2.700	0.870	-0.915	(159)	11.88	7.26	-8.82	.449

[a]No data were available for this category.

Table 6.21

Regression Results for Per Capita Consumption of Diesel Fuel by Mode, Developing Countries, Using Income and Price Measures as Explanatory Variables

Country groups	Coefficients: Constant	Coefficients: Log per capita income	Coefficients: Log price motor gas	N No. Obs.	t ratios: Constant	t ratios: Log per capita income	t ratios: Log price motor gas	$\bar{R}^2$
<u>All Transport</u>								
RGDP; P Gasoline	-5.116	1.227	0.087	(68)	-11.32	20.44	1.60	.861
GNP; P Gasoline	4.109	0.923	0.062	(67)	93.99	18.26	1.03	.834
RGDP; P Diesel	-5.265	1.249	0.023	(40)	-8.55	15.07	0.35	.855
GNP; P Diesel	4.134	0.938	-0.018	(39)	60.03	13.51	-0.24	.828
<u>Road Transport</u>								
RGDP; P Gasoline	-6.377	1.380	-0.090	(105)	-11.19	17.47	-0.93	.745
GNP; P Gasoline	3.991	1.075	-0.117	(105)	58.88	16.62	-1.15	.725
RGDP; P Diesel	-7.366	1.490	-0.179	(32)	-5.42	8.11	-0.71	.677
GNP; P Diesel	3.824	1.107	-0.294	(32)	27.96	7.20	-1.06	.621
<u>Rail Transport</u>								
RGDP; P Gasoline	-0.327	0.253	-0.235	(41)	-0.27	1.60	-0.71	.022
GNP; P Gasoline	1.564	0.274	-0.268	(41)	12.01	2.29	-0.84	.083
RGDP; P Diesel	-1.164	0.351	0.202	(21)	-0.77	1.74	0.75	.083
GNP; P Diesel	1.464	0.334	0.260	(21)	10.07	2.20	0.52	.156
<u>Water Transport</u>								
RGDP; P Gasoline	-8.290	1.317	-0.797	(37)	-4.23	4.90	-1.60	.379
GNP; P Gasoline	1.634	1.112	-0.936	(37)	8.18	5.73	-2.00	.461
RGDP; P Diesel	-8.309	1.338	0.139	(22)	-3.44	4.09	0.29	.452
GNP; P Diesel	1.734	1.115	-0.066	(22)	7.29	4.64	-0.14	.518

Chapter 7

Regression Analyses Using an Expanded Set of Explanatory Variables

Chapter 7 introduces a number of explanatory variables in addition to per capita income and price and uses those variables to explain most of the dependent variables considered in Chapter 6. Results for the full set of explanatory variables appear in Tables 7.1 through 7.13. Tables 7.14 and 7.15 present results limited to those variables having statistically significant coefficients, obtained by winnowing out nonsignificant variables through the comparison of a number of alternative equations for each dependent variable, in turn. Table 7.14 covers results for the first six categories of transport consumption: motor gasoline, gasoline per automobile, auto registration, truck registration, rail passenger travel and rail frieght shipped. Table 7.15 includes significant coefficients for the five categories of fuel use by mode: all modes, road, rail, air and water. The first 13 tables of the chapter follow the order shown for tables 7.14 and 7.15. However, two sets of tables appear for auto and truck registration respectively; the first set excludes motor gasoline prices while the second includes that variable.

Tables 7.1 through 7.13 present coefficients and t ratios for the world, developing country and industrial country samples, while tables 7.14 and 7.15 are limited to the developing countries only.

In addition to RGDP per capita, treated as our income measure, plus the most appropriate price measure, the explanatory variables included the following, listed by name and brief definition:

Road Density: Density of road network in kilometers of road network per square kilometer of area.

Population Density: Population divided by area in square kilometers.

Rank Change: A measure of relative per capita income growth consisting of per capita RGDP ranking in 1980 minus per capita RGDP ranking in 1960. The country of lowest income was ranked 1, and that of highest income was ranked 77. Hence, a positive rank change indicated a shift to a higher income position. (To allow the employment of the log form of the variable, Rank Change +25 was employed in practice, preventing the occurrence of a negative value.)

Year: Annual date, ranging from 1960 to 1982, and entered as 60 to 82.

Percent Urban: Percent of country population located in urban areas.

Percent Medium Age: The population of age 15-65 as a percent of the total population.

Percent in Largest City: The percent of the urban population located in the largest city in the respective country.

Some additional variables appeared in several of the equations. As indicated above, car and truck registrations were each related to the price of gasoline as well as to the price of new automobiles.

For a number of uses, it was hypothesized that an alternative mode could serve as a substitute, so per capita use of a competitive transport variable was introduced as follows:

given variable	competitive use
motor gasoline	rail passengers
automobiles	rail passengers
trucks	rail freight
rail passengers	automobiles
rail freight	trucks

All variables are measured in log form.

In reviewing the regression results we will first look for overall patterns by examining the behavior of the explanatory variables over all of the equations. We will then examine some of the individual regression equations to glean what additional information we can. In those investigations, comparisons will be made of patterns for developing versus industrial countries for the light that comparison sheds on transport energy consumption within the development process. The chapter concludes with a statement of the major findings of Part III of this report, embracing both chapters 6 and 7.

Effects of Independent Variables Across Equations

A sense of the overall effect of each independent variable can be obtained in relatively simple fashion by noting whether its effect is positive or negative for each of the 11 transport categories we have examined in this chapter. As a first step in developing this information, the number of positive versus negative coefficients was counted across Tables 7.1 through 7.13, excluding Tables 7.5 and 7.6 to avoid double-counting. (Those two tables were variants of Tables 7.3 and 7.4, respectively.) The results of those counts were as follows:

	Developing countries		Industrial countries	
	+	-	+	-
RGDP	8	3	8	3
Price	5	6	2	9
Road Density	9	2	10	1
Pop. Density	1	10	1	10
Rank Change	5	6	6	5
Competitive Mode	2	3	0	5
Year	7	4	7	4
Percent Urban	4	7	5	6
Percent Medium Age	4	7	4	7
Percent Large City	9	2	3	8

Additional information for the developing countries is obtained by counting positive and negative cases and, additionally, noting the nonsignificant cases, in Tables 7.14 and 7.15, which present results for significant cases only. Those counts are as follows:

	Developing Countries		
	+	-	Not Signif.
RGDP	8	3	0
Price Gasoline	6	5	0
Price Cars	0	2	0
Road Density	8	2	1
Pop. Density	1	9	1
Rank Change	2	2	7
Competitive Mode	0	2	3
Year	3	3	5
Percent Urban	2	5	4
Percent Medium Age	1	3	7
Percent Large City	6	2	3

It is immediately clear from these counts that Density of Road Network has a pronounced positive effect on transport levels and energy use in transport, and that Population Density has a pronounced negative effect. The first result no doubt is to be expected as expressing an obvious relationship in the case of motor gasoline use, road fuel use, all fuel use and in automobile and truck registrations: an expanded road network will encourage road transport. But it can be simplistic to view road construction as having a "negative" effect because it encourages fuel use, and also to see it as necessarily leading to reduced consumption of nonroad modes of transport. On the first point, if road construction pays for itself in terms of induced economic activity which yields more benefits than costs, then increased road construction has its justification. One of the two negative coefficients that occurs for Road Density in the developing countries is in gasoline use per car: as road density increases, gasoline use per car <u>decreases</u>. This suggests that an increased (and improved?) level of the highway network can improve fuel efficiency. On the second point, there is some evidence of a competitive effect, since the second of the two negative coefficients for the developing countries occurs in rail freight shipments (see Tables 7.8 and 7.14), while the negative coefficient for the industrial countries occurs in air transport fuel use (Table 7.12). But there is more evidence running in the opposite direction. Road Density has a positive effect on fuel use for most of the measures of alternative modes; for the developing countries, the positive effect occurs for rail passenger level, rail fuel use, air transport fuel use and water transport fuel use (Tables 7.7 and 7.11 through 7.15). It is plausible that infrastructure investment for other modes parallels that in roads, accounting for at least some of the positive association. Further, complementary as well as competitive relationships can occur between modes. If the road network increases, the possibility of rail and road connections ("piggybacking") increase, and access to ports and airports increases as well.

Population Density is negative in all cases for the developing countries except in its effect on gasoline per car. To speculate, that contrary result may exhibit the effect of congestion in reducing fuel efficiency. Population Density has negative effect in all cases for the industrial countries save in air transport fuel use. Perhaps concentration in large cities, making air transport more viable, explains that exception. To explain the generally negative impacts of population density on transport and fuel use, several hypotheses seem worth considering. First, the more the population is spread out, the longer the necessary trip lengths and length of shipments. Second, in large cities, travel on foot can often be substituted for travel by vehicle; often this substitution is economic, because travel and associated transport costs typically increase with city size. Third, higher density allows for more intensive use of transport facilities, as in mass transit.

The variables Percent Urban and Percent in Largest City are related to Population Density, and their effects complicate the picture, making the discernable pattern of relationships more ambiguous and harder to read. In the developing countries, Percent Urban tends to have a negative effect, reinforcing the Population Density effect. However, Percent in Largest City usually has a positive effect. If we summarize the patterns for fuel use exhibited in Tables 7.14 and 7.15, with 0 indicating no significant effect, + indicating a positive effect (fuel use increases as the variable increases) and - a negative effect, these results emerge:

	Gasoline	All Fuel	Road Fuel	Rail Fuel	Air Trans. Fuel	Water Trans. Fuel
Pop. Density	-	-	-	-	-	0
Percent Urban	0	-	0	0	-	+
Percent Largest City	+	+	0	+	+	+

No doubt, proponents of a policy of limiting entry to large cities may derive some comfort from the results for Percent in Largest City, but even if the positive result reflects the "waste" of traffic congestion, there is always the danger of suboptimization: the cure may be worse than the disease, in terms of giving up economic product and reducing economic welfare. Also note that in the industrial countries, the effect of both Percent Urban and Percent in Largest City is more often negative than positive, so the overall, net effect of urbanization appears to be negative. Table 7.9 is particularly relevant, since it exhibits results for all transport fuel use in the industrial countries. Here Population Density,

Percent Urban and Percent in Largest City all have negative and statistically significant coefficients. Hence, it seems clear from this case that increased urbanization eventually implies decreased transport energy use. Of course, further research on the net effects of urbanization in developing countries, and on how the urbanization process affects transport energy use, is recommended on the basis of these results.

The effect of income and price was discussed in detail in chapter 6. However, it seems worthwhile to review the apparently anomalous results appearing in the lists presented above. For the developing countries, negative income elasticities occur in three cases: gasoline per car, water transport fuel, and rail fuel. The last result was not statistically significant, but was retained for completeness of coverage; the water transport effect was questionable because of small sample size; and the gasoline per car effect may reflect intensive use of cars in poor countries. Positive gasoline price elasticities occurred in the following cases: all three rail use equations, water fuel use, automobile and truck registrations. It was hypothesized that the rail results involved substitution of rail for road transport given higher fuel prices; the water fuel use result was not statistically significant but was retained for completeness of coverage; and it was speculated that the auto and truck registration results might have involved a response to increased fuel efficiency of motor vehicles given higher prices. Given a great enough increase in fuel efficiency, the cost of gasoline per mile traveled may well have fallen. In any event, the vehicle price elasticity was negative for both cars and trucks, in line with expectations.

The time trend represented by Year was positive in seven cases and negative in four (in Tables 7.1 through 7.13). Of the four, three represented the rail use equations and one the water fuel use case. In tables 7.14 and 7.15, a statistically significant time trend occurred for both auto and truck registrations, and for fuel in road use. The railroad cases again were negative. Thus, there appears to be a trend in favor of road use and against rail use beyond the effects afforded by increases in per capita income. Hypotheses to explain this result include the following. It is possible that technological advance in road transport implies that more service is received per dollar of expenditure over time, and that this technological advance outweighs the advance (if any) occurring in rail and water transport. Stated another way, this hypothesis involves the argument that price of road transport involves overstatement that becomes worse as time passes because the quality of the product and its service have improved over time. A second hypothesis is that road transport has more net positive spillover effects aiding economic growth and development than do other forms of transport, building an implicit case for its increased use. For example, the nature of road transport is such that it can be presumed to yield improved access to more land area than do rail and water transport.

We turn now to the results for our three remaining explanatory variables: Competitive Mode, Percent Medium Age and Rank Change.

We have used the term Competitive Mode to refer to the effect of use of an alternative transportation mode on the use of a given mode, for example, the effect of rail freight use on number of truck registrations. As expected, the effect of the competitive mode was generally negative, although the effect seemed more pronounced for the industrial than for the developing countries. For the former, the coefficients of the competitive mode were negative in all five of the equations in which they appeared; for the latter, they were negative in three out of five cases (Tables 7.1 through 7.13). Only two of those five appeared in the set of variables with significant coefficients in Tables 7.14 and 7.15, but both were negative.

The remaining variables, Percent Medium Age and Rank Change, had only limited effect on results for the developing countries. It was expected that an increase in the percent in the medium age group (aged 15-65) would lead to greater transport use, but this happened only sporadically, and if anything, the general effect for that variable was negative. No doubt the demographic relationship is more complex than posited in the relatively simple hypothesis under which we introduced the variable, and future work might profitably explore the relationship.

A positive rank change indicates an upward movement in per capita income in relative terms, that is, a country with a positive rank change has had higher than typical growth in per capita income. Rank change was statistically significant for the developing countries in only four cases, with two coefficients positive, and two negative. The negative effects occurred for gasoline per car and fuel in rail use, while the positive effects occurred for automobile registrations and fuel for air transport. Those effects seem intuitively consistent with faster-than-average development, though cause and effect relations again must be a matter of speculation. If people expect higher incomes they may move more quickly from rail to road and air transport than would otherwise occur; alternatively, that movement might itself be part of a process generating higher incomes, touched on in brief fashion in our discussion of the time trend, above.

We conclude our survey of the effects of the explanatory variables across equations by comparing the level of agreement for developing and industrial countries in terms of the signs of coefficients. Agreement means the signs of the coefficients were the same (both were positive, or both were negative) and disagreement means the opposite (one sign was positive, one was negative). The number of cases in each category from that comparison was as follows:

	Agree	Disagree
RGDP	7	4
Price	6	5
Road Density	8	3
Pop. Density	9	2
Rank Change	2	9
Competitive Mode	3	2
Year	7	4
Percent Urban	7	4
Percent Medium Age	7	4
Percent Large City	5	6

There was generally good agreement, with Rank Change the major exception.

This area of disagreement was examined in detail by comparing coefficients in each equation. (Tables 7.5 and 7.6 were employed for automobiles and trucks because of higher significance levels and explained variance than occurred in Tables 7.3 and 7.4). These results emerged for the coefficient sign of Rank Change:

Dependent Variable	Developing Countries	Industrial Countries	Table Source
Gasoline	+	-	7.1
Gasoline/Auto	-	-	7.2
Automobiles	+	-	7.5
Trucks	-	+	7.6
Rail Passengers	-	+	7.7
Rail Freight	-	+	7.8
All Transport Fuel	+	-	7.9
Road Transport Fuel	+	-	7.10
Rail Transport Fuel	-	+	7.11
Air Transport Fuel	+	-	7.12
Water Transport Fuel	+	+	7.13

The developing country results seem very much in line with our hypotheses on the relationships between transport variables and development. Per capita purchase of gasoline, automobiles, all transport fuel, road transport fuel and air transport fuel were all positively related to high income growth, while per capita rail use and use of trucks were negatively related to growth in income. With respect to truck use, it was noted in Chapter 6 that development typically shifts the mix of trucks (including buses) and automobiles in favor of automobiles, and this result again is in line with that observation.

In contrast to the developing country results, however, the industrial countries show essentially the opposite effects for Rank Change. An enumeration of the rank change readings for the industrial countries helps in the formulation of hypotheses to explain these results. In order of rank change, we have these values:

Country	Rank Change 1960 to 1980
Japan	+15
France	+7
Spain	+4
Belgium	+4
W.Germany	+4
Finland	+3
Canada	+2
Italy	+1
U.S.	0
Denmark	-1
Netherlands	-1
Sweden	-1
Australia	-3
Switzerland	-4
U.K.	-5
New Zealand	-10

Two hypotheses emerge from this enumeration. First, there is probably a "catch-up" effect; countries that were lagging in transport technology and levels of use were also those "moving up the ladder" in terms of relative income; those countries include Japan, Spain and perhaps West Germany. Second, the readings for Japan and France probably were a major source of the Rank Change effect. Both of those countries have invested heavily in high speed rail transport; since considerable subsidy is involved, there is no assurance that the investment has been sound.

In any event, threre is a cautionary tale here: regression results must always be interpreted with care, recognizing that misinterpretations can easily occur.

Additional information of relevance appears in the following comparisons of coefficient signs for the trend variable, Year.

Dependent Variable	Developing Countries	Industrial Countries	Table Source
Gasoline	+	+	7.1
Gasoline/Auto	+	-	7.2
Automobiles	+	+	7.5
Trucks	+	-	7.6
Rail passengers	-	-	7.7
Rail Freight	-	-	7.8
All Transport Fuel	+	+	7.9
Road Transport Fuel	+	+	7.10
Rail Transport Fuel	-	+	7.11
Air Transport Fuel	+	+	7.12
Water Transport Fuel	-	+	7.13

Here, there is good agreement between results for developing and for industrial countries, thus tending to support the earlier speculations on the relationship between development and mode.

Results for Individual Regressions

(Individual Tables)

In this section we briefly consider each of the individual regression equations, selecting particular items of interest for discussion.

Gasoline Consumption (Table 7.1)

If we compare income and price elasticities appearing in Table 7.1 to the corresponding entries in Table 6.1, we find good agreement for the developing countries, but a marked falling off in elasticity levels for the industrial countries. This illustrates a common problem in regression analysis. Adding additional variables to an initial set of explanatory variables can cause considerable change in coefficient estimates for the initial variables, relative to the results obtained using only the initial variables. As noted earlier, the amount of change depends on the level of correlation between the initial and the additional variables. A further problem is that there may be several lines of causation that can obscure results. For example, if level of per capita income is a "cause" of investment in the road network, the effect of income on transport use can become obscured, and probably reduced because some of that "indirect" effect will be attributed to the road network. In the gasoline regression, in fact, Road Density is highly significant for the industrial countries, but is not statistically significant for the developing countries. This may be a factor in the observed changes. As we shall see below, low fuel price and income elasticities occur only for gasoline in the industrial countries, and do not occur for all fuel and fuel used in road transport. Hence, the gasoline result appears to be a statistical quirk, perhaps attributable to sampling variability.

Gasoline Use per Automobile (Table 7.2)

As noted in Chapter 6, increased income per capita is estimated to reduce gasoline consumption per car in the developing countries and increase it in the industrial countries. In addition to these disagreements, most of the variables in the equation have opposite signs for the two sets of countries. There is good agreement on the effect of price, with an elasticity of -0.6 in both cases. That estimate was exceedingly stable in the various alternative formulations examined; most were quite close to the -0.6 result. The general divergence in pattern probably reflects differing underlying conditions. In turn, this may imply that for fuel efficiency issues, effective policy varies between the two groups.

Automobile Registrations (Tables 7.3 and 7.5)

When the price of gasoline is excluded from the equation, there is a statistically significant positive time trend for both developing and industrial countries. The introduction of gasoline price makes that trend nonsignificant in both cases, although it does remain positive. The positive, albeit low, gasoline price elasticity observed for both developing and industrial countries is not easy to explain. As noted earlier, perhaps improved fuel efficiency in response to higher prices has made automobile purchase more attractive, since the effective price of gasoline use per mile may have fallen.

Truck Registrations (Tables 7.4 and 7.6)

The regression equations perform better in explaining truck registrations for the developing countries than for the industrial countries, both in terms of the signs of income and price elasticities, and in level of explained variance (.9 for the developing countries and .7 for the industrial). The price of gasoline does have a large negative elasticity (-.96) for the industrial countries, but for those countries, the price elasticity for car prices is positive, contrary to expectations. There is evidence in tables 6.10 and 6.11, above, that the use of adjusted price of cars improved estimates for the developing countries, but may have been inappropriate or harmful for the industrial country estimates. Adjusted price, or Price II, was obtained by scaling the initial price estimate, or Price I, by the ratio of RGDP to GNP. In both Table 6.10 and 6.11, the Price I elasticity is negative, while the Price II elasticity is positive for the industrial countries.

Rail Passengers (Table 7.7)

The equations for rail passenger use show generally good agreement of results between the developing and industrial countries. However, income elasticity is of relatively high magnitude for the former group (1.1) and is negative for the latter, symptomatic of an inferior good. Price elasticity is positive in both cases.

Rail Freight (Table 7.8)

Somewhat surprisingly, income elasticity is higher for the industrial than for the developing countries; a further surprise is that both elasticities are relatively high (2.6 and 1.8, for industrial versus developing countries, respectively). Price elasticity is positive for the developing countries, and negative, at -0.7, for the industrial. Perhaps as a matter of public policy, in response to higher fuel prices, rail subsidies were increased generally in developing countries, while only passenger rail traffic was given more favorable treatment in industrial countries. Consequently, rail fares (presumably) did not rise with fuel prices or even moved in a contrary direction. Of course, this is an empirical question, but it seems worth detailed examination.

Transport Fuel by Mode (Tables 7.9-7.13)

If we assemble the income and price elasticities for transport fuel by mode, including the gasoline estimates from Table 7.1, the following list is obtained.

	Transport Fuel					
	All Modes	Road	Rail	Air Transport	Water Transport	Gasoline
Income Elasticities						
Developing	1.2	1.2	-0.1	1.0	-1.1	1.5
Industrial	1.3	1.3	1.5	1.5	0.3	0.3
Price						
Developing	-0.1	-0.2	0.6	-0.5	0.3	-0.4
Industrial	-0.6	-0.6	-0.8	-0.9	-1.2	-0.1

The -0.1 result for the rail fuel income elasticity in developing countries does not square with the results for rail passengers and rail freight, above (in tables 7.7 and 7.8). It is possible, as noted earlier, that rail fares have not risen with fuel prices, because of government subsidy, helping explain the contradiction. Alternatively, the result may be a statistical quirk, paralleling what seems a statistical quirk for the gasoline income elasticity in the industrial countries. Given the much higher income elasticity for road transport for those countries, and the general level of income elasticity for the other modes, it seems reasonable to treat the gasoline estimate as an understatement.

With that comment as preamble, some key conclusions emerge:

(1) income elasticities are relatively high in both developing and industrial countries, ranging from abut 1.2 to 1.5; since they are above 1.0, an increase in per capita income will lead to a somewhat more than proportionate increase in transport energy use.

(2) Price elasticities are below 1.0 in both sets of countries, and are considerably lower in the developing than in the industrial countries. For a given price increase, the proportunate reduction in per capita consumption is much less. No doubt this has been a major source of difficulty for the developing countries over the last decade.

It is also of some interest to compare elasticities for road density and for the urbanization related variables between the country groups. Those elasticities are as follows:

	Transport Fuel					
	All Modes	Road	Rail	Air Transport	Water Transport	Gasoline
Road Density						
Developing	0.2	0.2	1.0	0.5	0.7	0.1
Industrial	0.2	0.2	0.01	-0.2	0.3	0.7

There is good agreement between country groups and across categories for all transport fuel and road fuel. The high value for gasoline for the industrial countries is likely an overstatement, perhaps balancing the understatement for income.

The Urbanization related elasticities are as follows:

	Transport Fuel					
	All Modes	Road	Rail	Air Transport	Water Transport	Gasoline
Developing Countries						
Population Density	-0.3	-0.3	-0.3	-0.7	-0.1	-0.2
Percent Urban	-0.2	0.1	-0.0	-0.9	2.9	0.01
Percent Largest City	0.2	0.1	0.4	0.7	1.1	0.3
Industrial Countries						
Population Density	-0.1	-0.2	-0.5	0.2	-0.1	-0.7
Percent Urban	-0.6	-0.9	0.2	-0.6	2.5	0.9
Percent Largest City	-0.1	-0.1	0.3	0.3	-0.3	-0.2

For all transport fuels in all modes, increased urbanization clearly reduces transport energy consumption in the industrial countries and probably reduces it in the developing countries. Effects on individual modes are not obvious but they generally appear to involve a net reduction in consumption, also.

Explained Variance

A measure of the level of success attained in explaining the dependent variables is given by $\bar{R}^2$, the explained variance. For the developing countries, $\bar{R}^2$ values obtained in tables 7.14 and 7.15 are shown in the following list. Essentially the same results were obtained in tables 7.1 through 7.13. The $\bar{R}^2$ values are arranged in descending order.

Equation	$\bar{R}^2$ Explained Variance
Road Fuel	.951
All Transport Fuel	.948
Motor Gasoline	.924
Auto Registrations	.917
Truck Registration	.889
Air Transport Fuel	.690
Rail Transport Fuel	.599
Gasoline per Auto	.592
Water Transport Fuel	.573
Rail Passengers	.573
Rail Freight	.485

An $\bar{R}^2$ value of 1.0 indicates a complete explanation and a value of 0 indicates no explanation has been afforded by the putative explanatory variable. In our equations, the explanation ranges from about half the variation in the dependent variable to 95 percent of that variation. There is a clustering of high $\bar{R}^2$ values for the road transport variables. Thus, road fuel, all transport fuel, motor gasoline, automobile registrations and truck registrations have $\bar{R}^2$ values at about .9 or above.

Lowest levels of explanation occurred for the rail use variables and water transport fuel, suggesting the need for additional explanatory variables or more and better data in those cases. Results for the industrial countries showed a good deal of similarity.

The results for the rail variables reinforce our earlier conclusion that additional information on rail fares and pricing policies would likely be of considerable help in analysis.

Conclusions

Major conclusions that can be derived from the results presented in chapters 6 and 7 will be enumerated in this section. Those conclusions will summarize statistical results and attempt to integrate the interpretations, insights and speculations based on those results. Because the statistical results contained occasional anomalies and contradictions, judgment has been used to arrive at patterns that appear consistent and reasonable. The conclusions will first be presented in capsule form, and then some of the key items will be amplified. The capsule conclusions are:

1. Per capita consumption of transport and of transport fuel increases somewhat more than proportionately as per capita income increases.
2. Per capita consumption falls less than proportionately as price increases. The price response is more limited in developing than in industrial countries.
3. In conjunction, the first two conclusions imply that world and developing country levels of transport energy consumption should increase considerably over time.
4. Our evidence suggests that higher energy prices have caused some shift from road to rail use in the developing countries.
5. Not surprisingly, alternative energy modes are usually competitive; increased use of one reduces the use of another.
6. Increased density of the road network implies general increases in transport consumption and fuel use, with increases not limited to directly related consumption categories. This suggests that there are complementary as well as competitive relationships between alternative modes. In the developing countries, fuel efficiency appears to increase with increased road density.
7. As urbanization increases, fuel use probably decreases.
8. Long term trends in use are running against rail use and in favor of road and air transport use.
9. Among the developing countries, higher than average income growth was associated with reduced rail consumption and increased auto registrations and air transport fuel consumption. Among the industrial

countries, however, exactly the opposite pattern prevailed. Cause and effect relations here are not obvious, but are likely to be important. Let us amplify some of the key points involved in these conclusions.

Income Elasticities

Income elasticities for transport and transport fuel are relatively high for both developing and industrial countries, in the sense of being somewhat above 1.0 in both cases. A given percentage increase in per capita income will generally lead to a somewhat more than proportionate increase in consumption. Best estimates of developing country income elasticities were derived in Chapter 6; carrying out a similar process for the industrial countries and comparing results yields this array of estimates:

	Income Elasticity Estimates	
	Developing Countries	Industrial Countries
Fuel		
Gasoline	1.4	1.3?
Road Fuel	1.3	1.3
All Transport Fuel	1.2	1.3
Air Transport Fuel	1.1	1.5
Rail Transport Fuel	0.2?	1.5
Water Transport Fuel	0?	0.3
Fransport Category		
Auto Registrations	1.65	1.3
Truck Registrations	1.1	0.8
Rail Passengers	1.0	-0.7
Rail Freight	1.5	2.6
Fuel Efficiency		
Gasoline/Car	-0.3	0.4

Question marks indicate both the exercise of judgment and some remaining concern about possibly anomalous results, subject to revision given better evidence.

The results indicate developing and industrial country elasticities are fairly close.

Within the developing countries, our evidence suggested some increase in transport income elasticities as income rose, though the pattern was not clear cut. For gasoline and for all fuel, these estimates were obtained:

	Income Elasticities for Developing Countries		
	Low Income	Medium Income	High income
Gasoline	1.2	1.4	1.5
All Fuel	0.85	1.3	1.1

These results, in combination with the similarity of income elasticities for developing and industrial countries suggest that developing country income elasticites will not fall, and will likely rise somewhat, as income increases.

It is likely that there is some approach to "saturation" of use of major forms of transport and transport fuel if income grows large enough; thus, the U.S. income elasticity for gasoline was estimated as 1.1, somewhat below the 1.3 estimated for the industrial countries as a whole. Obviously, developing countries are many decades away from that situation.

Price Elasticities

Price elasticities are generally relatively low (inelastic) for both developing and industrial countries, so a given price increase yields less than a proportionate change in consumption. Further, developing country energy fuel price elasticities are generally below those of industrial countries, and low income developing countries have lower price elasticities than high income countries. In conjunction, these results imply more responsiveness to price over time by the developing countries, assuming that their per capita incomes increase.

Again deriving industrial country estimates to parallel those for the developing countries, the following array of best estimates for price elasticities are obtained:

	Price Elasticity Estimates	
	Developing Countries	Industrial Countries
Fuel		
Gasoline	-0.4	-0.6?
Road Fuel	-0.2	-0.6
All Transport Fuel	-0.15	-0.6
Air Transport Fuel	-0.3	-0.9
Water Transport Fuel	0.2	-1.2
Rail Transport Fuel	0.8	-0.8
Transport category		
Auto Registrations	-0.65	-0.3?
Truck Registrations	-0.4	-0.2?
Rail Passengers	1.0	1.0
Rail Freight	1.5	-0.6
Fuel Efficiency		
Gasoline/Car	-0.6	-0.6

Fuel price elasticities are lower, but auto and truck registration elasticities are higher for the developing than for the industrial countries.

Density of Road Network

Although we confirmed the obvious that alternative modes are competitive, results for density of road network suggest that there are complementary relations between alternative modes as well, for increases in road density were associated with increases in most forms of transport and transport fuel use. The coefficients for road density can be viewed as elasticities in the same fashion as the coefficients for income and price. The estimated road density elasticities for major fuel uses were as follows:

	Developing Countries	Industrial Countries
Gasoline	0.1	0.1
Road Fuel	0.2	0.2
Rail Fuel	1.0	0.0
All Transport Fuel	0.2	0.2

Urbanization Process

The urbanization process is accounted for in our set of explanatory variables by population density, percent of population that is urban, and percent of the urban population located in the largest city. Our evidence suggests that these variables, in combination, have a net negative effect on fuel use.

Elasticities for those demographic variables are exhibited for the major fuels in the following lists, by country group, with Developing Countries indicated by Dev, and Industrial by Indl:

Major Fuel Use	Population Density		Percent Urban		Percent in Largest City	
	Dev.	Indl.	Dev.	Indl.	Dev.	Indl.
Road Fuel	-0.3	-0.2	0.1	-0.9	0.1	-0.1
Rail Fuel	-0.3	-0.05	-0.0	0.2	0.4	0.3
All Transport Fuel	-0.3	-0.1	-0.2	-0.6	0.2	-0.1

The negative effect seems manifest in the results for all transport fuel. That negative effect may occur because the efficiencies outweigh the frictions of higher density and urbanization, or because the frictions imply that the net cost of transport increases, forcing reductions in its use.

Rank Change

The higher the value for rank change, the more a country increased its relative income over the period 1960-1980. For the developing countries, improved income position brought increased spending on all transport fuels, on road fuel and on air transport fuels and decreased spending on rail fuel. The opposite pattern held for the industrial country, as shown by these elasticities:

	Developing Countries	Industrial Countries
Road Fuel	0.2	-0.8
Rail Fuel	-2.7	0.5
Air Transport Fuel	1.7	-1.9
All Transport Fuel	0.1	-0.7

Disentangling cause and effect relations here seems an important topic for future research.

Table 7.1

Regression Results Explaining Log Per Capita Consumption of Motor Gasoline, by Country Group, Using Expanded Set of Explanatory Variables

Explantory variable (in logs)	Coefficients			t ratios		
	World	Developing countries	Industrial countries	World	Developing countries	Industrial countries
Intercept	5.666	-1.371	-10.517	2.03	-0.35	-2.92
RGDP per capita	1.804	1.524	0.287	26.96	13.78	1.45
Price of gasoline	-0.396	-0.408	-0.059	-8.25	-5.97	-0.72
Road density	0.135	0.059	0.747	3.47	1.05	10.19
Population density	-0.176	-0.227	-0.653	-6.05	-5.49	-10.21
Rank change	-0.063	0.177	-0.377	-0.66	1.29	-2.74
Rail passenger km per capita	-0.124	-0.115	-0.346	-5.07	-3.62	-7.15
Year	0.112	0.741	0.823	0.27	1.24	1.74
Percent urban	-0.127	0.006	0.896	-1.76	0.06	4.52
Percent medium age	-0.511	0.137	3.135	-1.27	0.28	4.16
Percent in largest city	0.078	0.265	-0.213	1.97	3.58	-4.33
N: Number of observations	(271)	(150)	(121)	--	--	--
$\bar{R}^2$: Adjusted explained variance	.949	.936	.933	--	--	--

Table 7.2

Regression Results Explaining Log Gasoline Consumption per Automobile, by Country Group, Using Expanded Set of Explanatory Variables

Explantory variable (in logs)	Coefficients			t ratios		
	World	Developing countries	Industrial countries	World	Developing countries	Industrial countries
Intercept	4.984	4.211	0.420	1.97	1.15	0.18
RGDP per capita	-0.182	-0.305	0.395	-2.97	-3.58	4.01
Price of gasoline	-0.609	-0.587	-0.575	-14.41	-10.72	-11.98
Road density	-0.054	-0.108	0.187	-1.42	-1.78	4.52
Population density	0.017	0.147	-0.167	0.65	3.52	-5.43
Rank change	-0.122	-0.144	-0.247	-3.35	-3.41	-3.02
Year	0.957	0.380	-0.024	2.41	0.61	-0.08
Percent urban	0.081	0.238	-0.154	1.43	3.19	-1.44
Percent medium age	-0.516	-0.003	2.110	-1.41	-0.01	4.36
Percent in largest city	0.210	0.264	-0.094	5.39	4.46	-2.55
N: Number of observations	(347)	(195)	(152)	--	--	--
$\bar{R}^2$: Adjusted explained variance	.720	.589	.855	--	--	--

Table 7.3

Regression Results Explaining Log Per Capita Automobile Registrations, by Country Group, Using Expanded Set of Explanatory Variables, Excluding Gasoline Prices

Explantory variable (in logs)	Coefficients: World	Coefficients: Developing countries	Coefficients: Industrial countries	t ratios: World	t ratios: Developing countries	t ratios: Industrial countries
Intercept	-1.955	-3.781	-3.995	-0.66	-0.83	-1.14
RGDP per capita	1.615	1.599	1.324	15.24	10.22	8.45
Price of cars II (adjusted)	-0.623	-0.658	-0.160	-7.57	-4.19	-1.44
Road density	0.117	0.093	0.105	2.17	1.00	1.81
Population density	-0.184	-0.204	-0.112	-5.19	-3.44	-2.51
Rank change	-0.316	-0.052	-0.684	-3.25	-0.31	-6.00
Rail passenger km. per capita	0.067	0.091	-0.055	2.25	2.02	-1.44
Year	3.235	3.949	2.144	5.98	4.35	3.42
Percent urban	-0.138	-0.173	-0.039	-1.51	-1.36	-0.23
Percent medium age	-1.925	-2.330	-1.080	-3.76	-2.99	-1.59
Percent in largest city	-0.088	-0.064	-0.036	-1.77	-0.48	-0.64
N: Number of observations	(483)	(265)	(218)	--	--	--
$\bar{R}^2$: Adjusted explained variance	.927	.814	.846	--	--	--

Table 7.4

Regression Results Explaining Log Per Capita Truck Regristrations by Country Group, Using Expanded Set of Explanatory Variables, Excluding Gasoline Prices

Explantory variable (in logs)	Coefficients: World	Coefficients: Developing countries	Coefficients: Industrial countries	t ratios: World	t ratios: Developing countries	t ratios: Industrial countries
Intercept	-8.014	-12.435	-4.928	-2.92	-3.74	-1.06
RGDP per capita	0.825	0.927	-0.315	7.66	7.86	-1.26
Price of cars II (adjusted)	-0.085	-0.587	0.755	-1.13	-5.87	4.66
Road density	0.432	0.261	1.050	8.87	3.95	13.30
Population density	-0.401	-0.316	-0.790	-11.97	-7.55	-12.97
Rank change	-0.038	-0.071	0.638	-0.43	-0.61	4.13
Rail freight ton km. per capita	0.015	0.090	-0.003	0.57	3.17	-0.06
Year	1.288	3.247	-0.525	2.58	5.84	-0.55
Percent urban	0.124	0.072	1.071	1.47	0.78	4.99
Percent medium age	-0.245	0.143	-1.183	-0.58	0.27	-1.26
Percent in largest city	0.356	0.081	-0.080	6.88	0.83	-0.99
N: Number of observations	(511)	(275)	(236)	--	--	--
$\bar{R}^2$: Adjusted explained variance	.877	.868	.686	--	--	--

Table 7.5

Regression Results Explaining Log Per Capita Automobile Registrations, by Country Group, Using Expanded Set of Explanatory Variables, Including Gasoline Price

Explantory variable (in logs)	Coefficients			t ratios		
	World	Developing countries	Industrial countries	World	Developing countries	Industrial countries
Intercept	5.438	5.951	-8.487	1.32	1.17	-1.93
RGDP per capita	1.951	2.609	0.367	14.70	15.12	1.47
Price of cars II (adjusted)	-0.354	0.200	-0.154	-3.19	1.03	-1.08
Road density	0.076	0.089	0.337	1.30	1.10	3.90
Population density	-0.178	-0.487	-0.299	-4.42	-9.22	-4.20
Rank change	-0.171	0.648	-0.304	-1.28	3.17	-1.95
Rail passenger km per capita	0.036	-0.003	-0.251	1.07	-0.08	-4.60
Year	1.730	0.546	1.831	2.07	0.46	1.84
Percent urban	-0.376	-1.177	0.433	-3.11	-7.14	1.88
Percent medium age	-2.685	2.732	0.117	-4.52	-4.11	0.14
Biggest city as percent urban pop.	-0.137	0.049	-0.100	-2.55	0.36	-1.72
Price of gasoline	0.229	0.138	0.426	3.37	1.59	4.63
N: Number of observations	(231)	(111)	(120)	--	--	--
$\bar{R}^2$: Explained variance	.942	.936	.824	--	--	--

Table 7.6

Regression Results Explaining Log Per Capita Truck Registrations, by Country Group, Using Expanded Set of Explanatory Variables, Including Gasoline Prices

Explantory variable (in logs)	Coefficients			t ratios		
	World	Developing countries	Industrial countries	World	Developing countries	Industrial countries
Intercept	-0.749	6.523	-22.670	-0.14	1.17	-3.39
RGDP per capita	1.254	1.361	0.271	7.04	6.93	0.70
Price of cars II (adjusted)	0.364	-0.398	1.019	2.54	-2.12	4.34
Road density	0.393	0.301	0.989	5.44	3.37	9.25
Population density	-0.299	-0.373	-0.658	-5.80	-6.65	-8.18
Rank change	0.316	-0.025	0.791	2.12	-0.14	3.63
Rail passenger km per capita	0.060	0.023	-0.159	1.64	0.57	-2.44
Year	-0.933	1.007	-0.796	-0.86	0.84	-0.47
Percent urban	-0.001	-0.136	0.795	-0.01	-0.81	2.75
Percent medium age	-1.146	-2.509	2.584	-1.71	-3.81	2.11
Biggest city as percent urban pop.	0.490	0.169	-0.030	6.18	1.13	-0.32
Price of gasoline	0.043	0.347	-0.959	0.52	3.73	-7.89
N: Number of observations	(249)	(119)	(130)	--	--	--
$\bar{R}^2$: Explained variance	.814	.904	.730	--	--	--

Table 7.7

Regression Results Explaining Log Per Capita Rail Passenger Kilometers Traveled, by Country Group, Using Expanded Set of Explanatory Variables

Explantory variable (in logs)	Coefficients			t ratios		
	World	Developing countries	Industrial countries	World	Developing countries	Industrial countries
Intercept	-10.015	8.257	-34.360	-1.42	0.81	-5.90
RGDP per capita	0.068	1.097	-0.744	0.25	2.68	-2.02
Price of gasoline	0.623	0.979	1.188	5.35	6.15	10.26
Road density	0.367	0.201	0.354	3.75	1.38	2.51
Population density	-0.108	-0.499	-0.221	-1.42	-4.09	-1.79
Rank change	0.206	-0.327	1.353	0.85	-0.88	6.01
Automobiles per capita	-0.132	-0.383	-0.590	-1.23	-2.65	-4.06
Year	-4.449	-5.550	-2.487	-4.38	-3.72	-2.93
Percent urban	-0.246	-1.224	2.177	-1.35	-4.42	7.09
Percent medium age	6.881	4.833	7.579	7.42	3.95	6.41
Percent in largest city	0.126	0.045	0.139	1.25	0.23	1.51
N: Number of observations	(271)	(150)	(121)	--	--	--
$\bar{R}^2$: Adjusted explained variance	.705	.569	.864	--	--	--

Table 7.8

Regression Results Explaining Log Per Capita Rail Freight Ton Kilometers Shipped, by Country Group, Using Expanded Set of Explanatory Variables

Explantory variable (in logs)	Coefficients			t ratios		
	World	Developing countries	Industrial countries	World	Developing countries	Industrial countries
Intercept	44.566	43.909	19.826	5.07	3.26	2.16
RGDP per capita	1.433	1.773	2.599	5.81	3.70	7.10
Price of gasoline	1.084	1.759	-0.645	7.63	8.37	-3.28
Road density	0.145	-0.578	0.297	1.11	-2.73	1.76
Population density	-0.655	-0.527	-0.513	-6.85	-3.05	-4.01
Rank change	0.079	-0.545	1.325	0.28	-1.21	4.53
Trucks per capita	0.074	-0.036	-0.262	0.61	-0.17	-2.28
Year	-6.377	-7.324	-2.731	-4.87	-3.52	-2.14
Percent urban	-0.749	-0.991	0.962	-3.28	-2.93	-2.66
Percent medium age	-2.595	-1.073	-2.615	-2.20	-0.63	-1.59
Percent in largest city	-1.032	-1.326	-0.177	-7.46	-5.19	-1.42
N: Number of observations	(289)	(158)	(131)	--	--	--
$\bar{R}^2$: Adjusted explained variance	.626	.480	.823	--	--	--

Table 7.9

Regression Results Explaining Log Per Capita
Consumption of All Transport Fuel, by Country Group,
Using Expanded Set of Exploratory Variables

Explantory variable (in logs)	Coefficients			t ratios		
	World	Developing countries	Industrial countries	World	Developing countries	Industrial countries
Intercept	7.961	5.467	-3.351	3.90	2.32	-1.45
RGDP per capita	1.335	1.168	1.341	31.59	23.98	14.57
Price of gasoline	-0.106	-0.091	-0.626	-3.33	-2.56	-13.62
Road density	0.178	0.174	0.153	6.60	5.00	3.93
Population density	-0.219	-0.280	-0.116	-11.44	-10.87	-3.91
Rank change	-0.118	0.118	-0.703	1.90	1.59	9.59
Year	0.690	0.605	3.469	1.95	1.41	9.84
Percent urban	-0.280	-0.162	-0.584	-7.18	-3.89	-5.69
Percent medium age	-1.042	-0.685	-0.450	-4.19	-2.73	-1.00
Percent in largest city	0.034	0.193	-0.068	1.24	5.29	-2.00
N: Number of observations	(277)	(148)	(129)	--	--	--
$\bar{R}^2$: Adjusted explained variance	.956	.948	.946	--	--	--

Table 7.10

Regression Results Explaining Log Per Capita Consumption of
All Fuels in Road Transport by Country Group, Using Expanded Set
of Explanatory Variables

Explantory variable (in logs)	Coefficients			t ratios		
	World	Developing countries	Industrial countries	World	Developing countries	Industrial countries
Intercept	1.370	-0.862	0.177	0.48	-0.19	0.06
RGDP per capita	1.382	1.240	1.312	22.92	11.84	11.98
Price of gasoline	-0.206	-0.198	-0.557	-4.68	-3.14	-10.17
Road density	0.163	0.209	0.240	5.08	3.67	5.19
Population density	-0.226	-0.328	-0.201	-10.15	-8.60	-5.71
Rank change	-0.246	0.186	-0.759	-2.85	1.37	-8.70
Year	1.703	1.509	3.859	-3.75	2.00	9.20
Percent urban	-0.038	0.133	-0.895	-0.61	1.23	-7.33
Percent medium age	-0.666	-0.353	-1.235	-1.87	-0.72	-2.30
Percent in largest city	-0.047	0.061	-0.149	-1.38	0.89	-3.70
N: Number of observations	(240)	(111)	(129)	--	--	--
$\bar{R}^2$: Adjusted explained variance	.961	.949	.935	--	--	--

Table 7.11

Regression Results Explaining Log Per Capita Consumption All Fuels in Rail Transport, by Country Group, Using Expanded Set of Explanatory Variables

Explantory variable (in logs)	Coefficients			t ratios		
	World	Developing countries	Industrial countries	World	Developing countries	Industrial countries
Intercept	16.930	67.679	-4.798	2.37	5.32	-0.88
RGDP per capita	0.492	-0.145	1.481	3.23	-0.47	6.83
Price of gasoline	-0.145	0.633	-0.789	-1.12	3.01	-7.28
Road density	0.736	0.984	0.007	9.00	5.19	0.08
Population density	-0.550	-0.291	-0.048	-9.72	-3.28	-0.69
Rank change	-1.019	-2.791	0.501	4.93	-8.48	2.90
Year	-1.892	-9.570	0.634	-1.58	-4.20	0.76
Percent urban	-0.824	-0.003	0.192	-5.12	-0.01	0.79
Percent medium age	0.753	-3.452	-0.104	0.88	-2.86	-0.10
Percent in largest city	-0.066	0.430	0.343	-0.84	2.18	4.30
N: Number of observations	(217)	(88)	(129)	--	--	--
$\bar{R}^2$: Adjusted explained variance	.629	.594	.778	--	--	--

Table 7.12

Regression Results Explaining Log Per Capita Consumption of All Fuels in Air Transport, by Country Group, Using Expanded Set of Explanatory Variables

Explantory variable (in logs)	Coefficients			t ratios		
	World	Developing countries	Industrial countries	World	Developing countries	Industrial countries
Intercept	13.192	-21.479	5.089	1.57	-1.82	0.76
RGDP per capita	1.834	0.972	2.054	10.44	3.61	7.77
Price of gasoline	-0.075	-0.488	-0.918	-0.59	-3.05	-6.95
Road density	0.338	0.520	-0.202	3.61	3.56	-1.81
Population density	-0.320	-0.728	0.210	-4.93	-7.43	2.48
Rank change	-0.362	1.714	-1.850	-1.46	5.04	-8.79
Year	0.361	3.485	4.584	0.27	1.80	4.53
Percent urban	-1.416	-0.907	-0.582	-7.66	-3.25	-1.98
Percent medium age	-1.424	1.918	-4.169	-1.38	1.52	-3.22
Percent in largest city	0.295	0.721	0.299	3.00	4.10	3.08
N: Number of observations	(241)	(112)	(129)	--	--	--
$\bar{R}^2$: Adjusted explained variance	.666	.695	.791	--	--	--

Table 7.13

Regression Results Explaining Log Per Capita Consumption of Fuels in Water Transport, by Country Group, Using Expanded Set of Explanatory Variables

Explantory variable (in logs)	Coefficients			t ratios		
	World	Developing countries	Industrial countries	World	Developing countries	Industrial countries
Intercept	-13.685	-0.969	-50.016	-0.94	-0.04	-2.55
RGDP per capita	-0.164	-1.079	-0.333	-0.53	-2.00	-0.37
Price of gasoline	-0.127	0.262	-1.186	-0.42	0.57	-2.14
Road density	0.313	0.674	0.262	1.74	1.79	0.76
Population density	-0.142	-0.074	-0.129	-1.04	-0.34	-0.45
Rank change	0.386	0.387	0.113	0.96	0.58	0.20
Year	-1.755	-2.083	0.208	-0.69	-0.44	0.06
Percent urban	1.823	2.883	2.473	5.35	4.95	2.51
Percent medium age	3.726	-0.590	10.477	2.19	-0.24	2.99
Percent in largest city	0.252	1.129	-0.305	1.64	3.35	-1.15
N: Number of observations	(191)	(79)	(112)	--	--	--
$\bar{R}^2$: Adjusted explained variance	.605	.554	.172	--	--	--

Table 7.14

Regression Results for significant Coefficients Only, First Six Categories of Transport Consumption, All Developing Countries

Explanatory variable (in logs)	Motor gasoline	Gasoline per automobile	Autos	Trucks	Rail passenger kilometers	Rail freight ton kilometers
	Coefficients					
Intercept	1.666	5.843	-3.762	-9.075	3.072	34.238
RGDP per capita	1.428	-0.303	1.683	1.019	1.159	1.744
Price of gasoline	-0.357	-0.578	0.242	0.316	0.903	1.617
Price of cars II (adjusted)	--	--	-0.579	-0.623	--	--
Road density	--	-0.105	0.136	0.213	0.202	-0.614
Population density	-0.095	0.146	-0.379	-0.343	-0.535	-0.560
Rank change	--	-0.149	0.231	--	--	--
Competitive mode per capita[a]	-0.152	--	--	--	-0.423	--
Year	--	--	3.940	2.740	-5.028	-6.335
Percent urban	--	0.241	-0.231	--	-1.201	-0.978
Percent medium age	--	--	-2.408	--	5.305	--
Percent in largest city	0.450	0.267	-0.181	--	--	-1.465
N: Number of observations	(272)	(195)	(155)	(164)	(150)	(158)
$\bar{R}^2$: Adjusted explained variance	.924	.592	.917	.889	.573	.485
	t ratios					
Intercept	9.16	12.98	-0.90	-3.16	0.37	4.05
RGDP per capita	38.78	-3.86	16.50	18.12	3.36	5.21
Prices of gasoline	-8.54	-11.24	3.45	4.68	7.08	9.49
Price of cars II (adjusted)	--	--	-3.86	-6.94	--	--
Road density	-4.02	-1.84	1.91	3.37	1.63	-3.40
Population density	--	3.60	-8.06	-8.01	-4.71	-4.07
Rank change	--	-3.69	5.38	--	--	--
Competitive mode per capita[a]	-6.68	--	--	--	-3.09	--
Year	--	--	3.95	3.60	-3.68	-3.35
Percent urban	--	3.25	-2.72	--	-5.46	-2.96
Percent medium age	--	--	-4.88	--	4.88	--
Percent in largest city	9.84	4.57	-2.30	--	--	-6.71

--indicates not statistically significant.

[a]For given mode of road transport the corresponding rail transport mode was treated as competitive, with the reverse relation for each mode of rail transport. Thus, these pairs were specified:

Given mode	Competitive mode
motor gasoline	rail passenger kilometers
autos	rail passenger kilometers
trucks	rail freight ton kilometers
rail passenger km	autos
rail freight ton km	trucks

Table 7.15

Regression Results for Significant Coefficients Only, for Five Categories of Fuel Use by Mode, All Developing Countries

Explanatory variable (in logs)	All modes	Road	Rail	Air	Water
	Fuel Use by Mode				
	Coefficients				
Intercept	8.898	-1.263	67.699	1.356	-10.589
RGDP per capita	1.186	1.320	-0.147	1.059	-0.940
Price of gasoline	-0.050	-0.182	0.633	-0.323	0.215
Road density	0.162	0.169	0.985	0.591	0.556
Population density	-0.263	-0.318	-0.291	-0.718	--
Rank change	--	--	-2.790	1.549	--
Year	--	1.535	-9.575	--	--
Percent urban	-0.168	--	--	-0.831	2.677
Percent medium age	-0.809	--	-3.455	--	--
Percent in largest city	0.187	--	0.432	0.800	1.029
N: Number of observations	(148)	(117)	(88)	(112)	(79)
$\bar{R}^2$: Adjusted explained variance	.948	.951	.599	.690	.573
	t ratios				
Intercept	8.60	-0.50	5.45	0.70	-4.89
RGDP per capita	24.85	36.12	-1.18	4.08	-1.91
Price of gasoline	-1.79	-4.34	3.03	-2.39	0.73[a]
Road density	4.88	3.92	6.95	4.17	2.00
Population density	-11.13	-10.17	-3.31	-7.34	--
Rank change	--	--	-8.65	4.72	--
Year	--	2.62	-4.40	--	--
Percent urban	-4.19	--	--	-3.00	5.36
Percent medium age	-3.32	--	-2.99	--	--
Percent in largest city	5.22	--	3.68	4.65	3.39

--indicates not statistically significant.

[a]retained in equation although not significant, by convention.

Part IV

Case Studies of India and Ecuador

India and Ecuador offer strong contrasts. Per capita energy consumption of transport energy in Ecuador is ten times higher than in India although income per head is only 3 times higher. Differences in pricing policy account for the higher transport energy intensity of the Ecuadorian economy. Diesel and gasoline prices in Ecuador are among the cheapest in the world. On the other hand, in India gasoline is heavily taxed and diesel is quite close to international levels and in any event much higher in price than in Ecuador.

Chapter 8

The Case of India[1]

Although major improvements to the transport system have been made in the past, they have not been sufficient to keep pace with increasing economic activity. Insufficient throughput capacity and frequent delays still characterize many transport services in the country. Such conditions are typical of many developing countries but they are perceived to be more serious in India than elsewhere (with the possible exception of China whose transport system shares many similarities with India's). This central characteristic must be bourne in mind in interpreting past trends in transport energy consumption and speculating on future developments.

Trends in transport fuel use

In contrast to experience in many of the other developing countries, consumption of transport fuels in India has increased rather gradually over the past decade, by an annual average of about 2.6 percent (see Table 8.1). Moreover, some major shifts in consumption by the different transport sectors have taken place.

India is one of the few developing countries (China and Turkey are others) with an extensive railroad network. In 1971 railroads consumed almost 60 percent of all energy used in transport. In the subsequent

---

1. This chapter is based on a study of energy use in the India transport sector by Chauri Gadhock and Kapil Thukral of the Tata Energy Research Institute, New Delhi, India.

decade energy consumption by railroads fell steadily, and by 1982 it accounted for only 34 percent of total transport consumption.

In contrast to rail, consumption of energy in the other main transport sector--road--rose rapidly by an annual average of 7.7 percent from 1971 to 1982. By 1982 its share of total transport energy consumption had risen to 60 percent compared with 34 percent in the early 1970s. Virtually all of this increase took the form of diesel rather than gasoline--again a rather unusual development.

Finally, the two smaller transport sectors followed trends shared by many countries--a decline in the share of transport fuels accounted for by internal navigation, and an above average increase in air.

This shift in sectoral consumption was accompanied (see Table 8.2) by a considerable change in the mix of transport fuels. At the beginning of the period coal was the major fuel accounting for over 50 percent of the total. By 1983 its share had fallen to 25 percent (still much higher than other countries, except China). The share of petroleum products rose on the other hand from 46 to 71 percent of transport fuels. Among petroleum based transport fuels, the share of gasoline fell from 11 to 8 percent of total transport enegy consumption, an unusually low share for gasoline. By contrast diesel fuel increased its share of total transport energy consumption substantially from 29 to 50 percent; electricity which still plays a small role in transport, maintained its 1 percent share.

Changes in consumption of transport fuels are affected by a number of factors. The expansion in economic activity leads to a rise in transport activity (as indicated for example by increases in freight and passengers carried) and therefore, other things being equal, to an increase in the amount of energy used in transport. However, other things are not usually equal, and the trend to higher consumption as economic activity rises can be offset or reinforced by shifts from one transport mode to another, or by developments in the energy efficiency of each mode.

Transport activity levels and charges

Activity in both freight and passenger transport rose steadily over the period (1960 to 1980) for which data are available (see Table 8.3 and 8.4). Freight traffic which includes road and rail, though excludes the quantitatively small internal navigation and air freight, rose by an average of 3.6 percent a year from the early 60's to 1980 (see Table 8.3) more or less keeping track with the expansion of the economy. Thus the number of freight tons carried per million U.S.$ of constant GNP remained fairly steady over this period, though with some fluctuations. These fluctuations are believed to be due primarly to capacity constraints particularly in the railways. Freight transport costs probably remained constant in real terms over most of the period so that little change in freight could be ascribed to price changes. From 1980/81 to 1982/83, however, there was a sharp increase in tariffs to enable the railway sector to finance its modernization programs through internal resources, with minimal budgetary support in contrast to past procedures when expenditures were met from general budget revenues. It is too early to say at this point whether this quite sharp change in tariff policy has had an impact on rail traffic. It illustrates, however, the potential dilemma of railroad management. A reduction in subsidies leads to higher tariffs, thus encouraging a shift to road transport.

An interesting issue is whether different development strategies have differential impacts on the amount of freight activity. It is widely believed for example that heavy industry is more transport intensive than light industry and agriculture, and that an emphasis on rapid development of heavy industry would lead to a particularly sharp increase in transport activity relative to GNP. The period (the 1970s) covered by detailed data of freight transport suggests some change in emphasis from heavy to light industry and agriculture which may account for the rather lower freight traffic intensities in the mid-seventies compared with scattered data for previous years.

Passenger transport (see Table 8.4) expanded much more rapidly than freight. In the 1970s passenger kilometer in road and rail rose by an annual average of 6 percent (in contrast to freight transport's 3.5 percent rate). Air travel increased oven more rapidly by over 13 percent a year, but even so is a very small part of total passenger traffic. The increase in passenger transport was much greater than the rise in population, and passenger kilometers per capita more than doubled from 268 in 1966 to 682 in 1979. As Table 8.4 also shows, the increase in passenger transport was substantially higher--about twice as high--than the rise in GNP.

This sharp rise in passenger travel, up to 1980 at least, did not appear to be constrained by higher costs. Thus (from Table 8.4) both rail tariffs and diesel fuel costs remained fairly stable in this period. Gasoline prices however, rose sharply after 1974 and as shown below per

	1970	1973	1974	1975	1976	1979	1980	1982
Per capita consumption of motor gasoline (koe)	2.8	3.0	2.3	2.1	2.2	2.5	2.2	2.6
Gasoline prices (1975 $ per gal.)	0.75	0.87	1.92	1.60	1.35	1.46	1.63	1.42

capita consumption of gasoline fell in subsequent years by 25 percent from pre-1974 levels. A less sharp rise in prices in 1980 was associated with a smaller fall in consumption, but as inflation eroded these price rises, gasoline consumption has begun to rise again.

Because of the sharp increase in gasoline prices in 1974 while diesel prices were held constant, the gap between diesel and gasoline prices widened thus encouraging diesel consumption at the expense of gasoline. The effect of changes in gasoline prices on gasoline consumption for India over this period is estimated at -.36, that is a 10 percent increase in gasoline prices was associated with a 3.6 percent decline in consumption. For India gasoline consumption appears to be relatively insensitive to income changes with an income elasticity of 0.02 to 0.05 unusually low for a developing country. Thus there was a sharp fall in gasoline consumption after the 1973 price rise despite a steady rise in income.

Since 1980 both rail tariffs and diesel prices have risen sharply, though, as in the case of freight transport, it is too soon to see whether these cost increases have affected the level of travel.

Modal shifts

Trends in activity levels in the transport sector--the increase in freight and passenger kilometers associated with higher incomes--are therefore a factor leading to an increase in consumption in transport fuels. Consumption also depends on how the traffic is distributed among modes of varying energy intensity. If traffic switches from less to more energy intensive modes, energy consumption will go up even faster than the rate suggested by the overall growth in traffic. And, of course, vice versa.

In this context, a major development was the shift from rail to road, as, for a wide range of load and other assumptions rail traffic is less energy intensive than road. For passenger traffic the share of rail fell from 58 percent in 1961 to 40 percent in the early 1970s and the share of road rose from 42 percent to 60. Over the '70s there has been little change in shares with road now established as the major mode (see Table 8.5).

An interesting feature of India rail traffic is the large share of suburban (or commuting passengers), which accounted in 1983 for example for 55 percent of all rail passengers. As suburban distances are relatively small however their share of passenger kilometers is much lower (20 percent). The number of suburban passenger has rise much faster than long distance passengers suggesting that extensions and improvements to suburban railways have offered a viable alternative to commuting by road whether by bus, taxi or car. In recent years, however, the number of total passengers carried by rail has not increased which may signal some saturation in rail passenger transport.

In freight there was a less decisive but still pronounced shift from rail to road in the 1960s but since the early '70s rail has retained its two-third share of total freight carried. The failure of rail traffic to rise as rapidly as envisaged has important consequences for modernization, as several routes did not meet the traffic densities (20 mn gross tonne kilometers per route kilometer) required for electrification.

Our data on freight and passenger traffic by road stops at 1979 but there is evidence (a report of the Indian Energy Advisory Board) that from 1979 to 1983 a further, very rapid increase took place. The actual levels provided for 1983 in the Board report are well in excess of projections for that year made by experienced analysts only a few years previously. If the Board's data are comparable with the historical series, the last few years will have seen a new phase in the move from rail to road.

There are a number of reasons behind these developments. In India as throughout the world, there has been a move from rail to road reflecting the greater flexibility and therefore convenience of road transport especially for short haul freight. Indeed, the increasing average lead in rail transport (from 660 km in 1970-1 to 730 km in 1983) suggests that road is increasingly taking over short haul traffic. Though it is believed that both road and rail facilities are by now inadequate to deal promptly with the rising traffic, the rigidities in the rail sector are probably worse, leading more traffic to move to the road sector.

The changing structure of the economy may also have some influence. Railway networks were laid down to respond to well established traffic movements. As these movements change in response to economic development and changes in composition of imports and exports, the rail networks lose their usefulness and the new traffic patterns are frequently handled by the road network which is more suited to incremental expansion.

Government policy has also played a role. Though railways as the basic form of transport receive the single largest part of total public sector investments in transport (as high as 70 percent in the Third year Plan) the share of expenditures on roads and road transport has increased steadily and is now (in the Sixth Plan) at 39 percent, just short of the 42 percent devoted to rail (see Table 8.6).

Expenditures on rail transport have been to standardize gauges, extend the suburban lines (which carry some 20 percent of total rail passenger traffic), substitute diesel locomotives for steam and electrify certain densely travelled routes. As we shall see this development also has important implications for modal efficiencies.

Expenditures on road transport were devoted to increasing both total and surfaced road length. From the early 1950s to the mid 1970s total road increased by three and a half times. Surfaced road throughout the period has accounted for about 40 percent of total roads. The emphasis throughout the program has been on development of district and village roads rather than national and state highways. While this emphasis has improved access for rural areas the relative neglect of highways may have limited the further expansion of inter-city freight and passenger traffic.

An important aspect of road utilization is the provision of the road transport equipment, largely the responsibility of the private sector, although strongly influenced by government policy. The total number of motor vehicles in India increased fivefold from 1965 to 1982 (see Table 8.7) representing a substantial increase in vehicle ownership in relation to total population (from 2 per 000 population in 1965 to 8.7 in 1982). Vehicle ownership is nevertheless much lower than in many developing countries. Vehicle ownership is expensive--the present writer recently rode in India in a 27 year old Fiat which had been bought two years previously for the equivalent of US $2000. Import duties on cars are high, but, more important, importation for private purposes is virtually prohibited. Supplies are therefore limited to locally manufactured cars with low energy efficiencies. Recently, however, the government have permitted the manufacturers to seek foreign collaboration in manufacturing more energy efficient cars.

Vehicle operation is also expensive; gasoline prices are among the most expensive in the world due to high excise taxes. Diesel, on the other hand, is relatively cheap, and the increasing price differential between the two has led to an increase in diesel cars. It will be recalled from Table 8.1 that consumption of gasoline barely increased over the period while diesel rose sharply.

The impacts of this high cost regime on vehicle ownership is again illustrated in Table 8.7. Most categories of motor vehicles (cars, taxis, buses, trucks) rather more than doubled in number from 1965 to 1982. Two categories however increased tenfold. These are "other vehicles" including farm and special vehicles, and, quantitatively more important, two and three wheelers which are scooters and small taxi/utility vehicles. In 1965 two and three wheelers accounted for 20 percent of all vehicles. By 1982 their share had increased to 50 percent. The major increase in road transport equipment for private passenger use therefore took the form of scooters and three wheelers rather than cars and taxis.

There was also a rapid increase in the most energy intensive of all transport modes--air transport. The number of domestic passengers increased threefold from 1971 to 1983, and revenue passenger miles rose by an annual average of 13 percent over the same period.

Inland water ways and coastal shipping are relatively more efficient than land based modes. However, water bourne traffic has played a limited role. Freight traffic peaked in the early 1960s but has since declined sharply due to a number of factors such as vintage of existing fleet or tugboats, barges and tankers, lack of suitable terminal facilities, unsuitability of many rivers for mechanized craft, inadequate and time-consuming loading and unloading facilities.

In general, there has been a strong modal shift from rail to road in both passenger and to a lesser extent freight transport. From the data available this does not appear to have been a steady trend--in the ′70s the relative shares of both modes were quite stable--but over the longer period the trend seems well established. Furthermore, there has been a rapid rise in air transport and a decline in energy efficient inland waterways and coastal shipping. Together, these factors would be expected to lead to a further increase in transport energy consumption over and above the increase needed for higher activity levels.

Modal efficiencies

The final factor to consider is trends in energy efficiency of the different modes. Here evidence points to considerable improvements in some modal efficiencies, with an increase in railway energy efficiency (measured in 000 toe/bn gross ton kilometer) from 21 in 1973/4 to 12 in 1982/3--a rise of 43 percent in 9 years (see Table 8.8). It is interesting to note that the energy efficiencies of the different forms of rail traction did not rise and even fell substantially in the case of steam. The reason for the overall increase in efficiency is therefore a major switch in locomotive power from energy intensive coal to diesel and electric. Steam traction is highly energy intensive using in 1982/3 61,000 toe per bn gross ton kilometers compared with 3,000 for diesel and electric locomotion.

The extent of the switch from steam to diesel and electric is illustrated by the change in the composition of the locomotive stock. In the early seventies steam accounted for 86 percent of all locomotives but by 1983 their share had fallen to 70 percent. The decline in the share of traffic accounted for by steam is even greater, as steam locomotives are increasingly used in short hauls. This fact is largely responsible for the decline in energy efficiency of steam locomotion which took place from 1970/1 to 1982/3.

The change in means of locomotion shows up in the changing composition of fuels used by the railways in Table 8.1. Coal consumption fell in absolute terms from 1973 to 1983 and its share of the total declined from 90 to 75 percent. On the other hand, consumption of diesel and electricity both doubled. Even so, due to the much higher efficiencies of diesel and electricity the total amount of energy used by the railways declined over the period, despite the higher traffic. If this improvement in efficiency had not taken place energy consumption by the railwys would have been higher. The dieselization and electrification of the railways yields a once and for all improvement in efficiency. Once the process has been completed--and it is still some way from completion in India--consumption will normally start rising again.

From data available for road transport, it appears that efficiencies, that is the amount of fuel consumed per passenger or ton kilometer, have fallen. Total consumption of energy in road transport increased by about 90 percent in the 1970s whereas freight kilometers rose by about 25 percent and passenger kilometers by 60 percent. Efficiencies of road transport on average may have fallen by about 20-25 percent.

So far as passenger transport is concerned, the decline in fuel efficiencies could be due to partially offsetting faactors. On the one hand, part of the higher energy consumption in road transport is due to a move to private transport modes. This happens in all countries as incomes rise. On the other hand, this desire for private transport appears to have been accommodated at the cost of relatively small falls in average efficiencies, through the use of small three wheelers (with an average energy intensity of 625 btus per passenger kilometer) rather than cars and taxis (2000 btu).

In relative terms the most striking fall in efficiencies has been in air transport. The energy per available seat kilometer almost halved (from 0.083 litres to 0.049) from 1971 to 1983. This has been made possible by replacing high energy intensive turbo propulsion by jet aircraft such as the Airbus and Boeing 737 for domestic routes.

Conclusion

In conclusion, energy consumption in transport between 1971 and 1981, the period for which data are more readily available, rose by about 2.6 percent a year, lower than the rise in GNP and indeed lower than the rise in total energy consumption (4.2 percent). Contributing to this increase was the rise in all forms of transport activity--passenger and freight--in rail, road and air, though the first two are quantitatively by far the most important. Further contributions to higher total transport energy consumption derived from a distinct shift from rail to road passenger and freight transport and some lower efficiencies within the road transport sector. On the other hand, major efficiency savings in rail transport, and, though of lesser quantitative importance, in air transport, restrained the increase in consumption. Though they are not easy to quantify, these efficiency improvements may have saved two percentage points a year in the rate of increase in transport energy consumption.

Most of these developments have been closely affected by government policies in the form of investment in road and rail networks, changes in rail transport equipment, pricing policies for fuels and car ownership. The net result has been to hold back consumption in the transport sector by ensuring continued use of the railways, improving the efficiency of locomotion, and discouraging private car ownership. In the lastdecade or two this policy has met with some success at least as far as transport energy consumption is concerned. However, there are widespread reports of inadequate transport facilities and severe congestion on railroads, and inter-city highways. If economic development is not to be held back, further investments in the transport system will be necessary. Road transport can be expected to increase more rapidly than rail and the pressure for private passenger transport to grow. In future, however, there will not be the potential for dramatic savings from dieselization of the railways. In these circumstances the rate of increase in energy consumption in the transport sector could well accelerate.

Table 8.1

India: Energy Use in Transport

(000 toe)

	1971	1972	1973	1974	1975	1976	1977	1978	1979	1980	1981	1982	Avg. ann. increase (%)
Rail	8618	8452	7975	7851	8052	7591	7516	7085	6830	6980	6798	6732	-2.3
- coal	7887	7657	7182	7067	7147	6582	6462	6065	5689	5909	5635	5498	-3.3
- oil	591	637	661	652	745	822	856	832	943	877	947	1000	+4.9
- elec.	140	157	132	132	160	186	198	188	198	195	216	234	+4.8
Road	5073	5418	5845	6586	6911	7201	7738	8438	9528	10050	10625	11512	+7.7
- gasoline	n.a.	n.a.	1702	1627	1334	1364	1408	1485	1604	1584	1629	1711	0
- diesel	n.a.	n.a.	4143	4959	5577	5837	6330	6953	7924	8466	8996	9801	+10.0
Air	878	881	929	882	977	1044	1130	1250	1234	1214	1221	1239	+3.2
Water	303	222	89	177	219	225	197	200	287	199	234	217	-1.9
Total (including non-spec)	14872	14973	14938	15496	16159	16061	16581	16973	17879	18443	18878	19730	+2.6

Source: Energy Balances of Developing Countries 1971/82 International Energy Agency, OECD, Paris 1984

Table 8.2

India: Share of Different Fuels in Total Transport Energy Consumption

%

	1971	1972	1973	1974	1975	1976	1977	1978	1979	1980	1981	1982
Coal	53	51	48	46	44	41	39	36	32	32	30	28
Petroleum	46	48	51	54	55	58	60	63	67	67	69	71
Electricity	1	1	1	1	1	1	1	1	1	1	1	1

Source: Table 1.

Table 8.3

India: Freight Traffic

	1960/1	1965/6	1970/1	1971/2	1972/3	1973/4	1974/5	1975/6	1976/7	1977/8	1978/9	Annual Average increase
Road & rail freight traffic (bn tonne km)	122.7	171.9	193.4	199.2	203.5	189.4	205.3	221.3	232.8	240.0	231.0	3.6
GNP (bn '78 US$)	61.8	69.5	88.2	89.6	93.1	93.5	102.0	104.0	112.0	117.5	115.8	3.6
Freight (tkm per $ GNP)	1.985	2.473	2.193	2.223	2.186	2.026	2.013	2.128	2.079	2.043	1.995	0
Rail tariff (paise per ton km in '71 paises)	n.a.	n.a.	5.43	5.05	4.35	3.75	4.74	5.075	5.40	n.a.	n.a.	n.a.
Diesel price (1980 Rs/litre)	n.a.	n.a.	1.67	1.68	1.43	1.16	1.40	1.79	1.64	1.60	1.66	n.a.

Source: Annual Statistical Statements, Ministry of Railways, Gov't of India, various issues; Report of National Transport Policy Committe, 1980.

Table 8.4

India: Passenger Traffic

	1960/1	1965/6	1970/1	1971/2	1972/3	1973/4	1974/5	1975/6	1976/7	1977/8	1978/9	Annual Average increase (%)
Road & rail passenger Km (bn)	134.6	191.3	287.1	315.3	329.5	343.6	345.3	373.8	398.8	427.0	463.0	7.1
Domestic air passenger kms (bn)	n.a.	n.a.	1.5	1.8	2.2	1.9	2.2	2.6	2.9	3.4	4.1	13.4
Population (mn)	502.0	551.3	564.3	577.5	591.0	604.7	618.8	633.3	648.0	663.1	678.5	1.7
Per capita road & rail passenger kilometers	268	347	509	546	558	568	558	590	615	644	682	5.3
Road & rail (Pass. km per $75 GNP)	1.937	2.753	3.255	3.519	3.539	3.675	3.385	3.594	3.560	3.634	3.998	4.1
Rail tariff (paise per pass. km in 1971 paise)			2.79	2.57	2.18	1.94	2.48	2.50	2.46			
Gasoline price (1980 Rs/litre)			2.36	2.68	2.31	3.45	3.88	4.35	4.00	3.90	4.35	

Note: For diesel fuel prices see Table 8.3.

Source: Annual Statistical Statements, Ministry of Railways, Gov't. of India, various issues; Report of National Transport Policy Committee 1980, Annual Reports Indian Airlines.

Table 8.5

India: Change in Transport Modes

	1960/1	1965/6	1970/1	1971/2	1972/3	1973/4	1974/5	1975/6	1976/7	1977/8	1978/9	Annual Average increase (%)
Road & rail freight trans. (bn of km	122.7	171.9	193.4	199.2	203.5	189.4	205.3	221.3	232.8	240.0	231.0	3.6
<u>of which</u>												
rail (bn tkm)	87.7	116.9	131.5	133.2	134.3	122.4	134.3	148.3	156.8	163.0	152.5	3.1
road (bn tkm)	35.0	55.0	61.9	66.0	69.2	67.0	71.0	73.0	76.0	77.0	78.5	4.6
<u>of which</u>												
rail (%)	71	68	68	67	66	65	65	67	67	68	66	
road (%)	29	32	32	33	34	35	35	33	33	32	34	
Road & rail passenger trans. (bn pass kms).	134.6	191.3	287.1	315.3	329.5	343.6	345.3	373.8	398.8	427.0	463.0	7.1
<u>of which</u>												
rail (bn tkm)	77.6	96.3	118.1	125.3	133.5	135.6	126.3	148.8	163.8	177.0	193.0	5.1
road (bn tkm)	57.0	95.0	169.0	190.0	196.0	208.0	219.0	225.0	235.0	250.0	270.0	9.0
<u>of which</u>												
rail (%)	58	50	41	40	41	39	37	40	41	41	42	
road (%)	42	50	59	60	59	61	63	60	59	59	58	

<u>Source</u>: Annual Statistical Statements, Ministry of Railways, Gov't. of India, various issues; Report of National Transport Policy Committee 1980,

Table 8.6

India: Public Sector Expenditure on Transport Sector

(Rs bn current)

	First Plan (1951-6)	Second Plan (1956-61)	Third Plan (1961-66)	Annual Plans (1966-69)	Fourth Plan (1969-74)	Fifth Plan (1974-8)	Sixth Plan (1980-85)
Railways	2.2	7.2	13.3	5.1	9.3	15.2	51.0
Road transport	1.5	2.4	4.7	3.6	9.9	15.7	46.4
Other	0.6	1.4	1.8	1.6	6.0	9.9	23.4
Total transport	4.3	11.0	19.8	10.3	25.2	40.8	120.8
Total plan	19.6	46.7	85.8	66.5	157.8	289.9	975.0
Transport as percent of plan	22.1	23.5	23.1	15.6	16.0	14.1	12.4

Source: Report of the National Transport Policy Committee, Planning Commission, Gov't of India, 1980. Sixth Year Plan Document, Planning Commission, Gov't. of India, 1980.

Table 8.7

India: Motor Vehicle Registration

	Cars	Taxis	Jeeps	Buses	Goods[1] Vehicles	Other Vehicles	Two & Three Wheelers	Total
1965	396,293	31,762	-	70,470	241,840	64,162	201,920	1,006,447
1966	420,096	35,725	-	73,175	258,977	69,369	241,701	1,099,043
1967	443,629	38,321	-	76,033	266,190	80,347	285,701	1,190,412
1968	480,362	41,990	-	82,729	284,836	95,609	346,826	1,332,352
1969	526,787	51,355	-	87,436	303,524	99,738	419,431	1,488,271
1970	567,989	59,373	-	91,582	322,292	113,361	503,161	1,657,758
1971	539,475	60,446	82,584	93,907	342,557	133,668	612,658	1,865,315
1972	585,372	66,954	87,539	99,394	353,889	143,461	698,272	2,034,881
1973	579,779	67,916	65,892	102,991	362,462	205,865	777,246	2,182,151
1974	622,209	76,544	83,050	102,873	361,396	225,596	838,476	2,312,144
1975	626,838	77,104	92,866	112,940	367,673	236,370	936,338	2,450,129
1976	627,823	80,429	94,132	114,193	371,329	309,178	1,045,428	2,642,512
1977	630,925	79,519	98,364	114,656	373,396	347,365	1,235,137	2,879,362
1978	676,888	79,891	105,053	119,479	379,303	400,386	1,431,692	3,188,192
1979	722,511	82,999	119,414	126,671	411,610	416,088	1,678,142	3,557,435
1980	775,899	94,253	134,356	135,146	474,925	553,449	2,104,709	4,272,737
1981	888,880	n.a.	151,000	152,080	521,275	612,690	2,306,150	4,632,075
1982	907,445	n.a.	159,050	166,780	574,850	682,760	2,458,720	4,949,605

Source: Automotive Industry of India, Facts & Figures 1982. A Publication of All-India Automobile & Family Industries Association.

Table 8.8

India: Energy Intensity in Railway
('000 toe/billion gross t-km)

	Non-Suburban Passenger and Freight Traffic					
Year	Overall	Steam	Diesel	Electric	Suburban	All Railway Traffic
1970/71	NA	42.56	3.42	NA	10.43	NA
1971/72	NA	43.45	3.42	NA	9.98	NA
1972/73	NA	43.41	3.46	NA	9.32	NA
1973/74	20.87	47.54	3.56	3.78	9.37	20.54
1974/75	20.32	48.36	3.54	3.61	9.07	20.02
1975/76	18.80	47.06	3.48	3.63	9.36	18.54
1976/77	16.61	46.61	3.28	3.52	9.61	16.52
1977/78	16.45	48.66	3.41	3.55	9.70	16.27
1978/79	16.36	53.83	3.34	3.70	10.52	16.19
1979/80	15.64	55.74	3.25	3.93	10.56	15.50
1980/81	15.44	60.72	3.39	4.02	10.37	15.29
1981/82	13.15	61.29	3.47	3.58	10.29	13.07
1982/83	12.42	60.82	3.48	3.42	10.33	12.36

SOURCE: Railway Board.

Chapter 9

The Case of Ecuador[1]

It will be recalled from the previous Chapter that the rise in consumption of transport fuels in India over the last 10 years or so was exceptionally low compared with the average for other developing countries. Ecuador lies at the other extreme, having experienced a particularly rapid increase in consumption. As in the case of India, we shall analyze this trend in some detail as a basis for a discussion of policy issues.

Trends in transport fuel use

Consumption of transport fuels in Ecuador rose rapidly over the last 15 years (see Table 9.1) at an annual average of 10 percent, substantially in excess of the annual average rise in GDP of 6.7 percent. Unlike most countries transport energy growth rates accelerated after 1973 (to an annual average of over 16 percent before falling sharply to a still substantial 4 percent after 1980). In Ecuador the transport sector now accounts for over one half of total commercial energy consumption, again a much higher share than is typical in other countries. From many points of view, therefore, Ecuador differs markedly from the average country in its pattern of transport energy consumption.

Ecuador does, however, share one common feature, that is the importance of road transport which has accounted for between 60-70 percent of total transport energy consumption between 1969 and the present, rising

---

1. This case study is based on "Ecuador Transport Energy: Determinants and Policy" prepared by the Instituto Nacional de Energia (INE) Ecuador for Resources for the Future.

at an annual average rate of 9 percent a year. Again, the rise in consumption was particularly rapid between 1973 and 1980, and fell sharply after 1980. In the early 1970's gasoline dominated road transport fuels, accounting for 98 percent of the total. But consumption of diesel has risen rapidly and now accounts for 27 percent of the total (see Table 9.2).

Within the road transport sector passenger transport, public and private combined, account for about two-thirds of total road transport and freight for about one-third (see Table 9.3). The share of passenger is higher than in most developing countries where freight and passenger shares are about equal; it is very similar to the pattern of transport energy use in industrial countries. Within passenger traffic there has been a marked increase in the share of road transport energy used by private modes. In 1969 private passenger modes consumed 55 percent of all road passenger transport fuel, but by the early 1980s this share had risen to almost 70 percent. The share of public transport had fallen from 45 to 30 percent over the same period. This implies a very rapid rate of increase in energy consumption for private passenger traffic--on average 12 percent a year.

The next largest mode is <u>marine transport</u> which has grown rapidly over the last 15 years increasing its share of total transport fuel consumption from 20 percent to 30 percent in 1984 (see again Table 9.1). A more detailed breakdown indicates that much of this increase was accounted for by consumption of Ecuadorian vessels engaged in international (rather than coastal) trade. These figures may, however, include some illegal exports to neighboring countries whose petroleum product prices are substantially higher than in Ecuador. Such exports were estimated[2] at about 250 mtoe in 1978 or about 20 percent of total transport energy consumption.

Energy consumption in <u>air transport</u> rose broadly in line with total transport energy consumption and accounted for between 7 and 9 percent of the total. Finally, railways account for a negligible share of total energy consumption, especially in recent years as flooding has caused widespread damage on some lines. The small contribution of the railways in Ecuador is in marked contrast to India.

Transport activity levels

What were the trends underlying this exceptionally rapid increase in consumption of transport fuels, which as Table 9.2 shows was well in excess of both the population increase and the rise in GNP?

For Ecuador there are only sparse data on transport activity levels. These indicate a steady decline in rail freight carried by railways up to 1975 followed by a much more precipitous decline after 1975. Passenger rail kilometers remained constant at their fairly low levels. As in other countries, air passenger travel rose sharply in excess of the increase in GNP. In shipping there appeared to be a rapid increase in activity levels associated with rising foreign trade in the 1970s. There are no time series data on road freight and passenger traffic. However, the consumption data suggest for Ecuador the particularly rapid increase in passenger traffic which had bee noted in other developing countries. There is, however, an interesting variation in Ecuador. Thus, it is reported[3] that of the 11,000 kms. travelled per year by passenger car in urban areas some 20 percent was accounted for by mid day travelling to the house for lunch. In recent years public institutions, followed by businesses, have instituted the "Jornada unica" with an abbreviated lunch break which means that fewer workers are able to return home for lunch. Part of the time and kilometers saved may of course, be spent on additional leisure related driving. On balance, however, this trend to the shorter lunch break probably means that the rise in passenger kilometers by road is rather less than it would otherwise be. Within road passenger traffic, inter-city is the larger accounting for about 70 percent of total passenger kilometers. However, as much of this traffic takes place in (energy efficient) buses, inter-city traffic accounts for only one-third of total energy consumed in road passenger traffic. Increased urbanization will therefore tend to increase energy consumption in passenger transport.

For freight transport on the other hand, the rate of increase appears more rapid than that experienced in other countries. Thus the rise in energy consumed in freight traffic is almost as high as consumption in passenger traffic. Part of this apparent rapid rise in freight could be due to exceptionally rapid industrialization (industrial output rose by an annual average of 10 percent from 1965 to 1982) deliberately encouraged by incentives and protection.

Modal mix

Part of this high increase in road energy consumption for freight transport could also have been due to a switch of transport mode from energy efficient to energy intensive modes, as in the case of shifts from boats and railways to trucks. In Ecuador, however, road transport has always been predominant so that any shift from rail to road, though contributing to the increase in transport freight consumption would not have a major impact.

In passenger transport, however, modal aspects appear to be more important. As with freight there was probably some move from rail to road which would increase consumption but more important appears to have been a move from public to private forms of transport suggested by the much lower increase in energy consumption in public transport (see again Table 9.3).

Energy consumption per passenger kilometer in urban public transport is perhaps 5 times as energy efficient as private transport (see table 9.5) so that a switch from public to private transport leads to a significant increase in consumption.

The growing importance of private passenger transport is illustrated by the sharp rise in car ownership (see Table 9.6). Although there are important breaks in the series, all suggest a very rapid rise in car registration over the period. Thus the number of car registrations rose by 12 percent annually and pickups by almost 19 percent annually from 1965 to 1979. The rate of increase slowed after 1980 but still remained at a relatively high level of 7 percent. Ownership of light vehicles per 1000 population rose from 5 in 1965 to 22 in 1979, or a little higher depending on which series is used.

The relatively slower growth in public transport suggested in the energy consumption data is reflected by the much lower rate of increase in the public transport fleet (see Table 9.7). The public transport fleet increased at an average rate of 7 percent a year betwen 1965 and 1979 compared with 14 percent for cars and other light vehicles. Furthermore, within public road transport passengers were moving to smaller, more flexible (and more energy intensive) modes. Thus the number of buses (which carry 50 passengers) increased by about 3 percent a year while busetas (carrying 20) rose by 20 percent a year at least to 1980. Data for the years after 1979 are not readily comparable with the pre-1979 series. However, scattered data suggest a sharp fall in number of busetas due to govenment policy to promote the use of more energy efficient large buses.

Modal Efficiencies

Finally, energy consumption is also affected by changes in the efficiency of the different modes. An interesting point of comparison with India is the rapid rise in transport consumption in aviation in Ecuador which exceeds the number of passenger kilometers inferring perhaps that Ecuador has not yet been able to take full advantage of efficiency improvements in aircraft design.

However, as in other aspects of transport, road is the key sector. One of the striking features of the road transport sector is, until recently, its heavy dependence on gasoline as a transport fuel. In 1969, for example, gasoline accounted for 98 percent of all road fuels including consumption in cars, public transport vehicles and trucks. By the early 1980s, however, the share of diesel had risen from 2 to 20 percent of the total. Even so much (94%) of the public transport fleet and the lighter weight trucks (84%) still use gasoline. This change from gasoline to diesel though modest would contribute to the improved energy efficiency of road transport. Furthermore, there is some evidence of higher energy efficiency from the increasing share of both smaller cars and larger trucks in the road vehicle fleet in recent years.

On the other hand, congestion and poor traffic management in urban areas contributes to lower efficiencies. In Quito, for example, there are no bus-stops, and drivers stop wherever they see a passenger, thus impeding the flow of road traffic.[5]

To sum up, the roads are the most important transport sector for Ecuador. Consumption in both passenger and freight traffic grew exceptionally sharply in the 1970s and 1980s. While full data are not available it appears that the increase in energy consumption for passenger traffic is associated with a rise in passenger kilometers well in excess of the rise in GNP, and a marked switch from public to private transport modes. For freight, an unusually rapid rise in consumption appears to be mainly associated with high freight kilometers due, in turn, to rapid structural change. The rise in average truck size and increased dieselization would normally offset part of this increase.

Transport Policies

Part of the rapid increase in consumption of transport fuels was, therefore income related associated with the rapid pace of development following the oil price rises of 1973/74 and 1979/80. However, as noted before, transport energy consumption rose much in excess of the rise in income. This fact, and the high level of transport fuel consumption compared with other countries, is also related to low gasoline and diesel prices. These relationships were quantified in Table 6.7 of the regression analysis which showed Ecuador to have an annual elasticity of between .9 and 1.2 and a price elasticity of between -.26 and -.48.

Prices of transport fuels in Ecuador have always been one of the lowest in the world, in 1980 about 15 cents per gallon for regular gasoline (at the then current exchange rate). Prices through the 1960s and 1970s had declined in real terms, despite the rise in international prices of crude oil.

However, by the early ´80s the government, which is responsible for establishing prices of petroleum products, started to reverse its policy and to raise prices. In 1981 prices of regular gasoline were doubled and again increased very sharply in 1982. By 1984 prices were 5 or 6 times highe in nominal terms as in 1979. Inflation eroded half of that increase. Nonetheless by 1983 gasoline prices were still 2 to 3 times higher than in 1979. Diesel prices were also raised and are now about twice the level of 1979. Even at these high levels, however, prices of petroleum products are still substantially lower than international prices.

This increase in real prices of transport fuels was associated with a dramatic slowing in consumption. Before 1980 consumption of road transport fuels had been rising at an annual rate of 12 percent. From 1981 this fell to 2 percent. Not all of this decline can be attributed to high fuel prices; economic growth rates also declined. But higher prices contributed to this radical change in trend.

An unusual aspect of petroleum product pricing in Ecuador are differential rates charged to national and foreign entities. Prices of resid charged to international shipping companies were in 1984 5 times higher than prices to national companies and jet fuel almost 3 times higher. Even the relatively high prices charged to international entities are, however, probably lower than prices in other countries thus encouraging foreign shipping and aviation companies to maximize purchases in Ecuador. The effects of the two tiered market in certain transport fuels could well explain part of the unexpectedly rapid increase in fuel consumption by both air and maritime transport. And as noted earlier the large difference in prices of petroleum products between Ecuador and neighboring countries has encouraged illicit exports. The recent price increases have however discouraged these exports and made purchases by shipping and airlines less attractive.

A further change in policy which would be expected to affect consumption of transport fuels was a sharp change in policy with regard to vehicle ownership. Previous to 1980, for example, cars could be freely imported and prices had probably declined in real terms. In 1980, however, there was a marked increase in prices of automobiles partly due to a rise in c.i.f. costs (associated with the rise in value of the dollar in relation to the sucre) but also to a sharp increase in import taxes expecially on larger cars (see Table 9.8). A Ford Granada is now two and a half times more expensive in real terms as in 1980, and the more energy efficient Datsun just under twice as expensive. Since 1983, general imports of cars, pick-up and jeeps have been prohibited, except to those (international organizations, public institutions) with special licenses.

The effect of these measures as well as the decline in economic growth is reflected in the marked slowing in rates of increase in automobile registration after 1980, to 6 percent a year from 12 percent before. These policy changes have led to a change in the composition a well as the size of the vehicle fleet. Due to the higher tax rates imposed on larger cars the share of autos of less than 1200cc in total imports rose from 30 percent in 1977 to 38 percent in 1980, and the share of those over 4000cc fell from 24 to 17 percent, resulting in a more energy efficient stock of vehicles. On the other hand the import prohibition will delay the rapid adoption of new energy efficient automotive technologies in future.

The stock of heavy vehicles has also been affected by policy change. Since 1981 imports of vehicles with V8 engines have been banned. This means that imports of gasoline powered buses and trucks from the US have been replaced largely by diesel powered imports from Japan with higher fuel efficiencies. Besides measures regulating prices of transport fuels and vehicles, the government influences transport patterns and therefore transport energy consumption through its regulation of public transport.

While public transport is privately organized, fares are negotiated between the government and the companies. For political reasons the government wishes to keep fares as low as possible and requires depreciation of vehicle stock based on 1976 purchase prices even though prices have increased rapidly since then. Thus renewing the fleet is very expensive and tends to increase the lifetime of inefficient equipment.

Conclusion

From the survey of past trends, it appears that all of the factors which would be expected to lead to a rapid increase in consumption of transport fuels were present in Ecuador at least up until 1980. Rapid economic growth with emphasis on industrialization led to increased demand for both passenger and freight traffic. The poor development of alternative modes meant that this increase was concentrated in the relatively energy intensive road transport. The rapid increase in household income, low fuel prices, and the ready availability of foreign exchange to import cars led to a sharp increase in car ownership and a corresponding decline in the relative importance of the more energy efficient public passenger transport.

In the early 1980s, there was an important change in all of these factors. Economic growth came to an end, car imports were prohibited, and prices of both cars and transport fuels were sharply increased. This led to a sharp deceleration in transport energy growth rates though it is not clear whether general economic conditions or the new policy measures were the more important factors.

Future developments in transport energy consumption will depend on a number of factors. There are undoubted opportunities for increasing specific energy efficiencies through the substitution of smaller cars and the dieselization of the truck fleet. Higher prices should also induce behavioral changes such as reductions in kilometers driven in private cars, and more efficient maintenance and driving. (The National Energy Institute has distributed a leaflet on this topic to all car owners in the country.) On the other hand, the possibility of a shift to more energy efficient modes like rail is very limited. And a shift from private to public passenger transport will require major improvements and modernization of the public passenger transport fleet, (which has old equipment, high load factors, poor technical conditions) and improvement in urban traffic management, (bus stops, parking). Much will depend on government policies with regard to demand management and infrastructure development. A recent forecast of transport fuel consumption to 2000 indicate that rates of growth in transport energy consumption could be halved if firm demand management policies are adopted.

* * * * *

The Two Countries Compared

The two countries were purposely chosen for purposes of contrast. While both are developing countries, Ecuador has a much higher GDP per head than India and much lower energy prices (see Table 9.9). Thus in 1980, per capita GDP in Ecuador (measured in terms of purchasing power parities) was almost three times as high as in India. On the other hand, India's gasoline prices were 13 times higher than in Ecuador.

The effect of these differences is evident in the several measures of transport sector energy use and activity also given in Table 9.9. Thus per capita transport energy consumption in Ecuador is 10 times higher. The disparity in gasoline consumption is even greater (77 times higher in Ecuador) due to additional factors such as the absence of a significant railroad network in Ecuador and limited use of diesel fuels in road transport. The greater importance of road transport in Ecuador is illustrated again by differences in the numbers of cars and trucks relative to the population.

Of all the differences perhaps the most striking is the difference in prices of transport fuels. Ecuador is self-sufficient and even a net exporter of petroleum products and the Ecuadorian government has chosen to help prices of petroleum products to the domestic markets very low, well below international levels. On the other hand the government of India, although a significant producer, has traditionally imposed high taxes on gasoline. While diesel has not been taxed in India it has been priced near world levels and is much higher in price than in Ecuador. Although many factors contribute to differences in level of transport energy consumption among countries, prices differences account for a major part of the higher transport energy intensity of the Ecuadorian economy--over 200 toe per million dollar GDP in 1980 compared with 50 in India.

High fuel prices can affect levels of consumption through a number of mechanisms. Thus high gasoline prices cause car drivers to reduce kilometers driven and to be more careful in driving habits and maintenance. These are the short term effects which were observed in both India and Ecuador over time when gasoline prices rose sharply. In addition, high prices over the longer run influence the stock of transport equipment and even the development of different transport modes. In Ecuador, for example, traditionally low prices have facilitated travel and encouraged the rapid development of energy intensive private passenger travel. In India, on the other hand, high prices of transport fuels have contributed to lower levels of travel and have facilitated policy efforts to provide alternative energy efficient modes of travel.

Notes

2. "Energy Rationalization in the Ecuadorian Transport Sector" by Jan Jasewicz, mimeo U.N. Department of Technical Cooperation Project ECU/78/003, Quito, Ecuador, June 1981.

3. Plan Maestro de Energia "Analysis del Consumo de Energia en el sector transporte en el Ecuador" by Peter Kiblank, Instituto Nacional de Energia, Quito, Ecuador.

4. In 1982, for example, 14 bn passenger kilometers took place in private transport and 38 in public. If there had been a switch to private, holding the total constant, energy consumption would have risen by about 20 percent.

5. On balance, the overall efficiency of the Ecuadorian transport system is low. For example (see Kublank op cit.) the amount of energy per unit of activity in urban buses and road freight transport isover twice the average in France.

Table 9.1

Ecuador: Energy Consumption in Transport Sector

(000 tons oil equivalent)

											Annual Average Increase (%)			
	1969	1973	1974	1975	1979	1980	1981	1982	1983	1984	1969-73	1973-80	1980-84	1969-84
Road	331	466	552	614	1070	1160	1216	1291	1230	1280	8.9	13.9	2.5	9.4
Air	41	43	46	54	138	149	149	140	126	139	1.2	19.4	-1.2	8.5
Rail	8	8	8	11	7	8	n.a.	n.a.	n.a.	n.a.	0	0	n.a.	n.a.
M	90	64	86	153	291	371	380	455	416	566	-8.9	28.5	11.1	13.0
Total	470	580	692	832	1506	1688	1745	1886	1772	1985	5.4	16.4	4.1	10.1

Source: Estimates based on Instituto Nacional de Energia. The estimating procedure is given in this report. The above estimates exclude energy used by river transport, the armed forces, and pipelines. They will include part at least of illegal exports to neighboring countries.

Table 9.2

Ecuador: Consumption of Road Transport Fuels by Type

(000 toe)

											% Share		Annual Avg. Increase (%)		
	1969	1973	1974	1978	1979	1980	1981	1982	1983	1984	1969	1984	1969-73	1973-80	1980-84
Gasoline	326	435	505	793	880	954	990	1009	920	940	98	73	6.7	11.8	-0.2
Diesel	5	31	47	120	190	206	226	282	310	340	2	27	57.8	31.1	7.4
Total	331	466	552	913	1070	1160	1216	1291	1230	1280	100	100	8.9	13.9	1.4

Source: Same as for Table 9.1.

Table 9.3

Ecuador: Energy Consumption in Road Transport

(000 toe)

	1969	1973	1974	1975	1980	1982	1984	Annual Avg. Increase 1969-82
Passenger	225	326	377	424	738	827	n.a.	10.5
- private	123	215	270	311	510	560	n.a.	12.4
- public	102	111	107	113	228	267	n.a.	7.7
Freight	107	140	175	190	422	464	n.a.	11.9
Total	331	466	552	614	1160	1291	1280	9.4[1]

<u>Source</u>: Same as Table

[1] 1969 to 1984.

Table 9.4

Ecuador: Transport Energy Consumption per Capita and Relative to GNP

	1969	1973	1974	1975	1976	1977	1978	1979	1980	1981	1982	1983	1984	Annual Average Increase 1969-81
Total Trans. Energy Cons. per capita (koe)	81	89	103	121	121	159	169	194	211	211	221	202	219	8.3
GNP per cap (1975 $)	531	679	707	755	778	797	815	829	831	811	n.a.	n.a.	n.a.	3.6
Total trans. energy cons. (toe per mn 1975 $ GNP)	153	131	146	160	156	199	207	233	253	260	n.a.	n.a.	n.a.	4.5

Source: Energy data from Table 9.1, GNP data from project files based on World Bank.

Table 9.5

Ecuador: Energy Efficiencies in Various Road Transport Modes, 1981

(grams oil equivalent per passenger or ton km)	
Passenger cars (urban use)	69
Taxis (urban use)	167
Passenger cars (long distance)	23
Buses (urban use)	14
Buses (international)	9
Long distance (freight)	63

Source: Maestro de Energia Analysis de Consuno de Energia en El Sector Transporte en el Ecuador by P. Kublank, Instituto Nacional de Energia, Quito, 1982, p. 75.

Table 9.6

Ecuador: Light Vehicle Fleet[1]

	Cars (000)	Pickups (000)	light vehicle[2] (000)	Population (mn.)	Light vehicles per (000 pop.)
1965	11.4	9.0	26.1	5.13	5.1
1966	13.0	9.9	29.3	5.29	5.5
1967	14.2	11.8	33.7	5.45	6.2
1968	14.7	13.8	36.1	5.62	6.4
1969	16.4	16.1	40.8	5.79	7.0
1970	18.2	20.8	47.8	5.96	8.0
1971	20.2	26.8	56.9	6.13	9.3
1972	22.3	33.0	66.1	6.31	10.5
1973	24.0	37.6	72.4	6.50	11.1
1974	31.1	47.9	91.5	6.69	13.7
1975	37.3	55.1	106.4	6.89	15.4
1976	38.4	63.9	112.5	7.10	15.8
1977	47.1	88.1	145.4	7.32	19.9
1978	47.9	88.5	149.6	7.54	19.8
1979	55.0	101.9	171.7	7.78	22.1
1980	75.7	124.0	211.5	8.02	26.4
1981	83.4	136.2	232.6	8.28	28.1
1982	78.1	142.0	234.7	n.a.	n.a.
1983	91.1	151.1	259.7	n.a.	n.a.
1984	97.9	162.8	279.8	n.a.	n.a.
Annual Avg. inc. % 1965-79	11.9	18.9	14.4	3.0	11.0
Annual Avg. inc. % 1980-84	6.6	7.0	7.2	n.a.	n.a.

[1]Note break in series between 1979 and 1980.

[2]Include jeeps, station wagons.

Table 9.7

Ecuador: Public Transport Vehicles[1]

(numbers)

	Buses	Colectivas	Bustas	Total
1965	2824	1138	327	4289
1970	3828	1470	1299	6597
1975	3656	2618	1823	8097
1979	4131	2766	4579	11476
% increase ann. avg. 1965-79	2.8	6.5	20.7	7.3

[1]The capacity of buses is 50 passengers, Colectivas 30 passengers and Busetas 19 passengers.

Table 9.8

Ecuador: Prices of Road Vehicle, Gasoline and Diesel

(constant 1980 sucres)

Vehicles	1979	1980	1981	1982	1983	1984	1985	Annual increase % 1980-1985
Car	n.a.	633	912	n.a.	n.a.	n.a.	1566	19.9
Pick-up	n.a.	214	262	n.a.	n.a.	n.a.	413	14.1
Bus	n.a.	894	893	n.a.	n.a.	n.a.	1661	13.2
Truck	n.a.	2422	2031	n.a.	n.a.	n.a.	4700	14.2
Transport fuels (litre)								
Gasoline								
- super	5.3	4.7	11.8	13.3	15.4	10.3	n.a.	14.2
- regular	4.7	4.2	8.1	8.9	10.3	6.9	n.a.	8.0
Diesel	3.9	3.4	8.7	8.4	7.2	7.1	n.a.	14.1

Source: As from Table 9.1.

Table 9.9

India and Ecuador, Characteristics of Transport Energy, 1980

	India	Ecuador
Per capita GDP (1975 $ - purchasing power parity rates of exchange)	472	1300
Retail price gasoline (1975 $ per gallon)	1.63	0.12
Per capita transport energy consumption (koe)	26.6	266.1
Per capita consumption gasoline (koe)	2.2	168.6
Rail freight traffic (ton km per 000 $ GDP)	462	5
Rail passenger traffic (km per 000 $ GDP)	509	7
Cars per 000 population	1.3	8.1
Trucks and buses (000 population)	1.2	18.7
Urban population as % of total	24	46

Part V

Conclusion

On reasonable assumptions about trends in income and prices, and existing relationships between price and income and transport energy consumption, consumption of transport fuels is likely to grow rapidly in future and, given foreign exchange constraints, developing countries are likely to want to moderate this trend. The most promising areas appear to be increased energy efficiency of the vehicle fleet, improvements in alternatives to private passenger transport such as bus service, reduction in congestion, and improvements in truck load factors. Energy savings in these areas can be achieved through a consistent and mutually reinforcing set of market and regulatory interventions.

Chapter 10

Future Transport Energy Consumption and How It Can Be Influenced

The results of the regression analysis can be used to project future trends, to the year 2000, in transport fuels, gasoline, and car and truck registrations. The purpose of this exercise is to provide a background for the subsequent discussion of transport policy options.

A first step is to make some assumptions about trends in income and prices from our base year 1981 to 2000. For income, measured in terms of GDP per capita, projected rates of increase from the World Bank "A Model of World Energy Markets and OPEC Pricing" are used. These are as follows:

	Annual average increase in per capita GDP (%)	
	1980-1990	1990-2000
Oil importing developing countries	1.81	2.88
Non-OPEC oil exporting countries	1.84	2.74
Capital deficit OPEC	1.70	2.32
Capital surplus OPEC	0.22	2.72

These rates of increase applied to our categories of countries (which include both oil importers and exporters in each category) amount to a 56 percent increase in per capita GDP from 1981 to 2000 for the low income developing countries, 53 percent for the middle income countries and 54 percent for the high income developing countries.

In the World Bank study the price of OPEC oil "is assumed to decline slightly through the mid 1980s and then increase steadily to reach $37 per

barrell (in constant 1981 dollars) in 1990 and $56 in the year 2000."
Since the time of this forecast there has been a decline in the dollar price of oil so some reassessment of future trends in oil prices seems appropriate.

There are many views of future developments in crude oil prices over the next 15 years but they appear to coalesce around two scenarios. One is that dollar oil prices will decline in real terms from 1985 to 1990, stay constant in real terms from 1990 to 1995, and increase in real terms (say an average of 7 percent a year) from 1995 to 2000. The other view is that crude oil prices will stay constant in dollar terms from 1985 to 1990, and then increase in real terms (by about say 5 pecent a year) from 1990 to 2000. An illustration of these scenarios in comparable terms with the original World Bank estimates is given in Table 10.1.

Accepting the forecasts of scenario 1 and 2, the next step is to determine the level of transport fuel prices which correspond to the 2000 levels of crude oil prices. As we saw in Chapter 4, the five fold rise in the real price of crude oil from 1973 to 1981 was associated with an estimated 85 percent increase in gasoline prices in oil importing developing countries. In oil exporting countries prices typically remained constant in real terms or fell over this period.

The much lower rise in gasoline prices compared with crude oil prices was due to the relatively small share of crude oil in total pump prices. The other components of pump prices--refining and distribution costs, and taxes--remained constant in real terms. The reason for the decline in prices in oil exporting countries was largely government pricing policies providing oil to the domestic market at prices much below world market prices.

Future trends in gasoline prices in importing developing countries depend therefore not only on crude oil prices but also on trends in refining margins and distribution costs and taxes. It is assumed here that refining and distribution costs will remain constant to 2000.[1] The size of the tax component in real terms depends on government policies. In the oil importing developing countries these stayed constant in real terms between 1973 and 1981, nominal increases just keeping pace with the cost of living. If this trend continues into the future gasoline prices will range between $1.50 and $1.70 per gallon in 2000 (or an annual average increase of 0.8 to 1.6 from 1981 to 2000), depending on the rise in crude oil prices. We therefore start with this assumed rise in gasoline prices. This assumption is relaxed later to take into account alternative taxation policies.

Our assumptions do not take into account changes in the value of the dollar in terms of other currencies. Since 1980, the rise in the value of the dollar has offset declines in the international price of oil. It is widely assumed that a decline in the value of the dollar in terms of other currencies will occur in the future. In this case, the rise in gasoline prices will be less than assumed here.

Many of the oil exporting countries are committed to increasing prices of all petroleum products. A number of oil exporting countries have gasoline prices at about one half of the level of international prices by the year 2000. This would imply increases in real prices of gasoline of between 2.5 and 3.5 percent annually, the rate of increase assumed here.

Translating these assumptions to our three categories of countries, which again include both importers and exporters, we find that gasoline prices are estimated to rise by between 22 percent and 42 percent in low income countries, by 38 to 64 percent in the middle income countries and by

33 percent to 67 percent in the high income countries.

The projected increases in gasoline prices for the oil importing developing countries is much lower than in 1973 to 1981 when they increased by some 8 percent annually. In contrast, in the oil exporting countries gasoline prices are estimated to rise more rapidly in the future than in the past. The slower rate of increase in the oil importers is largely due to lower increases in crude oil prices. Prices in the oil exporters are estimated to grow more rapidly due both to the low base level but also due to the assumed changes in pricing policy.

Because of lack of data it has not been possible to develop equally reasoned price projections for cars and trucks. It is arbitrarily assumed that truck prices remain constant in real terms. For cars two alternatives are considered. First car prices are assumed to be constant in real terms and second that they rise by 50 percent in real terms from 1981 to 2000.

These assumed increases in incomes and gasoline prices (which are recapitulated in Table 10.2) are combined with selected price and income elasticities to derive per capita consumption of total transport fuels and gasoline, and ownership rates of cars and trucks in 2000. The results are given in Table 10.3.

Given our assumptions concerning price and income per capita, consumption of total transport energy would rise in all 3 categories of countries though more rapidly in the high income developing countries (about 2.5 percent a year in place of 1.9 percent in the low and medium income countries). These may be underestimates for the low income countries as the price and income elasticities incorporate the energy efficient technology introduced in railroads over the past fifteen years. Once the railroads are dieselized such dramatic savings will come to an end.

Consumption of gasoline rises more rapidly than total transport fuels by between 2 and 3.5 percent a year. This means that the share of gasoline in total transport fuels increases.[2]

A noticeable feature for both total transport fuels and gasoline but especially for transport fuels is the relatively small difference in consumption under the alternative price assumptions. This is due to the modest increase in prices and to the low price elasticities especially for total transport fuels.

Some additional sense of the sensitivity of our projections can be derived from table 10.4, which shows per capita consumption in the year 2000 relative to the base consumption in 1981 = 1.0), by transport category, developing versus industrial country grouping, and for three scenarios. The first scenario is a base case similar to that described above, with an increase in both per capita income and price of approximately 50 percent. The second scenario is an "optimistic" case of higher growth in income (a doubling of per capita income) and a lower price increase (25 percent), relative to the base case. The third scenario is a "pessimistic" case, with growth levels reversed (per capita income increases 25 percent and price doubles).

Prices refer to fuel prices in the case of fuel and of rail use, and to vehicle prices in the case of automobile and truck registrations. Trend effects are built into the projection, in the case of rail use and vehicle registrations.

The results suggest a fair amount of sensitivity to income and price changes combined in the developing countries for all fuel, gasoline, road fuel and vehicle registrations. However, as the following text table shows, for the developing countries much of this sensitivity stems from income rather than prices changes.

Individual effects of per capita income and price change on all transport fuel use is given in the following list:

Impacts on All Transport Fuel
Use of Specified Changes
in Per Capita Income and Price

Income Ratio	Impact on All Fuel Use	Price Ratio	Impact on All Fuel Use
	Developing Countries		
1.25	1.31	1.25	0.97
1.54	1.68	1.45	0.95
2.00	2.30	2.00	0.90
	Industrial Countries		
1.25	1.34	1.25	0.87
1.54	1.75	1.45	0.80
2.00	2.46	2.00	0.66

Higher income and price elasticities for the industrial countries relative to the developing countries are apparent in these results.

Both car and truck ownership rates are projected to rise rapidly--cars between 3 and 5 percent a year, and trucks between 3 and 3.5 percent. There appears to be, however, a considerable variation in car ownership rates stemming from differences in assumptions about car prices.

In a word, our assumptions about prices and incomes combined with an analysis of past experience and contrasting experience between countries suggest that the consumption of transport fuels and vehicle ownership will continue to rise rapidly, outstripping in most part the increase in economic activity; and that the expected rise in prices of transport fuels will not be sufficient to moderate this trend significantly. Our comparison of India and Ecuador does suggest that prices can be an important determinant of consumption, but the difference in gasoline prices between these two countries is far greater than the increase envisaged over the next 15 years and, in any event, intercountry comparisons are indicative of very long run adjustments.

Given the many unknowns it is not easy to judge how great a burden consumption at the projected level will be on the economies of these countries. However, a fifty percent increase in oil consumption combined with a fifty percent increase in the dollar price of oil implies, in the absence of reduced oil consumption in other sectors or substantially increased domestic oil production, a more than doubling of the oil import bills for the oil importing countries. Oil imports account at present for about 37 percent of export earnings, an unsustainably high level. The reduction of this share to a more manageable level, say about 20 percent would therefore require a sustained rapid growth in exports of over 10 percent annually--not an impossibly high level by 1960s and 1970s standards (when economic growth rates were also much higher) but higher than the 1980s levels, and very high in relation to projected GDP growth rates. Exports at this level will depend critically on the growth of markets in the industrial countries and access to these markets. Alternatively high oil imports could reduce economic growth rates. In either event, conservation of oil in all uses and especially in the transport sector is therefore likely to continue to be high on the policy agenda.

Our analysis leads to a number of conclusions relevant to policy. The first is that given low price elasticities, especially for total transport fuel, the magnitude of the price rises resulting from higher crude oil prices alone will not be sufficient to achieve significant savings in transport energy. It will be recalled that our gasoline price assumptions for the oil importing developing countries held taxes constant in real terms--the experience of the past 10 years. If, however, taxes were increased sharply (from 30 cents a gallon in 1975$ in 1981 to $1.10 in 2000) the price of gasoline would double, with significant effects on gasoline consumption. The results are illustrated for a number of countries in Table 10.5. Four price possibilities are given: (1) no rise in real prices from the 1981 level which assumes that real taxes on gasoline are allowed to erode thus offsetting the rise in crude oil prices; (2) and (3) the price rise assumed from Table 10.2 and (4) a 100 percent rise in prices implying a large real increase in taxes.

If real prices did not change over the period--an unlikely but not impossible situation in some countries--gasoline consumption would rise by 70 percent and over in most countries from 1981 to 2000. If at the other extreme taxes were increased so that prices doubled, consumption would increase by only 20 to 40 percent. The level of taxation could therefore have a substantial effect on gasoline consumption.

This effect could be reinforced by policies with regard to taxation of automobiles. Table 10.3 led to two conclusions. First, the rise in car ownership could be very rapid in the future, but second that the extent of the rise is reasonably sensitive to prices of automobiles. We have also seen from Table 5.5 that in many countries mixed signals are being offered to motorists in the form of cheap cars and expensive gasoline, or cheap gasoline and expensive cars. A consistent policy towards both cars and gasoline could achieve major savings in gasoline without causing unduly disruptive tax increases in either.

This last consideration is all the more important as major changes in the price of any one petroleum product affects the use of other petroleum products, sometimes in a socially unproductive manner. A wide gap in prices between (taxed) gasoline and (subsidized) kerosene can, for example, lead to substitution of kerosene for gasoline in transport with consequent diminution of performance and engine damage, as well as subvert policy objectives.

However, the more important example of substitution is between gasolne and diesel. suggested by the differences in price elasticities for gasoline (-0.4) and total transport fuels (-0.15) for the developing countries as a group. These elasticities imply that an increase in gasoline prices leads to a decline in gasoline use, but that part of this decline is compensated by increasing diesel use, so that total consumption of fuel use in transport falls by much less than the fall in gasoline consumption.

The potential for substitution has always existed. Indeed, in the early years of higher oil prices one of the standard prescriptions for saving energy in the transport sector was the substitution of diesel for gasoline powered passenger cars. (In many countries much of the freight fleet already consisted of diesel trucks). Mileage per gallon in diesel powered cars is in principle higher (about 45) than in gasoline powered vehicles (about 25) which means that major savings in transport fuels could be achieved by switching from gasoline in diesel cars. The drawback was that diesel cars were more expensive, were more sluggish and noisy, and were not commonly used so that servicing, parts, and even diesel fuel supplies were not as readily available as for gasoline cars. The drawbacks appeared to outweigh the efficiency advantages, and relatively few diesel powered cars were used.

However, in the ´70s the gap between diesel fuel and gasoline prices widened due to the almost universal effort in developing countries to keep diesel prices low. By 1981 gasoline prices in many developing countries were twice as high and more than diesel prices even though the border prices of both fuels were very similar, about $1.00 per gallon in 1981. This wide variation in prices, and perhaps the feeling that efforts would continue to be made to keep diesel prices low, led to accelerated use of diesel engined passenger cars in many countries (e.g. Costa Rica, Brazil, Tunisia).

At first sight this would seem an advantageous development, leading to the overall efficiency of the average transport fleet. Many countries have, however, found the benefits derived from higher efficiencies--not, in fact, as high as originally thought--were more than offset by other disadvantages. These include:

1. The high foreign exchange cost of diesel car imports.

2. The increase in car ownership or the premature scrapping of cars which come from the switch to the new technology (diesel).

3. The aggravation of refinery imbalance. The existing generation of refineries in developing countries was adapted to the pre-1973 product slate. The decline in the share of gasoline and the increase in share of diesel (together with a declining share of fuel oil which is the most substitutable petroleum product) changed the refinery configuration with the result that several developing countries which had previously been virtually in balance were obliged to import diesel, and export gasoline and fuel oil, often, as these were in small quantities, at distress prices.

4. Fundamentally, the wide gap in pump prices of gasoline and diesel which have, after all, very similar marginal costs leads to a misallocation

of resources. Even though the private decision to go diesel may be fully justified economically, the social cost of such misallocation may be considerable.

For these reasons several countries have acted to restrain diesel car use either by prohibiting imports as in Brazil or by prohibitive taxes on diesel cars. This experience underlines the need in pricing policy to recognize substitution possibilities within the transport sector (and outside). It also suggests that substitution may impose limits on the extent to which gasoline prices can be raised without also increasing diesel prices, which means in many cases reducing subsidies.

Our analysis so far underlines the importance of pricing policy (both level and structure) and its consistency with other elements of private passenger transport costs. Important though pricing policies are, low price elasticities combined with high income elasticities in the context of extreme foreign exchange constraints suggests that additional actions to moderate the rise in transport energy consumption will be needed.

Schematically three areas for saving transport energy can be identified--reducing the amount of transport services (measured in ton or passenger kilometers) relative to total output; changing the modal mix from energy intensive to less energy intensive transport modes; and increasing the efficiency of each mode (including introduction of new automotive technologies, improved load factors, improved operation of vehicles, improved infrastructure).

On the assumption that transport services are correctly priced, including all externalities, possibilities of reducing the amount of travel (that is passenger or ton kilometers) in order to save energy seem limited. The amount of freight kilometers are determined by the type and location of industry and markets. There is evidence of some reduction in the rate of increase in freight transport at higher levels of income as countries move from heavy to light industry and more regionalized development. However, at lower levels of income an increase in freight tonnage relative to GDP seems inevitable and efforts to alter this relationship through radical changes in development policy unrelated to comparative advantage could result in a reduction not only of transport energy consumption but also in overall economic efficiency. But we have also seen from the case studies of India and Ecuador, passenger energy transport and particularly private transport rises sharply in the earlier stages of economic development. Thus chapter 7 results, for example, suggest that in developing countries higher than average income growth is associated with higher than average growth in autos, gasoline and all transport use and lower than average growth in rail use. Part of this increase will be work related and therefore as difficult and as unproductive to reduce as freight transport. However, the other non-work part may well be responsive to higher costs of motoring. Thus chapter 6 also showed that a rise of 10 percent in gasoline prices leads to a decline in gasoline consumption per car of about 66 percent, presumably reflecting shorter and shorter trips. Projections of freight and passenger kilometers through the year 2000 based admittedly on incomplete data indicate a continued rise in the transport intensity in all categories of developing countries.

A major part of passenger travel is urban travel for work, household and leisure purposes. In Ecuador, for example, urban passenger transport accounts for 45 percent of total passenger kilometers and 54 percent of all the energy used in transport. The question therefore rises of whether it is possible through such actions as improvement in the telephone systems, re-siting of wholesale and retail markets and places of employment, to minimize trip distances between home, work, school and shopping. These possibilities are of particular interest to developing countries where urban area increases very rapidly. As little work has been done on the energy implications of different urban design it is not possible to assess the extent of energy savings wich could be derived from such a strategy. However, results from Chapter 7 suggest that in some circumstances the net effect of increased urbanization is to reduce energy consumption. Cities after all serve many functions (political, social and economic) which may conflict with the narrower aim of energy conservation. On the other hand, traffic congestion is of increasing importance to cities, as we shall see later, and plans to reduce congestion often appear to reduce energy consumption if not necessarily passenger or vehicle kilometers.

A second possibility in reducing consumption of transport energy lies in switching traffic from less to more energy efficient modes. Energy efficiency (measured in toe per ton or passenger kilometer) varies considerably between the different transport modes. Generally, for freight, pipelines, river transport and rail are the most energy efficient, followed by road and then by air. For passenger transport, buses and railways are the most energy efficient followed by cars and then by airplanes. Table 10.6 gives some indication of the range of efficiencies in the main transport modes. In theory, therefore, a switch in traffic from energy intensive road to energy efficient rail would result in a saving in energy for a given transport of freight or passengers. Some of the results in Chapter 6 and 7 were interpreted as indicating that just such a switch occured in recent years, though a long term downward trend in use was also manifest. This downward trend was clearly confirmed in the case studies of India and Ecuador.

Customers, whether passengers or those wishing to send freight, decide on which mode to use on the basis of cost, convenience and speed rather than energy intensity which represents after all only one element of cost. It is true that for freight, rail is usually cheaper than road transport over a given distance, but such initial cost advantage can easily be outweighed by the greater flexibility of road transport which obviates expensive transshipments. For passengers, rising incomes are associated with a move to energy intensive modes such as passenger cars and air. Again this trend was confirmed in the two case studies.

The robustness of these trends away from the energy efficient to the more energy intensive modes is confirmed by experience in virtually all countries. Even in India, with an exceptionally good rail network and major investments in rehabilitation and improvement, the share of freight and passengers transported by rail has declined. It may, however, be possible in some countries to arrest this decline in future or at least to slow it. Rail is particularly well suited to the transport of heavy density freight over long distances without much transshipment (such as iron ore in Brazil) and for passenger traffic in heavily travelled corridors (such as the suburban railways in Bombay). The improvement of such facilities could result in a stabilization of rail's share in transport facilities, with consequent savings in energy. The aim would therefore be a multi-modal transport system with each mode transporting the traffic to which it was most suited.

Such an aim implies integrated transport planning in which policies towards the different branches of the transport sector--typically in the past developed as ad hoc responses to particular problems--are coordinated to produce the most efficient transport network. Examples of such a policy would be the coordination of investment plans to improve long distance freight routes on railways, and reconsideration of truck regulation. In many countries, as truck transport began to attract traffic from the railways, governments regulated such traffic in order to protect the position of the railways. Deregulation of trucking could result in a more intensive and therefore more efficient use of the truck fleet.

The above applies to those countries with a rail network. Many of the developing countries, however, commenced their development during the age of road transport and rely entirely on road transport. For such countries, Ecuador is an example, the possibilities of modal switch are limited, if indeed they exist at all. The high capital costs--and high energy costs--of building railways and the stringent and limiting conditions for their cost effective operation imply that few railways for freight haulage will be built in future. For passenger traffic the situation is rather different especially in densely populated cities where places of work and residence are widely separated. In such cases metros or suburban railways are possible options. Several (often heavily subsidized) new passenger railways have been built or are under consideration (Mexico City, Seoul) but their effectiveness in saving energy, especially as much energy is used in their construction, depends on two main factors. First, load factors must be high. A suburban railway or metro with low load factors is a highly energy intensive (as well as financially unsound) mode of transport. Second, if average energy intensity is to be reduced passenger railways must attract passengers from private cars, rather than urban buses which, under a wide range of operating conditions and load factor assumptions are more energy efficient than railways. Metros and suburban railways could, of course, save transport energy indirectly by reducing congestion. Further, if urban railways help in improving access to work opportunities some increase in energy intensity may be worthwhile in the interest of wider development objectives.

Experience with existing or newly constructed urban rail projects should give some indication of the balance of these trends and identify the most important parameters in determining their success or failure. However, for many countries this option does not realistically exist. In these cases savings in transport energy must come from the improved efficiency of the different transport modes, in particular the predominant road transport sector.

There are several aspects of improved efficiency in road transport. The first, which could equally well qualify as a modal switch, lies in the composition of the passenger road vehicle fleet. This consists of buses of various sizes, taxis, the multitude of motorized and unmotorized two or three wheelers available for hire, motorcycles and private cars. The energy intensity of the "modes" varies considerably from zero in the case of non-motorized forms to 60-80 grams oil equivalent per passenger mile in passenger cars in urban use. Such a range offers the possibility of saving transport energy by switching to less energy intensive passenger modes, in particular from the private car to public transport such as taxis and buses.

Our analysis suggests that the demand for the flexibility and convenience in transport has led and will continue to lead to a rapid increase in passenger car ownership. To moderate these trends will involve policies which add to the cost of private motoring while simultaneously promoting the attractiveness of the alternatives.

As we have seen earlier, government action in the form of taxes (or subsidies) on transport fuels and equipment is an important element in determining the cost of transport to the final consumer. Other fiscal interventions concern rate structure and user costs, that is charges for using transport facilities such as road and railways. Road taxes are imposed on car and truck operators to help defray the costs of the damage done by road traffic and also to help pay for improvements to the road network.

A variation on user cost is to tax access to or use of congested areas. One method is to impose high parking fees. This approach probably does not lead to a major increase in the total cost of operating a car. However, it is believed that out-of-pocket expenses exercise a strong influence on decisions to use a car so that high parking charges may have a disproportionately large effect on car use.

A more systematic approach to providing strong disincentives to use congested areas has been introduced in Singapore consisting of an Area License scheme supplemented by higher parking fees and a park and ride program. The Area License scheme permits entry to the restricted downtown zone between 7:30 a.m. and 10:15 a.m. to car pools with 4 or more occupants, buses and commercial vehicles, and license holders at a cost of $50 for a monthly license. At the same time, parking charges at public car parks in the restricted area have been increased sharply and restructured to encourage short term and discourage all day parking. The net result of this scheme has been a reduction in total traffic of 44 percent during the restricted period. As the purpose of the scheme was to relieve congestion rather than save transport fuel no specific estimate of energy savings attributable to this scheme was made. However, on the basis of this traffic reduction, the increase in load factors and the higher speeds achieved during the restricted hours, savings of some 30 percent are probable.

Efforts to moderate increases in private passenger transport by increasing its costs are enhanced by parallel efforts to improve the attractiveness of alternatives. A good example is India where the development of three wheelers appears to have been successful in providing relatively cheap, flexible transport at energy costs much less than those of taxis or passenger cars. These forms of transport in many countries are at present illegal or actively discouraged. A change in this policy could contribute to energy savings.

The bus service is the backbone of the urban passenger transport system in virtually all countries. There are widespread reports of unsatisfactory service despite typically high subsidies. It is important to improve bus service not only to discourage energy intensive private travel but also to assist the large majority of the population which are entirely dependent on bus services. On the basis of recent experience two approaches (not mutually exclusive) to improved bus service appear promising. The first is city wide integration of bus systems such as the city of Curitiba in Brazil where, through a combination of zoning, bus express lanes, organization of feeder buses to the express buses, easy transfer, and restriction of urban center to passenger cars, the speed and coverage of the urban bus system was greatly improved. As in the case of Singapore the purpose of the scheme was not first and foremost to save transport energy but rather to improve the flow of the system. However, like Singapore there is every evidence of a substantial energy saving.

Even short of a revamping of the entire bus network there is increasing evidence of late of the need to reconsider the organization of bus services. In many countries bus services are owned and operated largely by public authorities often incurring substantial deficits. For example in Calcutta, Istanbul and Bangkok public bus companies cover only about 60,37 and 72 pecent of total costs with revenue, the remainder being made up by government grants. Despite such subsidies service is often poor. In these cities it was found that private bus companies using small buses but with high load factors are able to provide better service at a lower overall cost. A graphic example is Istanbul where a minibus owner makes about $1,100 profit per year per bus compared with a loss of $64,000 per publicly operated bus.[3] Such comparison suggest the need for increasing the role of private operators in bus systems. Although the direct energy savings (as opposed to total resource savings) may not be increased, the improvement of the bus service could lead to important indirect savings by encouraging bus rather than car travel.

A second way of providing intra-modal energy savings is through energy efficiency of transport equipment. The dramatic example of energy savings in railroad locomotion was documented for India. Most of the other countries with an extensive rail network have already benefitted from the efficiency gains of moving from coal to diesel or electric locomotion. Future improvements in these countries and others without rail networks will come largely from increased efficiencies in road transport equipment and to a lesser extent airplanes.

There is undoubtedly a major potential for increased efficiencies in passenger cars. Substantial increases in efficiency have already taken place over the last 10 years and further increases are likely by the end of the century. The question for the developing countries is how to ensure the adoption of the new technologies and how rapidly these new technologies can be introduced given the typically low scrapping rates of vehicle fleets.

Higher gasoline prices increase the incentive to use more energy efficient cars, although as we have seen earlier, in the substitution of diesel for gasoline powered cars, the limits of price incentives must be recognized. Other policy incentives include higher import duties or license fees on energy intensive cars. Here again there can be drawbacks to this system. Thus, pick-up trucks are typically taxed lower than cars on the basis that they are used in "productive" i.e. agricultural and industrial activities rather than for private passenger transport. However, as in Costa Rica, a widening gap between car and pick-up truck prices can encourage the purchase of pick-up trucks in place of standard passenger cars, thus leading to an overall fall in energy efficiency. These types of reasons have lead some governments to impose energy efficiency standards on both domestic and imported cars.

While many countries have policies in place which encourage the use of energy efficient cars, other policies such as high import duties on all cars or even import prohibition slows the rate of replacement which is, in any event, slower than in industrial countries related to the low cost of repairs and less emphasis on technological and luxury features.

We have already seen in the India case study the effect of improved technology on consumption of energy in air transport. This is expected to continue as the high share of fuel costs in total aircraft operating costs provides incentives both to manufacturers and airline companies.

Transport energy consumption can also be reduced through the more intensified use of the existing transport fleet. Many trucks run less than fully loaded and return empty. In Taiwan, for example, the average load factor in trucks is estimated at 35 percent. Although increased energy costs will encourage higher load factors there is frequently a lack of information about the availability of loads which could be improved by the organization of freight terminal facilities. Regulation of the trucking industry can also lead to low average load factors if it encourages the rapid growth of "own account" transport unable to take loads on return trips.

In passenger transport, load factors, especially in private passenger cars, could also be improved through differential tolls, special traffic lanes and instituting systems that encourage commuter car pooling such as the Singapore Area Licensing Scheme.

* * * * *

In conclusion, we have seen that on reasonable assumptions about trends in income and prices, and existing relationships between price and income and transport energy consumption, consumption of transport fuels is likely to grow rapidly in future and, given foreign exchange constraints, developing countries are likely to want to moderate this trend. The most promising areas appear to be an increase in efficiency of the vehicle fleet, improvements in alternatives to private passenger transport such as bus service, reduction in congestion, and improvements in truck load factors. Energy savings in these areas can be achieved through a consistent and mutually reinforcing set of market and regulatory interventions. Pricing policy is important, but the effect of higher prices is limited particularly in the poorer countries, by low price elasticities. As development proceeds, however, pricing measures are likely to become more effective.

The last word must be on the heterogeneity of the developing countries. The emphasis in the poorer countries must be to provide adequate transport services for productive activities. Low incomes mean that there is not yet a high demand for private passenger transport. In the richer developing countries the need to moderate the demand for private passenger transport is much greater.

Footnotes

1. It is assumed that gasoline and diesel prices remained constant in real terms in our countries between 1981 (our base year) and 1985 on the basis that the fall in the dollar price was offset by the strengthening of the dollar.

2. The discussion in this paper concentrates on total transport energy, gasoline and diesel. However, other forms of transport energy, electricity for trains and trolley buses and fuel oil for maritime and railroad use are also used and included in the total even though there are insufficient data for a detailed discussion of the other fuels.

3. A.A. Walters, Cost and Scale of Bus Services, World Bank Staff Working Paper No. 325, (Washington, D.C., World Bank).

Table 10.1

Projections of Real Cost of Crude Oil

(1981$ per barrel)

	1985	1990	1995	2000	% increase annual 1985 to 2000
World Bank in World Energy markets	32	37	(47)[1]	56	3.8
Scenario 1	32	29	29	41	1.7
Scenario 2	32	32	41	52	3.3

[1]interpolated value.

Table 10.2

Increases in Price and Income and
Price and Income Elasticities

	Increase in Income 1981-2000 (%)	Income Elasticity	Increase in Prices 1981-2000 (%)	Price Elasticity	Time Trend
Total transport Fuels					
1. Low income dev. countries	56	0.85	22-42	0.0	
2. Middle income dev. countries	53	1.3	38-64	-0.2	
3. High income dev. countries	54	1.1	33-58	-0.1	
Gasoline					
1. Low income dev. countries	56	1.2	22-42	-0.5	
2. Middle income dev. countries	53	1.4	38-64	-0.4	
3. High income dev. countries	54	1.5	33-67	-0.3	
Car Ownership					
1. Low income dev. countries	56	1.7	0-50	-0.6	0.5
2. Middle income dev. countries	53	1.5	0-50	-0.6	0.5
3. High income dev. countries	54	1.6	0-50	-0.6	0.5
Trucks					
1. Low income dev. countries	56	1.2	0	-0.6	0.5
2. Middle income dev. countries	53	1.1	0	-0.4	0.5
3. High income dev. countries	54	1.0	0	-0.5	0.5

Table 10.3

Per Capita Consumption of Transport Fuels, Gasoline, Car and Truck Ownership Rates 1981 and 2000

	1981	2000	Annual increase %
Total Transport Fuels (koe)			
1. Low income developing countries	26.6	37.93	1.9
2. Middle income developing countries	83.2	131.0-135.6	2.4-2.6
3. High income developing countries	250.2	392.7-399.5	2.4-2.5
Gasoline (koe)			
1. Low income developing countries	3.6	6.4-6.9	3.0-3.5
2. Middle income developing countries	41.6	61.4-65.8	2.1-2.4
3. High income developing countries	136.6	217.5-229.1	2.5-2.8
Cars (# per 1000 pop.)			
1. Low income developing countries	1.7	3.5-4.4	3.9-5.1
2. Middle income developing countries	11.4	18.8-23.9	2.7-4.0
3. High income developing countries	68.2	119.1-151.9	3.0-4.3
Trucks (# per 1000 pop.)			
1. Low income developing countries	1.4	2.7	3.5
2. Middle income developing countries	6.9	12.0	3.0
3. High income developing countries	23.0	39.9	2.9

Table 10.4

Alternative Projections of Transport Variables
to Examine Sensitivity of Projections
Per Capita Consumption in 2000 Relative to 1981

	Base Case		High income, Low price increase		Low income, High price increase	
	Dev.	Indl.	Dev.	Indl.	Dev.	Indl.
All Fuel	1.59	1.40	2.22	2.15	1.18	0.88
Gasoline	1.58	1.40	2.41	2.15	1.04	0.88
Road Fuel	1.63	1.40	2.35	2.15	1.16	0.88
Rail Fuel*	0.59	1.58	0.55	2.64	0.73	0.90
Autos*	2.26	1.88	3.78	2.76	1.31	1.30
Trucks*	1.77	1.31	2.51	1.67	1.24	1.04
Rail Passengers*	0.90	0.68	1.00	0.49	1.00	1.08
Rail Freight*	1.12	1.50	1.32	3.24	1.32	0.72
Gasoline/Car	0.70	0.95	0.71	1.15	0.61	0.72

Underlying Projections for Cases:	Level in 2000 Relative to Level in 1981	
	Income	Price
Base Case	1.54	1.45
High Income, Low Price	2.00	1.25
Low Income, High Price	1.25	2.00

*Projection includes effect of time trends; year elasticity set as follows:

	Dev.	Indl.
Autos	2.0	1.0
Trucks	1.35	0
Rail Fuel	-5.0	0.6
Rail Passengers	-5.0	-2.5
Rail Freight	-6.0	-2.7

Table 10.5

Consumption of Gasoline Per Capita for Selected Countries under different Gasoline Price Consumption

(koe)

		2000			
	1981	No change in real prices	Low price assumption	High price assumption	100% price increase
Country					
Low Income Dev.					
Bangladesh	0.53	0.90	0.83	0.77	0.6
India	2.48	4.23	3.92	3.64	3.0
Kenya	18.83	32.11	29.78	27.63	22.72
Middle Income Dev.					
Colombia	126.9	236.7	196.3	182.3	179.4
Ecuador	163.5	277.1	229.7	213.4	210.0
Jamaica	86.8	161.8	152.3	143.4	122.7
Morocco	17.0	31.8	29.9	28.2	24.1
Philippines	29.6	55.3	52.0	49.0	41.9
Thailand	34.2	63.8	60.0	56.5	48.3
High Income Dev.					
Brazil	65.4	128.2	121.6	116.2	103.4
Chile	119.7	233.4	202.8	191.9	189.6
Costa Rica	61.3	119.5	114.2	109.2	97.1
Gabon	66.9	117.7	102.3	96.8	95.6
Portugal	82.4	160.6	153.5	146.7	130.5

Table 10.6

Energy Efficiencies of Different Types of Transport
(gram oil equivalent/unit km.)

Freight	
Oil pipeline	1 - 2
River boat	6 - 15
Unit trains	7 - 9
Ordinary trains	10 - 14
Road - long haul	15 - 60
- medium haul	35 -100
- short haul	100 -300
Passenger	
Buses - city	14 - 20
- inter-city	11 - 20
Express trains	12 - 17
Local trains	22 - 27
Suburban railways	20 - 22
Two wheelers - small	18 - 25
- large	35 - 50
Metros	25 - 45
Car	58 - 80
Short and medium haul air	65 -220

Source: Adapted from J.M. Beauvais and J.P. Pillet, Transports et Energies: Nouveaux Enjeux, Paris, Enertrans, April 1981.

Appendix 1

Documentation of Data Series

A. Country Coverage

B. Derivation of Variables in Data Set

A. COUNTRY COVERAGE

The countries covered in this study are :

Low Income Developing

Bangladesh
Burma
P. R. China
Ghana
India
Kenya
Malawi
Pakistan
Zaire
Zambia

Middle Income Developing

Bolivia
Cameroon
Colombia
Dominican Republic
Ecuador
Egypt
Honduras
Indonesia
Iran
Ivory Coast
Jamaica
Korea
Morocco
Nigeria
Peru
Philippines
Thailand
Tunisia
Turkey

High Income Developing

Algeria
Argentina
Barbados
Brazil
Chile
Costa Rica
Cyrpus
Gabon
Greece
Hong Kong
Iraq
Israel
Malaysia
Mexico
Panama
Portugal
Singapore
South Africa
Syria
Taiwan
Trinidad & Tobago
Uruguay
Venezuela
Yugoslavia

High Income Oil Exporters

Kuwait
Libya
Saudi Arabia

Eastern bloc

Czechoslovakia
German Democratic Republic
Hungary
USSR

Industrial

Australia
Belgium
Netherlands
New Zealand

Canada	Spain
Denmark	Sweden
Finland	Switzerland
France	United Kingdom
Italy	USA
Japan	W. Germany

Data for all countries were not available for all variables. Information on the country coverage of each table is given at the end of each Table.

Though a large number of countries are included in our data set it is important to realize that the income based category totals consists of an average of selected countries and do not because of lack of data include all countries which qualify for each category. In some tables category total are not given due to lack of data for a sufficient number of countries in that category.

Definition of Income Categories

As stated in the text the definition of the categories is basically that of the World Bank in its Annual Report of 1983. However, basing historical categories on a single year has the disadvantage of ignoring the fact that countries could change categories over time because of differential rates of economic growth. As many of the series are for relatively small periods of time in practice this is not a major problem. Even over longer periods of time (say since 1960) the classification showed considerable robustness. An alternative categorization was therefore developed based on changing income rank of countries over a 20 year period 1960 to 1980 (see Table 1.A.1). The categories were very similar with only one of two differences. The Cameroon whose income rose sharply in recent years due to oil developments would, under this alternative categorization, be included as a Low Income Developing countries. Ghana, on the other hand, despite declining economic performance would be in the Middle Income Developing category.

For simplicity, the Summary Tables use the first formulation while the second categorization is using the regression analysis.

For information, the unweighted average income of our groups of countries is given in Table 1.A.2.

Table 1.A.1

Changes in Income Rank of Countries

(1 = lowest per capita income)

	Average Rank	Rank change 80-60	Sum of rank over 3 years
Malawi	1	1	13
Burma	2	1	16
Zaire	3	-2	18
Bangladesh	4	-1	22
Indonesia	5	6	26
Kenya	6	-1	27
India	7	-2	29
Pakistan	8	0	31
China	9	5	43
Cameroon	10	-1	45
Thailand	11	+8	47
Philippines	12	-3	47
Egypt	13	7	48
Jordan	14	-7	57
Bolivia	15	0	58
Morocco	16	+6	59
Zambia	17	-16	60
Honduras	18	-7	60
Nicaragua	19	-2	71
Ivory Coast	20	0	76
Ecuador	21	+1	77
Tunisia	22	+9	98
Korea	23	15	78
Ghana	24	-24	78
Syria	25	+17	80
Dominican Republic	26	-8	81
Iran	27	-1	95
Algeria	28	0	98
Taiwan	29	+22	98
Brazil	30	+2	99
Colombia	31	-11	106
Malaysia	32	+2	108
Peru	33	-15	109
Turkey	34	-6	109
Jamaica	35	-21	111
Iraq	36	+11	114
Panama	37	-6	121
Brabados	38	1	122
Costa Rica	39	-8	123
Gabon	40	+33	131
Singapore	41	+12	132
Hong Kong	42	+24	134

Mexico	43	-5	138
Portugal	44	+1	138
South Africa	45	-11	139
Chile	46	-10	144
Cyprus	48	-1	146
Greece	19	+4	158
Argentina	50	-9	161
Venezuela	51	-10	165
Uruguay	52	-13	166
Trinidad & Tobago	53	1	169
Libya	74	15	224
Kuwait	77	0	234
Saudi Arabia	64	20	197
Hungary	54	-6	169
USSR	55	-1	169
Czechoslovakia	60	-4	192
Federal Rep. of Germany	63	-4	197
Spain	56	+4	171
Italy	58	+1	182
Japan	59	+15	187
New Zealand	61	-10	194
Finland	62	+3	196
United Kingdom	65	-5	198
Belgium	66	+4	202
Netherlands	67	-1	204
France	68	+7	209
Australia	69	-3	215
Denmark	70	-1	217
West Germany	71	+4	217
Switzerland	72	-4	223
Sweden	75	-1	225
Canada	73	+2	223
United States	0	0	231

Appendix Table 1.A.2

Definition of Categories of Countries
by Income level, 1980
(GNP/GDP per capita 1975 US$)

	Average Income	
	RGDP	GNP
Low Income Developing	494	152
Middle Income Developing	1341	530
High Income Developing	2599	1482
High Income Oil Exporting	n.a.	n.a.
Centrally Planned Economies*	4074	n.a.
Industrial Countries	6498	7095

Source: See appendix 1B

*GNP data not available for Centrally Planned Economies on a comparable basis. Alternative estimates of income per head for these countries on a comparable basis are available (see Chapter 2) and used in other tables.

B. Derivation of Variables in Data Set

ENDEVA

Individual Country Entries

Variable

1. Country code.

2. Year.

3. Railway traffic-passenger km in millions.

4. Railway traffic - net ton km in millions.

   Sources for variables 3 and 4:

   UN Statistical Yearbooks

   1970, 1973, 1974, 1975 on:1981 Yearbook

   1971, 1972:1979/80 Yearbook

   1965-1969:1975 Yearbook

   1961-1964:1970 Yearbook

   1960:1969 Yearbook

   Note: Values can vary between Yearbooks. We endeavored to use the latest entries available.

5. GNP in million of 1975 dollars, 1960 to 1980: from computer printout obtained from World Bank by Joy Dunkerley; 1981: data from Mr. Chander of the World Bank to Harry Broadman of Resources for the Future.

6. Consumption of motor gasoline in 1,000 metric tons, 1960, 1980-82, Table 21, p. 377 of United Nations, 1982 Energy Statistics Yearbook; 1970-1979: Table 35, p. 686 of United Nations, 1979 Energy Statistics Yearbook.

7. Consumption of aviation gasoline, 1960, 1980-82: table 20, p. 358 of United Nations 1982 Energy Statistics Yearbook; 1970-1979: table 34,

p. 663 1979 Energy Statistics Yearbook; for 1961-69, the UN did not publish separate series for motor gasoline and aviation gasoline. Total gasoline is given, consisting of motor gasoline, aviation gasoline and gasoline from plants for years 1950-74 in United Nations, World Energy Supplies 1950-1974, Table 12, p. 375.

1961-69 consumption of motor gasoline is obtained by subtracting aviation gasoline from total gasoline, where aviation gasoline 1961-69 is obtained by interpolating.

For some countries, discrepancies occur in the 1970-74 data for motor gasoline obtained in this fashion when compared to the "original" given data ("direct" entries). Consequently, care was taken in splicing series together, making the 1961-69 entries consistent with the "direct" entries.

World and Continent Totals (for ENDEVA)

Railway traffic variables do not appear. The UN does not list world and continental totals, and the sum of individual countries would not help because data for many countries do not appear.

GNP in billions of current dollars was obtained from the World Bank Atlas, employing various issues covering 1965 and 1970-81. These data were deflated to constant dollars using the U.S. Consumer Price Index. GNP coverage for 1960-64 and 1966-69 was obtained by splicing into the World Bank series estimates based on GNP indexes for the world and continents obtained from the UN Statistical Yearbook for various years. In the UN data, Asia includes Indonesia, Cyprus and Turkey. The World Bank series were adjusted to establish consistency within these classifications. In the UN data, Southern Europe includes Yugoslavia, which was transferred to

Eastern Europe to be consistent with our treatment of Yugoslavia as falling in Communist Europe.

Motor gasoline and aviation gasoline were obtained from the same sources as those listed for individual countries. For some years only gasoline consumption totals were available. In those years aviation gasoline was estimated by interpolation from years in which it was given, and where necessary there was an accounting for "gasoline from plants" a very minor component of the total. Aviation gasoline itself is a minor component of total, amounting to about 3 percent of the world total in 1960, 1 percent in 1970 and 1/2 of 1 percent in 1980. Then motor gasoline was obtained as the net of total gasoline minus aviation gasoline and plant gasoline.

ENDEVA
Year Coverage

Country Code	Name	Railway Traffic Passenger km	Freight net ton km	GNP million 78$	Consumption Motor gasoline	Aviation gasoline
101	Algeria	60-77	60-77	60-81	60-82	60-82
601	Argentina	60-80	60-80	60-81	60-82	60-82
201	Bangladesh	60-76	60-76	60-81	72-82	72-82
501	Barbados	-	-	60-81	60-82	60-82
602	Bolivia	61-71, 73-80	61-71, 73-80	60-81	60-82	60-82
603	Brazil	60-80	60-80	60-81	60-82	60-82
202	Burma	60-80	60-78	60-81	60-79	60-82
604	Chile	60-80	60-80	60-81	60-82	60-82
605	Colombia	60-80	60-80	60-81	60-82	60-82
503	Costa Rica	60-63, 66-74,76	60-74,76	60-81	60-82	60-79
302	Cyprus	-	-	60-81	60-82	60-82
606	Ecuador	60-80	60-80	65-81	60-82	60-82
103	Egypt	62-80	62-79	60-81	60-82	60-82
104	Gabon	-	-	60-81	60-82	60-82
204	Hong Kong	60-80	60-80	60-79	60-82	60-82
205	India	60-80	60-80	60-81	60-82	60-82
206	Indonesia	60-80	60-80	60-81	60-82	60-79
207	Iran	60-78	60-78	-	60-82	60-82
208	Iraq	60-78	60-78	60-79	60-82	60-82
209	Israel	60-80	60-80	60-81	60-82	60-82
106	Ivory Coast	60-78,80	60-78,80	60-81	60-82	60-82
506	Jamaica	60-77	60-77	60-81	60-82	60-82
211	Jordan	-	-	71-81	60-82	60-82
107	Kenya	-	-	60-81	60-82	60-82
212	Korea	60-80	60-80	60-81	60-82	60-69, 80-82
213	Kuwait	-	-	62-81	60-82	60-82
108	Libya	-	-	60-81	60-82	60-82
109	Malawi	60-63, 67-80	60-80	60-79	64-82	70-82
214	Malaysia	60-80	60-80	60-81	70-82	70-79
507	Mexico	60-80	60-80	60-79	60-82	60-82
110	Morocco	60-80	60-80	60-81	60-82	60-82
111	Nigeria	60-74	60-74	60-81	60-82	60-82
215	Pakistan	60-80	60-80	60-81	60-82	60-82
508	Panama	-	-	60-81	60-79	60-79
607	Peru	60-77	60-77	60-81	60-82	60-82
216	Philippines	60-80	60-80	60-81	60-82	60-82
217	Saudi Arabia	61-74	61-74	63-81	60-82	60-82
218	Singapore	-	-	60-67	60-82	60-82
220	Taiwan	60-69	60-69	60-81	-	-
221	Thailand	60-80	60-80	60-81	60-82	60-82
113	Tunisia	60-80	60-80	61-81	60-82	60-82
608	Uruguay	65-67, 69-78	65,67-78	60-81	60-82	60-82
609	Venezuela	60-78	60-78	60-81	60-82	60-82
114	Zaire	62-73,76	62-73,76	60-81	60-82	60-82
115	Zambia	-	-	60-81	60-82	60-82

Country Code	Name	Railway Traffic Passenger km	Freight net ton km	GNP million 78$	Consumption Motor gasoline	Aviation gasoline
502	Canada	60-78	60-78	60-81	60-82	60-82
510	United States	60-78	60-78	60-81	60-82	60-82
210	Japan	60-78	60-78	60-81	60-82	73-82
701	Australia	-	60-77	60-81	60-82	60-82
702	New Zealand	60-80	60-80	60-81	60-80	60-80
304	Finland	60-78	60-78	60-81	60-82	60-82
305	France	60-78	60-78	60-81	60-82	60-82
306	W. Germany	60-78	60-78	60-81	60-82	60-82
308	Italy	60-78	60-78	60-81	60-82	60-82
309	Netherlands	60-78	60-78	60-81	60-82	60-82
312	Sweden	60-78	60-78	60-81	60-82	60-82
313	Switzerland	60-80	60-80	60-81	60-82	60-82
314	United Kingdom	60-78	60-78	60-81	60-82	60-82
403	Hungary	60-78	60-78	-	60,70-82	-
402	German Dem. Rep.	60-78	60-78	-	60,70-82	-
404	USSR	60-78	60-78	-	60,70-82	-
301	Belgium	60-78	60-80	60-81	60-82	60-82
102	Cameroon	60-80	60-80	60-81	60-82	60-82
203	China	77-80	70-71, 77-80	-	60,70-82	-
303	Denmark	60-80	60-80	60-79	60-82	60-82
504	Dominican Rep.	-	-	60-81	60-82	60-82
105	Ghana	60-72	60-72	60-81	60-82	60-82
505	Honduras	-	-	60-81	60-82	60-82
310	Portugal	60-80	60-80	60-81	60-82	60-82
112	South Africa	-	60-80	60-81	60-82	60-70,80-82
219	Syria	60-80	60-80	60-81	60-82	75,80-82
509	Trinidad & Tobago	-	-	60-81	60,70-82	Sporadic
222	Turkey	60-80	60-80	60-81	60-82	60-69,80
307	Greece	60-80	60-80	60-81	60-82	60-72
311	Spain	60-78	60-80	60-81	60-82	60-82
401	Czechoslovakia	60-69	60-69	70-78	-	-
405	Yugoslavia	60-69	60-69	60-79	-	-
000	World	-	-	60-81	60-82	60-82
100	Africa	-	-	60-81	60-82	60-82
200	Asia	-	-	60-81	60-82	60-82
300	Europe-Free Mkt.	-	-	60-81	60-82	60-82
400	Europe-Communist	-	-	60-79	60-82	60-82
500	North & Cent. America	-	-	60-81	60-82	60-82
600	South America	-	-	60-81	60-82	60-82
700	Oceania	-	-	60-81	60-82	60-82

ENDEVB

Individual Country Entries

Variable

1. Country code.

2. Year.

3. RGDP*; Real Gross Domestic Product per Capita Adjusted for Changes in the terms of trade. Source: R. Summers and A. Heston, Data Table appearing in "Improved International Comparisons of Real Product and Its Composition, 1950-80," The Review of Income and Wealth, Series 30, No. 2, June 1984, pp. 207-262, and addendum to Data Table for 1981. Values are in 1975 U.S. dollars.

   Note that RGDP (Real Gross Domestic Product per Capita) was employed for Eastern European Communist Countries.

4. Population in thousands. From Summers and Heston (as shown above) for almost all years and countries. Data for 1982 was derived using their 1981 figure times the (1982/1981) value obtained from the World Bank, World Development Report, 1983 and World Development Report, 1984. Countries not appearing in Summers and Heston were obtained as follows. Kuwait, Libya and Saudi Arabia data for 1970 to 1982 were obtained from R. Chander of the World Bank (through Harry Broadman of RFF), while data for 1960 to 1969 were obtained from the UN 1970 Demographic Yearbook. Hungary for 1982 was obtained from the UN 1982 Demographic Yearbook.

5. Passenger cars in thousands.

6. Trucks and buses (commercial vehicles) in thousands.

   Primary source: UN data from various UN Statistical Yearbooks. Same coverage as for ENDEVA railway traffic.

1970, 1973, 1974, 1975 on: 1981 Yearbook

1971, 1972: 1979/80 Yearbook

1965–1969: 1975 Yearbook

1961–1964: 1970 Yearbook

1960: 1969 Yearbook

Major Secondary Source: "World Motor Vehicle Registration" tables in Motor Vehicle Manufacturers Association, Motor Vehicle Facts and Figures, annual, 1962 through 1984. Additional data obtained from International Road Federation, World Road Statistics, various issues, and for U.S., from data obtained from U.S. Federal Highway Administration.

7. Density of road network in kms per square km. From International Road Federation, World Road Statistics, Table 1, various issues.

8. Registration code.

9. Density code.

For variables 5 and 6, and for 7, various adjustments and reconciliations between sources were necessary. The codes document those adjustments. The registration and density codes are defined, in turn, as follows.

8. Registration code

0: UN data accepted as is.

1: Motor Vehicle Manufacturers (MVM) data accepted as is.

2: Interpolation.

3: Inference from internal data, both cars and commercial vehicles.

4: Inference from internal data, cars only.

5: Inference from internal data, commercial vehicles only.

6: Inference from outside information.

7: In UN data a definitional change appears to occur, and this was then built into previous years.

8: MVM data adjusted to be consistent with UN data for continents.

9: MVM data accepted despite a major inconsistency with UN data; available evidence suggests the MVM data were more accurate.

Additional detail on codes

1. The UN data coverage often stopped around 1977, although some series had coverage to 1980. The MVM data were then drawn on for coverage to 1982, with reconciliation as necessary to make MVM consistent with UN data.

2. Interpolation occurred when there were missing values that occurred between two years with consistent data. For example, MVM listed registrations for Cyprus for 1978 and 1982, which appeared consistent with one another; intervening years were not given, so 1979, 1980 and 1981 were derived by interpolation.

3, 4 and 5. Inferences. An inconsistency occurred in an original series, which can be inferred from preceding and following entries to the 3, 4 or 5 entries, that is, 0 or 1 occurring before or after 3, 4 or 5 entries indicates the original source. Changes were made to impose consistency. In a few cases, discrepancies were quite large, and again, an attempt was made to develop the most reasonable values given the available information. A phone conversation with Mr. Evers of MVM (who is responsible for the MVM series) on December 5, 1984 yielded the information that in some countries, registration data can show marked revisions over time.

As an example of an extreme case and the inference employed, consider these data for the Philippines, in thousands:

	Cars	Trucks and buses	Total
1978 UN	464.0	369.8	833.8
1981 Int. Road Fed.	318.1	382.5	700.6
1980 MVM	550.0	500.0	1050.0
1981 MVM	849.1	916.4	1765.5
1982 MVM	344.6	524.1	868.7

Reconciliation of these data was carried out as follows. The MVM 1982 total was accepted as consistent with the 1978 UN total, and earlier year totals. The 1978 UN proportionate distribution was assumed applicable in 1982 and applied to the MVM total to obtain the amounts for each category. Then 1979, 1980 and 1981 values were obtained by interpolation.

6. Primary reliance was placed on International Road Federation or U.S. Federal Highway Administration data in making inferences.

8. For continents, totals only, MVM data were relied on, but were made consistent with UN data.

9. Density Code

0. Data accepted as is.
1. Minor change to impose consistency, e.g., round-off procedure may vary between years. Made consistent.
2. Large change to impose consistency. For example, Argentina was given as

1968	.07
1969	.07
1970	.07
1971	.07
1974	.11

1975	.11
1976	.07
1977	.07
1978	.07

The 1974 and 1975 values were changed to .07.

3. A major change was made. For example, in the case of Australia there was an apparent decimal point error, so 1.27 was changed to .127.

5. Interpolation, where this appeared clearly justified.

7. Anomalies but explainable by territorial change, i.e., changes in a country's borders.

8. Contradictory data and no basis for inference. Set equal to zero (not available).

9. Filling in of a "not available" with an unchanged value that occurs both before and after the date of the "not available" entry.

Codes 4 and 6 were not used.

World and Continent Totals (for ENDEVB)

Population was obtained from issues of the United Nations *Demographic Yearbooks* and *Statistical Yearbooks*. In practice, the most recent yearbooks were drawn on directly for the years they covered. Disagreements often occurred between population data in the most recent yearbooks and data listed in earlier yearbooks, presumably reflecting revisions and refinements based on improved reporting and estimation. Given the discrepancies for the years in common, corresponding changes were made in the data appearing in the earlier yearbooks but not in the most recent, to fill in all of the years in the series.

Passenger car and truck and bus registrations were obtained from the same sources drawn on for the individual country registrations. UN data were employed for most of the entries, with entries for the most recent years obtained from MVM data made consistent with the UN series (code 8 is employed to indicate that an adjustment was made in the MVM data, in variable 8, the registration code).

RGDP* and the road density variable were not available at the continental and world level

<u>Year Coverage for ENDEVB</u>

Absence of coverage is as follows:

RGDP*, 1982 - not available, all countries

RGDP* for all years, not available for Libya, Kuwait, Saudi Arabia

RGDP* for 1981, not available for Hungary, German Democratic Republic, USSR, China, Czechoslovakia and Yugoslavia

RGDP* also not available for world and continents, all years

Density of road network not available for continents and world.

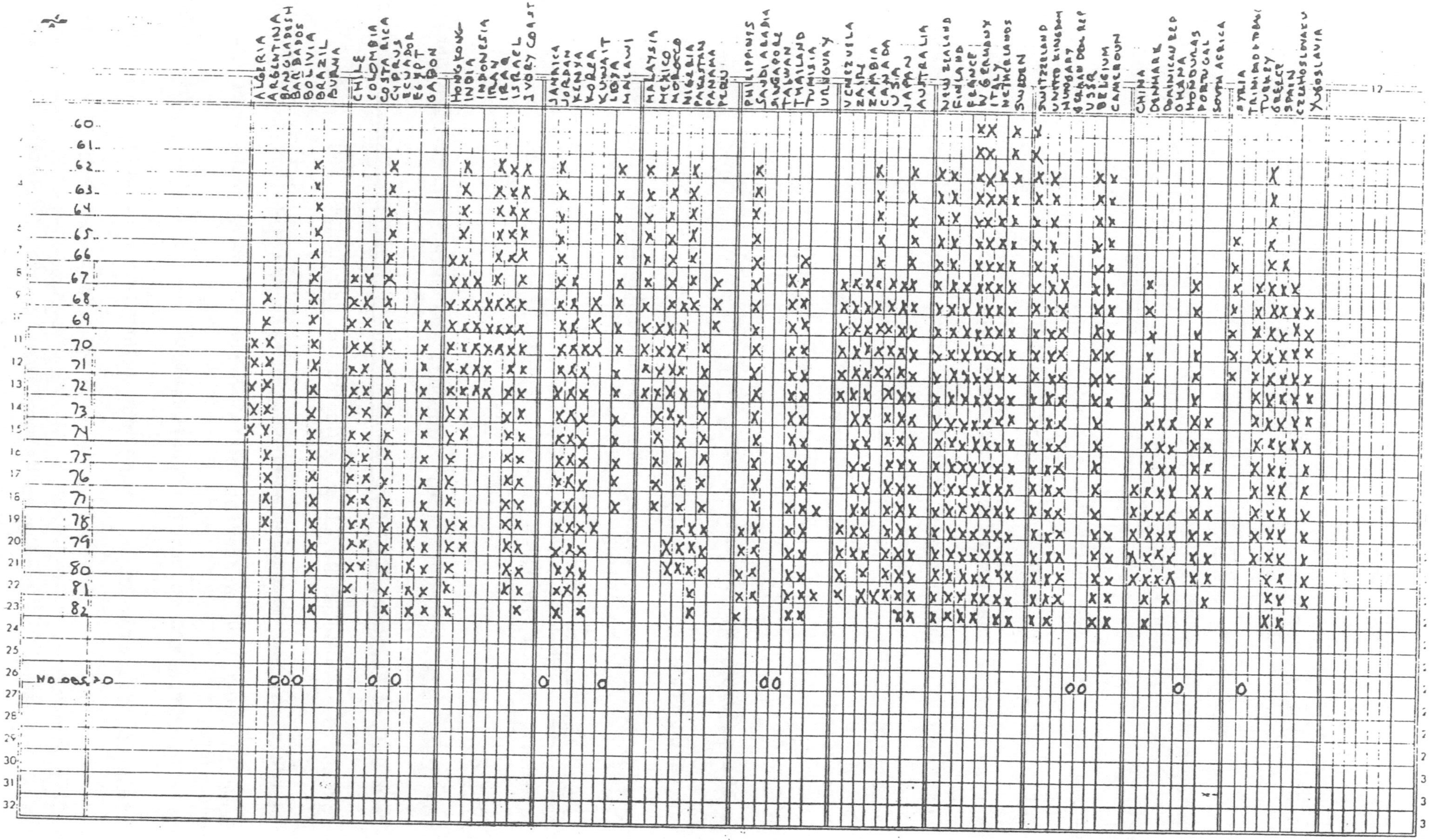

COVERAGE ON DENSITY OF ROAD NETWORK IN ENDEVB

RENDEVA

Variable

1. Country code.
2. Year.
3. Quantity of fuel used in total transportation.
4. Quantity of fuel used in road transportation.
5. Quantity of fuel used in rail transportation.
6. Quantity of fuel used in air transportation.
7. Quantity of fuel used in water transportation.
8. Nonspecified use of fuel in transportation.
9. Units code.

For the majority of countries, data were available from 1971 to 1982 and were taken from:

(1) International Energy Agency, OECD, Energy, Balances of Developing Countries 1971/82, Paris 1984.

(2) International Energy Agency, OECD, Energy Balances of OECD Countries 1971/82, Paris 1984.

(3) For Costa Rica, Cyprus, Israel, Jordan, and Malawi, data were obtained from United Nations, Energy Balances 1977-80 and Electricity Profiles 1976-81 for Selected Developing Countries and Areas, New York, 1983. In addition, for several countries, source (1) only listed amounts used in total transportation while source (3) gave amounts of fuel used by different modes of transportation for 1977-1980. The proportions of fuel used in each mode was determined from source (3) and applied to the total given in source (1). The countries for which this procedure was used are: Gabon, Ivory Coast, Philippines, Saudi Arabia, Tunisia and Uruguay.

(4) Some data for the Dominican Republic, Honduras and Trinidad and Tobago were available from OLADE (Latin American Energy Organization), Energy Balances for Latin America, Quito, Ecuador, Nov. 1981.

Variable 9: code indicating units

1: data for variables 3-8 are in 1000 tons of oil equivalent (TOE). Sources (1) and (2).

2: data for variables 3-8 are in terajoules. One terajoule = 23.5 tons of oil equivalent (TOE). Source (3).

3: data for variables 3-8 are in 1000 TOE. Source (4).

Note: not available is coded as 0.

"actually zero" is coded as 0.1.

RENDEVA

Year Coverage

Code	Name	Total transport	Quantity of Fuel Used by Mode Road	Rail	Air	Water	Not spec.	Code 1
101	Algeria	71-82	-	-	-	-	-	71-82
601	Argentina	71-82	71-82	71-82	71-82	75-82	71-82	71-82
201	Bangladesh	72-81	-	-	-	-		72-81
501	Barbados	77-80	77-80	77-80	77-80	-	77-80	77-80
602	Bolivia	71-81	-	-	-	-	-	71-81
603	Brazil	71-82	-	-	-	-	-	71-82
202	Burma	71-81	-	-	-	-	-	71-81
604	Chile	71-82	-	-	-	-	-	71-82
605	Colombia	71-81	-	-	-	-	-	71-81
503	Costa Rica	77-80	77-80	-	77-80	-	77-80	77-80
302	Cyprus	77-80	77-80	-	77-80	-	77-80	77-80
606	Ecuador	71-82	-	-	-	-	-	71-82
103	Egypt	71-82	71-82	-	71-82	-	71-82	71-82
104	Gabon	71-81	77-80	-	77-80	-	77-80	71-82
204	Hong Kong	71-82	71-82	-	71-82	71-82	71-82	71-82
205	India	71-82	71-82	71-82	71-82	71-82	71-82	71-82
206	Indonesia	71-82	71-82	71-82	71-82	71-82	-	71-82
207	Iran	71-82	71-82	-	71-82	-	71-82	71-82
208	Iraq	71-82	-	-	-	-	-	71-82
209	Israel	77-80	77-80	77-80	77-80	-	77-80	77-80
106	Ivory Coast	71-81	77-80	80	77-80	-	77-80	71-82
506	Jamaica	71-81	77-80	77-80	77-80	-	77-80	71-82
211	Jordan	77-80	-	-	77-80	-	77-80	71-82
107	Kenya	71-82	71-82	71-82	71-82	71-82	-	71-82
212	Korea	71-82	71-82	71-82	71-82	71-82	71-82	71-82
213	Kuwait	71-82	71-82	-	71-82	-	71-82	71-82
108	Libya	71-81	-	-	-	-	-	71-81
109	Malawi	77-80	77-80	78-80	77-80	-	77-80	77-80
214	Malaysia	71-82	71-82	-	71-82	-	71-82	71-82
507	Mexico	71-82	71-82	71-82	71-82	71-82	71-82	71-82
110	Morocco	71-81	-	-	-	-	-	71-81
111	Nigeria	71-82	71-82	71-82	71-82	71-82	71-82	71-82
215	Pakistan	71-82	71-82	71-82	71-82	-	71-82	71-82
508	Panama	71-81	-	-	-	-	-	71-81
607	Peru	71-81	-	-	-	-	-	71-81
216	Philippines	71-81	77-80	-	77-80	77-79	77-80	71-81
217	Saudi Arabia	71-82	77-80	-	77-80	-	-	71-82
218	Singapore	71-82	71-82	-	71-82	-	-	71-82
220	Taiwan	71-82	-	-	-	-	-	71-82
221	Thailand	71-82	71-82	-	71-82	-	71-82	71-82
113	Tunisia	71-81	77-80	-	77-80	-	77-80	77-80
608	Uruguay	71-81	-	-	77-80	-	77-80	71-82
609	Venezuela	71-82	71-82	-	71-82	-	71-82	71-82
114	Zaire	71-81	-	-	-	-	-	71-81
115	Zambia	71-81	-	-	-	-	-	71-81

RENDEVA (continued)

Code	Name	Total transport	Quantity of Fuel Used by Mode					
			Road	Rail	Air	Water	Not spec.	Code 1
502	Canada	71-81	71-81	71-81	71-81	71-81	71-81	71-81
510	United States	71-81	71-81	71-81	71-81	-	71-81	71-81
210	Japan	71-81	71-81	71-81	71-81	71-72, 74-81	71-81	71-81
701	Australia	71-81	71-81	71-81	71-81	79-81	80	71-81
702	New Zealand	71-81	71-81	71-81	71-81	71-81	71-81	71-81
304	Finland	71-81	71-81	71-81	71-81	71-81	71-81	71-81
305	France	71-81	71-81	71-81	71-81	71-81	71-81	71-81
306	W. Germany	71-81	71-81	71-81	71-81	71-81	71-81	71-81
308	Italy	71-81	71-81	71-81	71-81	71-81	71-81	71-81
309	Netherlands	71-81	71-81	71-81	71-81	71-81	71-81	71-81
312	Sweden	71-81	71-81	71-81	71-81	71-81	71-81	71-81
313	Switzerland	71-81	71-81	71-81	71-81	71-81	71-81	71-81
314	United Kingdom	71-81	71-81	71-81	71-81	71-81	71-81	71-81
403	Hungary	-	-	-	-	-	-	-
402	German Dem. Rep.	-	-	-	-	-	-	-
404	USSR	-	-	-	-	-	-	-
301	Belgium	71-81	71-81	71-81	71-81	71-81	71-81	71-81
102	Cameroon	-	-	-	-	-	-	-
203	China	-	-	-	-	-	-	-
303	Denmark	71-81	71-81	71-81	71-81	71-81	71-81	71-81
504	Dominican Rep.	73,74, 76,78,80	-	-	-	-	-	-
105	Ghana	-	-	-	-	-	-	-
505	Honduras	70,72, 74,76	-	-	-	-	-	-
310	Portugal	71-81	71-81	71-81	71-81	71-81	71-81	71-81
112	South Africa	-	-	-	-	-	-	-
219	Syria	-	-	-	-	-	-	-
509	Trinidad & Tobago	70,72,73 76,79	-	-	-	-	-	-
222	Turkey	71-81	71-81	71-81	71-81	71-81	71-81	71-81
307	Greece	71-81	71-81	71-81	71-81	71-81	71-81	71-81
311	Spain	71-81	71-81	71-81	71-81	71-81	71-81	71-81
401	Czechoslovakia	-	-	-	-	-	-	-
405	Yugoslavia	-	-	-	-	-	-	-

RENDEVB

Variable

1. Country code.

2. Year.

3. Retail price of regular gasoline in dollars per gallon.

4. Retail price of auto diesel fuel in dollars per gallon.

5. Retail price of distillate fuel in dollars per barrel.

   Sources of retail prices for petroleum products, as of July in each year:

   1965, 1969-1975: Bureau of Mines, Department of Interior, International Petroleum Annual.

   1976-1978: Energy Information Administration, DOE, International Petroleum Annual.

   1979-1982: Energy Information Administration, DOE, International Energy Annual.

6. Diesel fuel used in total transportation.

7. Diesel fuel used in road transportation.

8. Diesel fuel used in rail transportation.

9. Diesel fuel used in air transportation.

10. Diesel fuel used in inland and coastal waterways.

   Sources for diesel fuel measures:

   (1) United Nations, Energy Balances 1977-1980 and Electricity Profiles 1976-1981 for Selected Developing Countries and Areas, New York, 1983.

   (2) International Energy Agency/Organization for Economic Cooperation and Development, Energy Statistics 1976/1980, Paris, 1982.

(3) International Road Federation, World Road Statistics, various issues.

11. Source code for diesel fuel

1. Data from UN. Unit of measure: terajoule.
2. Data from International Energy Agency OECD. Unit equals 1000 metric tons.
3. Data from International Road Federation. Unit equals 1000 metric tons.
4. Data derived by inference from International Road Federation Information. Unit equals 1000 metric tons.
5. Data for fuel used in total transportation is from UN (terajoules) but data used for fuel used in road transportation is from International Road Federation (1000 metric tons).

Notes on Variables

Additional information on price series was obtained from DOE personnel (Bernadette Michalski 252-9412, and Harold Wiseman, 252-1158). They noted that retail prices were reported for a particular city in each country and might not be fully representative of prices in the rest of the country. Information was obtained from embassy filling out of questionnaire and may vary in quality between countries.

For diesel fuel use, UN employed "inland and coastal waterways" as a category while OECD used "internal navigation". Latter source covered UK, US, France, Japan, W. Germany, Greece, Turkey, Portugal and Spain.

RENDEVB

Year Coverage

Code	Name	Retail Price of Fuel: Regular gasoline	Retail Price of Fuel: Auto diesel	Retail Price of Fuel: Distillate fuel	Quantity of Diesel Fuel (quantity in aviation always is zero): Total transport	Road	Rail	Water	Source
101	Algeria	-	-	-	-	-	-	-	-
601	Argentina	65,70-82	78-82	75-79,81-82	77-80	65,70-80	77-80	77-80	65,70-82
201	Bangladesh	-	-	-	-	-	-	-	-
501	Barbados	-	-	-	77-80	77-80	77-80	77-80	77-80
602	Bolivia	65,70-82	80-82	75-82	-	-	-	-	-
603	Brazil	65,70-82	78-80, 82	75-77,82	77-80	77-80	77-80	77-80	77-80
202	Burma	65,70-81	80-81	75-79,81	-	-	-	-	-
604	Chile	65,70-82	78-82	75-77,79, 81-82	77-80	77-80	77-80	77-80	77-80
605	Colombia	65,70-82	79-82	75-79,81	-	-	-	-	-
503	Costa Rica	-	-	-	77-80	77-80	77-80	77-80	77-80
302	Cyprus	-	-	-	77-80	77-80	77-80	77-80	77-80
606	Ecuador	70-74, 77-80, 82-83	80, 82-83	77-79	-	-	-	-	-
103	Egypt	-	-	-	-	-	-	-	-
104	Gabon	-	-	-	-	-	-	-	-
204	Hong Kong	-	-	-	-	65,70-80	-	78-80	65,70-80
205	India	65,70-82	78-82	75-82	77-80	65,70-72 77-80	77-80	77-80	65,70-82
206	Indonesia	70-83	-	-	77-80	65,70,71, 73,77-80	77-80	77-80	65,70-82
207	Iran	65,70-81	80-81	75-79,81	-	-	-	-	-
208	Iraq	-	-	-	-	65,70,71	-	-	-
209	Israel	65,70-83	80-83	78-83	77-80	77-80	77-80	77-80	77-80
106	Ivory Coast	-	-	-	77-80	77-80	77-80	77-80	77-80
506	Jamaica	65,70-83	80-83	75-79, 81-83	77-80	77-80	77-80	77-80	77-80
211	Jordan	-	-	-	77-80	-	-	-	77-80
107	Kenya	65,70-81	78,79, 81	75-77,81	77-80	65,70-80	77-80	77-80	65,70-80
212	Korea	79,83	79,83	79,83	77-80	78-82	-	-	77-82
213	Kuwait	-	-	-	-	-	-	-	-
108	Libya	-	-	-	-	-	-	-	-
109	Malawi	-	-	-	77-80	65,70-80	77-80	-	65,70-80
214	Malaysia	-	-	-	-	73,76,77	-	-	73,76,77
507	Mexico	65,70-83	78-83	75-83	77-80	-	-	-	77-80
110	Morocco	65,70-83	80-83	75-79,81-83	-	65,70-81	-	-	65,70-81
111	Nigeria	-	-	-	77-80	77-80	77-80	77-80	77-80
215	Pakistan	65,70-83	78, 80-83	75-77	-	65,70-72	-	-	65,70-72
508	Panama	65,70-83	78-83	75-77,81	-	-	-	-	-
607	Peru	65,70-83	80-83	75-83					
216	Philippines	65,70-82	78-82	75-77,80-81	77-80	77-80	-	77-80	77-80
217	Saudi Arabia	65,70-82	79, 81-83	75-79,82-83	77-80	-	-	-	77-80
218	Singapore	71-82	78-82	75-79,81-82	-	-	-	-	-
220	Taiwan	-	-	-	-	-	-	-	-
221	Thailand	65,70-82	78-82	75-77,80-82	77-80	70,71, 73-76, 81,82	-	-	70-82
113	Tunisia	65,70-79, 82	78-79	75-79	77-80	77-80	-	-	77-80
608	Uruguay	65,70-78, 80,81	78,80, 81	75-78	77-80	-	-	-	77-80
609	Venezuela	65,70-82	78-81	75-77, 80-82	77-80	-	-	-	77-80
114	Zaire	-	-	-	-	70,73,78	-	-	70,73,78
115	Zambia	-	-	-	-	-	-	-	-

RENDEVB (continued)

		Retail Price of Fuel			Quantity of Diesel Fuel (quantity in aviation always is zero)				
Code	Name	Regular gasoline	Auto diesel	Distillate fuel	Total transport	Road	Rail	Water	Source
502	Canada	65,70-83	78-83	75-77,80	-	70,71, 72-75, 78-81	-	-	70,71, 72-75 78-81
510	United States	65,70-83	78-83	75-83	76-80	65,70-81	65,70-81	-	65,70-81
210	Japan	65,70-83	78-83	75-77, 80-83	76-80	65,70-82	76-80	76-80	65,70-82
701	Australia	65,70-83	78-83	75,77,81-83	-	78-82	-	-	78-82
702	New Zealand	-	-	-	-	81-82	-	-	81-82
304	Finland	65,70-82	78-82	75-77,80-82	-	65,70-72	-	-	65,70-82
305	France	65,70-80	78-80	75-77,79	76-80	65,70-80	76-80	76-80	65,70-80
306	W. Germany	65,70-80	78-80	75-79	76-80	65,70-80	76-80	76-80	65,70-80
308	Italy	65,70-83	78-83	75-83	-	75-76, 79-80	-	-	75-76,79-80
309	Netherlands	65,70-83	78-83	75-80	-	65,70-82	-	-	65,70-82
312	Sweden	65,70-83	78-83	75,77,79-83	-	65,70-82	-	-	65,70-82
313	Switzerland	65,70-81	79-81	75,77-80	-	65,70-82	-	-	65,70-82
314	United King.	65,70-81	78-81	75-77,80	76-80	65,70-81	76-80	76-80	65,70-81
403	Hungary	-	-	-	-	65-78	-	-	65-78
402	German Dem. Rep.	-	-	-	-	-	-	-	-
404	USSR	-	-	-	-	-	-	-	-
301	Belgium	65,70-82	78-82	75-78,80-82	-	65,70-82	-	-	65,70-82
102	Cameroon	-	-	-	-	80-81	-	-	80-81
203	China	-	-	-	-	78-80	-	-	78-80
303	Denmark	65,70-82	79-82	75-79,81-82	-	-	-	-	-
504	Domin. Rep.	70-81	78-81	75-77,80-81	-	-	-	-	-
105	Ghana	65,70-82	78-82	75-77,81-82	-	-	-	-	-
505	Honduras	-	-	-	-	-	-	-	-
310	Portugal	65,70-82	80-82	75-79,81-82	76-80	76-80	76-80	76-86	76-80
112	South Africa	65,70-82	78-82	75-77,79-82					
219	Syria	-	-	-	-	-	-	-	-
509	Trinidad & Tobago	-	-	-	-	-	-	-	-
222	Turkey	65,70-82	78-82	75-82	76-79	76-79	76-79	76-79	76-79
307	Greece	65,70-82	79-82	75-82	76-80	76-80	76-80	76-80	76-80
311	Spain	65,70-82	78-82	75-79,81-82	76-80	76-80	76-80	76-80	76-80
401	Czechoslovakia	-	-	-	-	-	-	-	-
405	Yugoslavia	65,70-80, 82	79,80, 82	75-80	-	-	-	-	-

XENDEVA

Variable

1. Country code.
2. Projected population in millions, 1982. Source:

   World Bank, World Development Report, 1984, Oxford University Press for the World Bank, July 1984, Table 1, "Population Projections," p. 192. Note: all variables in XENDEVA obtained from World Development Report, 1984 (WDR).
3. Projected population in millions, 1990.
4. Projected population in millions, 2000.

   WDR, Table 19, "Population Growth and Projections," p. 254.
5. Projected population in millions, 2050.
6. Hypothetical size of stationary population, in millions, WDR, Table 19, p. 254.
7. Year of stationary population. Obtained by adding 60 to "Assumed year of reaching net reproduction rate of 1.0" as shown in WDR, Table 19, p. 254. (More detail appears below.)
8. Area in thousand square kilometers. WDR "Basic Indicators", p. 218.

The WDR defines a stationary population as one in which age-and sex-specific mortality rates have not changed over a long period, while age-specific fertility rates have simultaneously remained at replacement level (net reproduction rate equals 1.0). In such a population, the birth rate is constant and equal to the death rate, the age structure is also constant, and the growth rate is zero. A population tends to grow even after fertility has declined to replacement level because past high growth rates will have produced an age distribution with a relatively high proportion of women in, or still to enter, the reproductive ages. Consequently, the birth rate will exceed the death rate and the growth rate will remain positive for several decades. A population takes 50-75 years, depending on initial conditions, before its age distribution fully adjusts to changed fertility rates. Here, we employed a figure of 60 years as an approximate midpoint between 50 and 75 years, to obtain our estimated year of stationary population. (Based on WDR, p. 281.)

Year and Variable Coverage

All population projection data not available:

Barbados, Cyprus, Gabon, Taiwan

Year 2050 population projection not listed:

Canada, U.S., Japan, Australia, New Zealand, Finland, France, W. Germany, Italy, Netherlands, Sweden, Switzerland, UK, Hungary, German Dem. Rep., USSR, Belgium, Denmark, Portugal, Greece, Spain, Czechoslovakia, Yugoslavia.

XENDEVB

Variable

1. Country code.

2. Year.

3. Urban population as percent of total population.

4. Percent of urban population in largest city.

5. Percent of urban population in cities of over 500,000 persons.

6. Number of cities of over 500,000 persons.

Variables 3,4,5 and 6 from World Bank, World Development Report 1984, Table 22, p. 260. Variable 3: 1960, 1982. Variables 4,5 and 6: 1960, 1980. For 1970, variable 3 only from World Bank, World Tables, second edition, 1980, Table 1, p. 437. (Special cases: Cyprus, Gabon & Taiwan--variable 3 for 1960, 1970 and 1980 from World Tables source.)

7. Dependency ratio in percent for 1960, 1980, 2000. World Bank, World Development Report, 1984, Table 2, p. 194.

8. Age structure--age 0-14 as percent of total 1960, 1970 and most recent estimate: 1980 (MRE).

9. Age structure--age 15-65 as percent of total 1960, 1970, MRE = 1980 and 1982.

10. Age structure--age 65+ as percent of total 1960, 1970 and MRE.

"Most recent estimate" treated as equivalent to 1980. Sources: for 1960, 1970 and MRE: World Bank, World Tables, Table 1, p. 436. For 1982, age 15-65, from World Bank, World Development Report, Table 21, p. 258.

Variable 3:

Urban population as % of total population.

Countries with 1960 and 1982, missing 1970 entry. This occurred because 1970 value was inconsistent. Boliva, Burma, Malawi, Panama, Zaire.

Countries with 1960, 1970 and 1980 values, 1980 rather than 1982. This occurred because _World Tables_ had data on country, but _World Development Report 1984_ did not: Cyprus, Gabon, Taiwan. Those 3 countries also did not have entries for variables 4,5 and 6.

Country with no entries for variables 3,4,5 & 6: Barbados.

Countries with variable 4 (% in largest city) not listed: Zambria, Trinidad and Tobago.

Variable 9:

Age structure--age 15-65 as % of total

Not available for 1982: Cyprus, Gabon, Taiwan.

XENDEVC

Variable

1. Year

2. Monthly consumer price index, July value. For use in deflating gasoline prices. 1967=100 in series. Source: BLS, Monthly Labor Review, various issues.

3. Annual Consumer Price Index, 1967=100. Source: BLS, Monthly Labor Review, various issues and U.S. Statistical Abstract, 1984, Table 809, p. 493.

4. Average car price, in U.S. current dollars. Weighted average price of domestic and import car sales.

5. Import car price, in U.S., current dollars.

   Source of Variables 4 and 5: Motor Vehicle Manufacturers Association, Motor Vehicle Facts and Figures, 1984 edition, p. 42.

6. Automobile price index: consumer price index for new cars. Source: BLS, Monthly Labor Review, various issues.

7. Regulation cost per new car: cost imposed for safety and emission regulations in the United States. Source: same as Variables 4 and 5.

XENDEVD

Variable

1. Country code

2. Country name

3. Rank. Ranking based on average ranking for per capita RGDP over the periods 1960, 1970 and 1980. RGDP per capita was sorted by rank order, running from lowest to highest level (1 through 77) for 1960, 1970 and 1980. Those values were summed and then a rank order was applied to the sum, again running from lowest to highest. Source of per capita RGDP reading: ENDEVB. (Note RGDP* has been referenced as RGDP in text for ease of exposition.)

4. Rank change. 1980 RGDP per capita rank minus 1960 RGDP per capita rank. If a country improved its relative income position, its rank change was positive.

5. Sum rank. Sum of 1960, 1970 and 1980 RGDP per capita rankings.

6. Small car tax rate: tariff duties, sales taxes, and all other auto taxes as percent applied to import value before taxes.

7. Medium size car tax rate; tariff duties sales taxes and all other auto taxes as percent applied to import value before taxes. Source of variables 6 and 7: Developed from data in Overseas Department, S.M.M.&T. Ltd., Customs Tariff Service, London, 1981.

Appendix 2

Statistical Tables 1 - 17

Appendix Table 1

PER CAPITA FUEL CONSUMPTION IN TRANSPORT BY INCOME CATEGORY
(KG of oil equivalent per person)

		YEAR							
		71	73	74	75	78	79	80	81
CAT	CNAME								
LOW INC DEV	BANGLADESH	.	1.5	2.9	3.7	3.6	3.7	5.4	4.7
	BURMA	18.4	14.8	17.4	14.4	16.7	18.2	18.7	18.5
	CHINA	.	.	.	.	.	.	.	.
	GHANA	.	.	.	.	.	.	.	.
	INDIA	26.4	25.3	25.6	26.1	25.6	26.4	26.6	26.6
	KENYA	53.8	58.5	62.8	58.2	61.6	56.7	57.2	59.9
	MALAWI	.	.	.	.	14.8	14.7	15.6	.
	PAKISTAN	27.4	20.1	21.8	20.2	29.9	32.5	36.3	35.4
	ZAIRE	18.0	16.8	17.8	17.1	18.2	19.6	18.4	18.6
	ZAMBIA	64.2	66.9	67.2	72.8	71.8	75.0	64.9	68.3
MIDDLE INC DEV	BOLIVIA	67.5	83.2	87.0	112.9	155.4	130.0	121.7	115.6
	CAMEROON	.	.	.	.	.	.	.	.
	COLOMBIA	120.2	131.0	143.8	137.6	155.9	158.5	145.0	154.3
	DOMINICAN REP	.	120.6	123.6	.	112.5	.	106.7	.
	ECUADOR	97.7	124.9	145.3	152.0	216.4	244.5	266.1	264.0
	EGYPT	38.2	50.1	59.0	59.9	72.7	74.7	77.4	77.5
	HONDURAS	.	.	53.2	.	.	.	.	.
	INDONESIA	19.0	23.4	26.7	29.6	38.8	40.7	44.4	46.7
	IRAN	117.5	172.7	197.2	236.9	251.9	206.4	215.0	175.4
	IVORY COAST	79.6	77.2	73.9	74.7	98.9	62.4	84.8	70.6
	JAMAICA	372.1	343.7	321.9	310.3	225.8	220.8	187.2	167.6
	KOREA	83.5	80.6	74.8	66.0	124.2	145.3	128.3	142.2
	MOROCCO	44.9	53.5	53.0	49.0	56.0	78.6	69.3	67.3

(CONTINUED)

		YEAR							
		71	73	74	75	78	79	80	81
CAT	CNAME								
MIDDLE INC DEV	NIGERIA	13.6	28.4	32.5	39.9	38.1	39.0	43.8	37.5
	PERU	143.2	146.9	141.3	156.4	125.9	127.4	126.4	117.9
	PHILIPPINES	62.2	60.0	51.4	54.1	47.8	55.2	49.0	44.2
	THAILAND	65.9	84.2	72.6	76.1	88.8	93.2	94.2	86.7
	TUNISIA	104.6	121.7	130.4	132.8	176.0	179.7	175.5	191.3
	TURKEY	97.5	117.3	118.0	132.3	143.4	128.2	124.6	100.5
HIGH INC DEV	ALGERIA	63.9	80.9	84.2	96.6	127.3	138.3	148.1	135.6
	ARGENTINA	388.8	407.3	388.9	368.6	359.6	352.5	378.6	379.1
	BARBADOS	.	.	.	.	303.1	286.6	302.9	.
	BRAZIL	141.6	177.0	183.6	188.4	201.2	208.2	195.5	189.0
	CHILE	249.0	241.7	201.5	178.9	199.5	202.9	224.4	223.3
	COSTA RICA	.	.	.	.	212.8	208.5	189.7	.
	CYPRUS	.	.	.	.	291.8	304.6	315.2	.
	GABON	304.0	352.9	311.5	301.9	631.5	350.0	438.2	483.9
	GREECE	233.0	296.4	238.0	235.4	405.0	419.6	430.9	433.9
	HONG KONG	237.4	259.3	271.4	256.3	308.8	325.9	320.5	334.3
	IRAQ	57.9	61.5	64.9	54.4	104.0	117.4	111.3	95.1
	ISRAEL	.	.	.	.	330.3	329.5	323.0	.
	MALAYSIA	44.3	54.5	64.7	53.8	59.1	59.8	78.6	74.4
	MEXICO	206.7	227.1	235.0	230.4	264.8	298.4	327.9	348.9
	PANAMA	277.5	289.3	309.8	333.3	282.9	280.0	248.9	258.8
	PORTUGAL	207.1	241.2	230.3	242.0	268.5	277.1	264.7	275.7
	SINGAPORE	169.2	239.9	242.5	283.6	334.9	356.5	358.0	354.5

CONTINUED)

		YEAR							
		71	73	74	75	78	79	80	81
CAT	CNAME								
HIGH INC DEV	SOUTH AFRICA	.	.	.	.	.	.	.	.
	SYRIA	.	.	.	.	.	.	.	.
	TAIWAN	30.3	31.4	34.0	37.1	42.1	43.1	43.7	43.5
	TRINIDAD & TOBAGO	.	266.0	.	.	.	460.2	.	.
	URUGUAY	202.1	208.8	191.5	193.7	202.4	220.7	226.4	226.8
	VENEZUELA	291.3	317.3	367.0	365.9	656.8	668.5	670.6	599.2
	YUGOSLAVIA	.	.	.	.	.	.	.	.
HIGH INC OIL EXP	KUWAIT	773.0	750.6	754.2	804.4	1191.4	1186.0	1362.2	1688.5
	LIBYA	133.2	200.1	243.1	248.1	336.6	376.3	414.4	411.3
	SAUDI ARABIA	172.1	192.9	229.8	283.6	506.2	570.6	676.9	748.7
EASTERN BLOC	CZECHOSLOVAKIA	.	.	.	.	.	.	.	.
	GERMAN DEM REP	.	.	.	.	.	.	.	.
	HUNGARY	.	.	.	.	.	.	.	.
	USSR	.	.	.	.	.	.	.	.
INDUSTRIALIZED	AUSTRALIA	854.5	935.7	967.2	994.9	1341.3	1181.6	1181.5	1207.4
	BELGIUM	469.5	518.5	488.2	516.3	580.5	612.7	599.8	588.1
	CANADA	1390.8	1587.3	1631.5	1637.5	1758.5	1812.2	1846.7	1690.8
	DENMARK	653.2	701.2	634.9	689.7	721.0	713.7	662.7	663.4
	FINLAND	467.5	536.5	522.4	575.4	562.8	604.2	601.7	605.4
	FRANCE	448.4	522.3	514.7	529.1	591.8	612.0	617.0	624.0
	ITALY	316.3	355.8	344.3	343.9	397.1	433.7	428.4	426.1
	JAPAN	342.5	415.9	406.7	393.7	465.0	477.1	418.0	410.3

(CONTINUED)

		YEAR							
		71	73	74	75	78	79	80	81
CAT	CNAME								
INDUSTRIALIZED	NETHERLANDS	501.1	554.7	514.4	544.7	604.5	603.1	611.5	608.8
	NEW ZEALAND	662.0	755.0	756.6	702.3	790.6	774.0	798.2	778.8
	SPAIN	263.5	323.5	316.8	340.4	405.1	400.2	403.7	399.4
	SWEDEN	583.4	640.5	640.1	666.7	758.5	747.9	717.9	706.2
	SWITZERLAND	620.3	672.4	643.7	614.1	633.1	633.5	667.2	681.0
	UNITED KINGDOM	500.9	552.0	531.4	524.5	586.9	600.6	604.4	583.7
	UNITED STATES	1776.8	1946.8	1887.2	1930.0	2160.7	2112.5	1999.0	1929.8
	W GERMANY	500.5	533.9	511.5	532.8	635.6	660.8	672.6	654.5

Appendix Table 2

PER CAPITA FUEL CONSUMPTION IN ROAD TRANSPORT BY INCOME CATEGORY
(KG of oil equivalent per person)

		YEAR							
		71	73	74	75	78	79	80	81
CAT	CNAME								
LOW INC DEV	BANGLADESH	.	0.0	0.0	0.0	0.0	0.0	0.0	0.0
	BURMA	0.0	0.0	0.0	0.0	0.0	0.0	0.0	0.0
	CHINA	.	.	.	.	.	.	.	.
	GHANA	.	.	.	.	.	.	.	.
	INDIA	9.0	9.9	10.9	11.2	12.7	14.0	14.5	15.0
	KENYA	20.4	20.9	24.6	19.6	23.1	19.8	17.9	20.9
	MALAWI	.	.	.	.	14.1	14.0	14.8	.
	PAKISTAN	17.8	11.2	11.1	11.1	14.3	15.6	16.9	19.7
	ZAIRE	0.0	0.0	0.0	0.0	0.0	0.0	0.0	0.0
	ZAMBIA	0.0	0.0	0.0	0.0	0.0	0.0	0.0	0.0
MIDDLE INC DEV	BOLIVIA	0.0	0.0	0.0	0.0	0.0	0.0	0.0	0.0
	CAMEROON	.	.	.	.	.	.	.	.
	COLOMBIA	0.0	0.0	0.0	0.0	0.0	0.0	0.0	0.0
	DOMINICAN REP	.	0.0	0.0	.	0.0	.	0.0	.
	ECUADOR	0.0	0.0	0.0	0.0	0.0	0.0	0.0	0.0
	EGYPT	35.4	45.4	53.7	55.6	69.1	69.9	73.3	73.8
	HONDURAS	.	.	0.0	.	.	.	.	.
	INDONESIA	16.7	21.1	22.7	24.6	35.2	37.2	40.5	42.9
	IRAN	36.8	48.5	57.8	70.3	78.1	62.3	60.4	40.9
	IVORY COAST	0.0	0.0	0.0	0.0	88.9	56.6	72.4	0.0
	JAMAICA	0.0	0.0	0.0	0.0	199.1	188.4	173.5	0.0
	KOREA	54.3	55.1	46.9	38.5	78.7	89.5	79.5	89.7
	MOROCCO	0.0	0.0	0.0	0.0	0.0	0.0	0.0	0.0

(CONTINUED)

CAT	CNAME	71	73	74	75	78	79	80	81
		YEAR							
MIDDLE INC DEV	NIGERIA	10.6	23.3	28.2	33.5	36.2	37.1	42.0	35.7
	PERU	0.0	0.0	0.0	0.0	0.0	0.0	0.0	0.0
	PHILIPPINES	0.0	0.0	0.0	0.0	34.6	36.7	35.0	0.0
	THAILAND	24.5	27.8	29.4	31.4	37.5	36.7	34.8	31.1
	TUNISIA	0.0	0.0	0.0	0.0	136.4	147.6	162.4	0.0
	TURKEY	62.9	76.6	78.8	94.4	107.5	98.3	98.1	83.5
HIGH INC DEV	ALGERIA	0.0	0.0	0.0	0.0	0.0	0.0	0.0	0.0
	ARGENTINA	333.6	353.1	331.6	311.1	310.6	312.5	334.3	334.6
	BARBADOS	.	.	.	.	295.1	278.5	290.6	.
	BRAZIL	124.3	155.9	158.3	163.6	174.2	176.5	168.3	158.3
	CHILE	187.4	188.0	153.7	138.1	153.8	162.5	184.3	182.4
	COSTA RICA	.	.	.	.	195.1	192.1	175.1	.
	CYPRUS	.	.	.	.	289.5	302.0	312.6	.
	GABON	0.0	0.0	0.0	0.0	294.4	153.7	329.1	0.0
	GREECE	134.6	162.2	135.7	139.2	235.6	238.4	243.3	258.0
	HONG KONG	88.8	95.5	103.5	87.4	121.1	123.4	119.4	128.8
	IRAQ	0.0	0.0	0.0	0.0	0.0	0.0	0.0	0.0
	ISRAEL	.	.	.	.	323.8	323.4	316.9	.
	MALAYSIA	32.2	41.1	51.7	12.0	44.4	48.7	66.0	60.4
	MEXICO	187.9	206.8	211.2	207.3	244.3	273.6	301.9	322.8
	PANAMA	0.0	0.0	0.0	0.0	0.0	0.0	0.0	0.0
	PORTUGAL	135.8	157.1	152.4	168.8	200.6	210.6	200.8	209.3
	SINGAPORE	108.1	135.3	121.3	132.9	136.6	143.1	153.5	163.4

(CONTINUED)

		YEAR							
		71	73	74	75	78	79	80	81
CAT	CNAME								
HIGH INC DEV	SOUTH AFRICA	.	.	.	.	.	.	.	.
	SYRIA	.	.	.	.	.	.	.	.
	TAIWAN	0.0	0.0	0.0	0.0	0.0	0.0	0.0	0.0
	TRINIDAD & TOBAGO	.	0.0	.	.	.	0.0	.	.
	URUGUAY	0.0	0.0	0.0	0.0	0.0	0.0	0.0	0.0
	VENEZUELA	263.7	289.9	319.9	320.9	571.3	584.4	586.5	546.1
	YUGOSLAVIA	.	.	.	.	.	.	.	.
HIGH INC OIL EXP	KUWAIT	456.5	457.5	465.2	476.7	541.3	558.9	693.1	593.6
	LIBYA	0.0	0.0	0.0	0.0	0.0	0.0	0.0	0.0
	SAUDI ARABIA	0.0	0.0	0.0	0.0	367.7	403.1	484.7	0.0
EASTERN BLOC	CZECHOSLOVAKIA	.	.	.	.	.	.	.	.
	GERMAN DEM REP	.	.	.	.	.	.	.	.
	HUNGARY	.	.	.	.	.	.	.	.
	USSR	.	.	.	.	.	.	.	.
INDUSTRIALIZED	AUSTRALIA	726.1	791.2	813.1	832.7	1189.4	943.4	935.8	959.8
	BELGIUM	373.3	418.9	387.9	427.6	491.4	524.8	512.1	495.5
	CANADA	1056.2	1210.6	1251.9	1288.2	1400.9	1500.8	1204.0	1152.8
	DENMARK	417.3	428.3	390.9	426.9	461.7	464.7	449.0	434.4
	FINLAND	396.1	452.8	437.1	486.2	489.5	522.9	516.6	520.7
	FRANCE	378.9	445.9	438.1	451.7	514.0	526.5	532.8	541.9
	ITALY	267.4	308.1	294.9	305.6	349.9	385.9	384.8	382.0
	JAPAN	229.7	268.6	262.2	275.1	316.0	327.8	319.4	323.8

(CONTINUED)

		YEAR							
		71	73	74	75	78	79	80	81
CAT	CNAME								
INDUSTRIALIZED	NETHERLANDS	353.8	387.2	368.3	397.5	481.0	472.5	484.4	490.8
	NEW ZEALAND	522.6	640.9	661.2	605.2	678.1	662.5	489.3	500.0
	SPAIN	170.7	209.6	193.9	219.4	306.4	291.4	283.8	286.1
	SWEDEN	457.4	503.1	532.4	555.6	643.2	635.2	610.2	596.1
	SWITZERLAND	492.1	526.6	501.6	476.6	483.5	483.4	513.5	533.3
	UNITED KINGDOM	383.0	427.3	415.5	406.6	457.2	467.5	472.9	459.4
	UNITED STATES	1458.5	1626.1	1582.2	1626.0	1850.3	1789.2	1681.6	1630.3
	W GERMANY	409.5	441.9	423.9	453.0	547.2	567.2	580.5	560.4

Appendix Table 3

PER CAPITA MOTOR GASOLINE CONSUMPTION (KGOE/person)

		YEAR					
		60	65	70	75	80	82
CAT	CNAME						
LOW INC DEV	BANGLADESH	0.0	0.0	0.0	0.8	0.7	0.6
	CHINA	3.0	0.0	3.8	9.0	10.4	10.3
	GHANA	22.0	17.2	19.4	25.4	22.5	20.9
	INDIA	2.0	2.4	2.8	2.1	2.2	2.6
	KENYA	15.2	10.7	15.7	19.5	20.4	15.3
	MALAWI	0.0	4.9	6.2	6.9	9.6	7.8
	PAKISTAN	4.7	6.2	7.1	3.8	7.5	7.2
	ZAIRE	10.4	8.9	5.9	7.9	7.5	6.8
	ZAMBIA	0.0	28.9	35.1	38.5	32.3	26.8
MIDDLE INC DEV	BOLIVIA	32.8	41.3	56.1	76.8	79.3	85.2
	CAMEROON	9.4	8.1	13.9	15.5	40.6	49.2
	COLOMBIA	71.9	82.4	97.3	110.3	125.1	126.2
	DOMINICAN REP	26.3	16.4	48.1	65.9	52.0	42.3
	ECUADOR	51.8	55.1	65.5	103.7	168.6	179.4
	EGYPT	11.0	13.1	16.1	38.7	33.8	34.5
	HONDURAS	21.0	20.9	33.2	30.5	27.0	26.8
	INDONESIA	15.5	11.9	10.3	13.9	20.4	23.4
	IRAN	21.9	21.7	42.2	89.9	101.0	85.7
	IVORY COAST	25.9	35.5	30.4	30.1	42.6	27.9
	JAMAICA	47.9	125.2	187.7	141.6	100.2	81.9
	KOREA	6.2	6.4	21.8	15.2	21.7	15.1
	MOROCCO	25.1	20.2	22.3	22.5	19.9	18.5
	NIGERIA	5.0	6.5	8.3	16.7	34.3	34.0

(CONTINUED)

CAT	CNAME	60 PCMGAS	65 PCMGAS	70 PCMGAS	75 PCMGAS	80 PCMGAS	82 PCMGAS
		YEAR					
MIDDLE INC DEV	PERU	58.8	67.9	88.5	106.3	70.3	62.9
	PHILIPPINES	32.0	37.0	50.4	43.8	32.6	23.7
	THAILAND	15.0	18.4	19.3	33.7	38.3	35.5
	TUNISIA	19.5	14.6	15.0	25.0	25.9	27.7
	TURKEY	15.9	16.5	29.4	46.6	39.5	44.6
HIGH INC DEV	ALGERIA	35.2	20.1	33.9	44.6	69.9	79.4
	ARGENTINA	101.3	160.0	183.1	165.5	215.3	206.3
	BARBADOS	74.4	93.0	156.2	272.0	218.3	213.1
	BRAZIL	46.8	57.8	79.4	101.3	69.7	58.6
	CHILE	81.2	102.3	132.0	90.8	105.9	116.8
	COSTA RICA	38.0	39.0	47.0	65.5	62.5	61.3
	CYPRUS	116.4	126.9	170.1	130.4	164.6	180.0
	GABON	22.8	35.7	49.2	37.0	58.4	97.4
	GREECE	29.4	41.2	79.0	112.0	157.9	170.8
	HONG KONG	23.0	19.7	25.0	26.7	42.0	51.4
	IRAQ	35.8	36.2	43.7	40.8	94.1	86.7
	ISRAEL	105.0	131.7	168.2	206.9	203.2	240.4
	MALAYSIA	0.0	0.0	54.5	55.5	98.4	104.9
	MEXICO	100.6	103.2	131.5	150.6	210.4	213.1
	PANAMA	80.7	89.3	114.3	149.0	0.0	0.0
	PORTUGAL	24.4	34.1	61.6	91.1	76.6	87.8
	SINGAPORE	48.6	71.7	107.5	132.7	153.7	169.1
	SOUTH AFRICA	97.9	110.1	130.1	155.2	134.5	144.5

(CONTINUED)

CAT	CNAME	60	65	70	75	80	82
		YEAR					
HIGH INC DEV	SYRIA	30.3	22.5	33.5	58.1	75.0	65.6
	TAIWAN	0.0	0.0	0.0	0.0	0.0	0.0
	TRINIDAD & TOBAGO	135.0	0.0	184.9	209.0	0.0	0.0
	URUGUAY	102.8	111.0	92.6	76.1	81.0	75.1
	VENEZUELA	208.3	250.1	297.8	376.8	490.1	456.8
	YUGOSLAVIA	0.0	0.0	0.0	0.0	0.0	0.0
HIGH INC OIL EXP	KUWAIT	630.5	601.9	449.2	477.1	695.7	731.6
	LIBYA	49.9	55.5	105.8	198.1	293.9	318.1
	SAUDI ARABIA	41.6	64.7	66.3	166.8	386.9	386.9
EASTERN BLOC	CZECHOSLOVAKIA	0.0	0.0	0.0	0.0	0.0	0.0
	GERMAN DEM REP	13.5	28.0	111.1	155.5	198.8	194.3
	HUNGARY	19.2	35.3	65.0	111.9	140.0	.
	USSR	114.6	148.9	192.2	253.5	265.5	275.4
INDUSTRIALIZED	AUSTRALIA	432.3	553.1	642.2	752.8	797.2	762.0
	BELGIUM	126.5	174.1	241.3	305.2	317.3	290.9
	CANADA	705.0	823.1	975.9	1194.3	1231.0	1090.1
	DENMARK	192.0	343.5	324.9	331.2	350.6	304.4
	FINLAND	82.8	151.1	245.8	304.6	304.1	323.7
	FRANCE	137.1	191.1	263.0	322.4	340.3	378.7
	ITALY	57.6	123.7	207.4	220.0	230.7	226.6
	JAPAN	47.7	85.8	156.2	202.9	234.8	240.0
	NETHERLANDS	113.2	165.9	249.2	284.1	387.6	316.5
	NEW ZEALAND	411.7	410.1	533.5	577.6	558.2	0.0

(CONTINUED)

CAT	CNAME	YEAR 60	65	70	75	80	82
INDUSTRIALIZED	SPAIN	19.7	41.8	80.1	136.3	164.8	136.8
	SWEDEN	228.7	369.6	367.4	423.6	455.5	477.0
	SWITZERLAND	160.9	266.4	360.6	408.6	466.5	490.5
	UNITED KINGDOM	160.7	215.6	276.4	301.4	355.2	360.1
	UNITED STATES	994.6	1091.6	1297.3	1432.4	1391.7	1326.1
	W GERMANY	106.9	178.1	270.4	347.3	417.2	402.9

Appendix Table 4

RAIL FREIGHT TRAFFIC PER GDP (NET TONS * KM PER 000 $ OF GDP)

		YEAR				
		60	65	70	75	80
CAT	CNAME					
LOW INC DEV	BANGLADESH	68	60	41	26	.
	BURMA	136	110	91	39	.
	CHINA	.	.	454	.	494
	GHANA	52	48	33	.	.
	INDIA	388	565	512	462	428
	KENYA	.	.	.	.	.
	MALAWI	165	116	165	144	113
	PAKISTAN	373	264	219	203	157
	ZAIRE	.	263	280	.	.
	ZAMBIA	.	.	.	.	.
MIDDLE INC DEV	BOLIVIA	.	100	82	88	102
	CAMEROON	38	45	49	66	78
	COLOMBIA	46	44	40	30	17
	DOMINICAN REP	.	.	.	.	.
	ECUADOR	35	19	10	5	.
	EGYPT	.	155	134	66	.
	HONDURAS	.	.	.	.	.
	INDONESIA	35	29	19	13	8
	IRAN	118	92	69	57	.
	IVORY COAST	86	85	75	59	51
	JAMAICA	38	48	36	45	.
	KOREA	195	236	213	175	138
	MOROCCO	258	179	187	149	158

(CONTINUED)

RAIL FREIGHT TRAFFIC PER GDP (NET TONS * KM PER 000 $ OF GDP)

		YEAR				
		60	65	70	75	80
CAT	CNAME					
MIDDLE INC DEV	NIGERIA	56	52	34	.	.
	PERU	43	38	27	21	.
	PHILIPPINES	12	6	2	2	1
	THAILAND	88	82	77	61	50
	TUNISIA	313	305	262	155	141
	TURKEY	151	147	113	106	54
HIGH INC DEV	ALGERIA	161	99	93	64	.
	ARGENTINA	345	263	205	133	109
	BARBADOS	.	.	.	.	.
	BRAZIL	192	233	150	299	320
	CHILE	153	161	124	104	70
	COSTA RICA	39	15	6	.	.
	CYPRUS	.	.	.	.	.
	GABON	.	.	.	.	.
	GREECE	31	34	29	31	22
	HONG KONG	4	6	4	5	3
	IRAQ	119	97	109	98	.
	ISRAEL	50	44	45	29	51
	MALAYSIA	88	91	90	45	38
	MEXICO	279	258	229	246	229
	PANAMA	.	.	.	.	.
	PORTUGAL	74	55	42	33	33
	SINGAPORE	.	.	.	.	.

(CONTINUED)

RAIL FREIGHT TRAFFIC PER GDP (NET TONS * KM PER 000 $ OF GDP)

		YEAR				
		60	65	70	75	80
CAT	CNAME					
HIGH INC DEV	SOUTH AFRICA	1157	1196	1030	1006	1409
	SYRIA	34	18	17	11	30
	TAIWAN	260	199	.	.	.
	TRINIDAD & TOBAGO	.	.	.	.	.
	URUGUAY	.	51	33	36	.
	VENEZUELA	1	1	0	0	.
	YUGOSLAVIA	601	549	.	.	.
HIGH INC OIL EXP	KUWAIT	.	.	.	.	.
	LIBYA	.	.	.	.	.
	SAUDI ARABIA	.	.	.	.	.
EASTERN BLOC	CZECHOSLOVAKIA	1020	1165	.	.	.
	GERMAN DEM REP	708	749	683	667	.
	HUNGARY	580	620	602	613	.
	USSR	3368	3368	3271	3498	.
INDUSTRIALIZED	AUSTRALIA	329	358	371	369	.
	BELGIUM	219	187	166	124	133
	CANADA	1329	1338	1348	1278	.
	DENMARK	84	66	62	66	40
	FINLAND	382	316	301	263	.
	FRANCE	392	334	273	207	.
	ITALY	134	102	89	69	.
	JAPAN	332	220	138	86	.

(CONTINUED)

RAIL FREIGHT TRAFFIC PER GDP (NET TONS * KM PER 000 $ OF GDP)

		YEAR				
		60	65	70	75	80
CAT	CNAME					
INDUSTRIALIZED	NETHERLANDS	93	74	58	37	.
	NEW ZEALAND	227	213	225	245	217
	SPAIN	115	98	85	68	66
	SWEDEN	348	346	357	290	.
	SWITZERLAND	191	188	192	142	190
	UNITED KINGDOM	168	118	111	81	.
	UNITED STATES	886	858	808	723	.
	W GERMANY	257	221	219	155	.

Appendix Table 5

RAIL PASSENGER TRAFFIC PER GDP (KM PER 000 $ OF GDP)

CAT	CNAME	YEAR 60	65	70	75	80
LOW INC DEV	BANGLADESH	159	124	82	156	.
	BURMA	266	298	266	348	273
	CHINA	.	.	.	.	120
	GHANA	40	67	58	.	.
	INDIA	418	468	476	509	605
	KENYA	.	.	.	.	.
	MALAWI	68	.	50	52	39
	PAKISTAN	492	329	273	296	319
	ZAIRE	.	91	100	.	.
	ZAMBIA	.	.	.	.	.
MIDDLE INC DEV	BOLIVIA	.	73	68	59	83
	CAMEROON	28	27	38	47	29
	COLOMBIA	36	24	9	14	6
	DOMINICAN REP	.	.	.	.	.
	ECUADOR	19	12	14	7	.
	EGYPT	.	274	262	257	222
	HONDURAS	.	.	.	.	.
	INDONESIA	220	216	76	47	51
	IRAN	90	42	46	27	.
	IVORY COAST	89	133	111	126	104
	JAMAICA	23	22	20	21	.
	KOREA	316	339	279	244	283
	MOROCCO	70	41	37	43	37

(CONTINUED)

RAIL PASSENGER TRAFFIC PER GDP (KM PER 000 $ OF GDP)

CAT	CNAME	YEAR 60	65	70	75	80
MIDDLE INC DEV	NIGERIA	20	23	21	.	.
	PERU	24	14	11	16	.
	PHILIPPINES	48	37	25	24	8
	THAILAND	180	156	143	147	159
	TUNISIA	113	118	87	71	71
	TURKEY	154	113	113	68	65
HIGH INC DEV	ALGERIA	58	60	67	41	.
	ARGENTINA	357	240	197	179	146
	BARBADOS	.	.	.	.	.
	BRAZIL	233	206	106	54	46
	CHILE	150	148	115	112	54
	COSTA RICA	24	.	19	.	.
	CYPRUS	.	.	.	.	.
	GABON	.	.	.	.	.
	GREECE	89	67	64	51	40
	HONG KONG	56	34	23	25	22
	IRAQ	81	44	39	31	.
	ISRAEL	80	54	35	29	16
	MALAYSIA	76	56	46	55	50
	MEXICO	82	55	45	31	29
	PANAMA	.	.	.	.	.
	PORTUGAL	209	215	190	215	202
	SINGAPORE	.	.	.	.	.

(CONTINUED)

RAIL PASSENGER TRAFFIC PER GDP (KM PER 000 $ OF GDP)

CAT	CNAME	YEAR 60	65	70	75	80
HIGH INC DEV	SOUTH AFRICA	.	.	.	.	.
	SYRIA	13	14	14	10	20
	TAIWAN	457	368	.	.	.
	TRINIDAD & TOBAGO	.	.	.	.	.
	URUGUAY	.	84	69	47	.
	VENEZUELA	1	2	1	1	.
	YUGOSLAVIA	444	414	.	.	.
HIGH INC OIL EXP	KUWAIT	.	.	.	.	.
	LIBYA	.	.	.	.	.
	SAUDI ARABIA	.	.	.	.	.
EASTERN BLOC	CZECHOSLOVAKIA	444	404	.	.	.
	GERMAN DEM REP	415	290	252	257	.
	HUNGARY	525	505	438	365	.
	USSR	382	348	348	338	.
INDUSTRIALIZED	AUSTRALIA	.	.	.	.	.
	BELGIUM	300	220	161	141	115
	CANADA	51	45	31	17	.
	DENMARK	196	155	125	114	104
	FINLAND	184	125	103	128	.
	FRANCE	220	198	159	165	.
	ITALY	260	192	160	168	.
	JAPAN	1124	968	634	591	.
	NETHERLANDS	213	161	126	117	.

(CONTINUED)

RAIL PASSENGER TRAFFIC PER GDP (KM PER 000 $ OF GDP)

		YEAR				
		60	65	70	75	80
CAT	CNAME					
INDUSTRIALIZED	NEW ZEALAND	83	60	46	36	29
	SPAIN	139	148	121	112	•
	SWEDEN	165	130	97	102	•
	SWITZERLAND	350	303	255	237	257
	UNITED KINGDOM	191	164	148	117	•
	UNITED STATES	36	23	13	10	•
	W GERMANY	189	149	117	106	•

Appendix Table 6

PER CAPITA GNP (1975 $)

		YEAR				
		60	65	70	75	80
CAT	CNAME					
LOW INC DEV	BANGLADESH	67	73	75	64	74
	BURMA	90	100	97	99	120
	CHINA	.	.	.	.	.
	GHANA	371	378	379	335	296
	INDIA	113	118	133	137	148
	KENYA	196	185	235	258	287
	MALAWI	93	100	111	139	.
	PAKISTAN	116	145	178	182	211
	ZAIRE	187	216	237	244	194
	ZAMBIA	380	466	473	452	381
MIDDLE INC DEV	BOLIVIA	280	313	335	392	407
	CAMEROON	261	281	324	352	462
	COLOMBIA	453	481	550	667	780
	DOMINICAN REP	408	393	480	630	673
	ECUADOR	.	470	540	755	831
	EGYPT	175	218	226	267	375
	HONDURAS	332	340	364	362	414
	INDONESIA	152	147	183	229	286
	IRAN	.	.	.	.	.
	IVORY COAST	502	606	671	704	872
	JAMAICA	854	956	1141	1180	872
	JORDAN	.	.	.	460	698
	KOREA	331	397	581	799	1053

(CONTINUED)

PER CAPITA GNP (1975 $)

CAT	CNAME	YEAR 60	65	70	75	80
MIDDLE INC DEV	MOROCCO	373	391	428	513	560
	NIGERIA	350	371	413	493	550
	PERU	420	518	565	645	562
	PHILIPPINES	270	305	329	386	439
	THAILAND	190	232	301	361	454
	TUNISIA	.	436	507	732	889
	TURKEY	551	621	759	969	978
HIGH INC DEV	ALGERIA	897	764	990	1042	1246
	ARGENTINA	1175	1352	1545	1729	1726
	BARBADOS	781	1032	1400	1551	1930
	BRAZIL	579	626	784	1133	1343
	CHILE	969	1098	1201	1077	1445
	COSTA RICA	790	837	1010	1181	1348
	CYPRUS	890	1133	1552	1184	2240
	GABON	1568	1913	2457	4806	2927
	GREECE	1030	1483	2043	2543	3044
	HONG KONG	797	1183	1620	2037	.
	IRAQ	638	849	870	1223	.
	ISRAEL	1603	2126	2642	3213	3061
	MALAYSIA	469	576	669	831	1084
	MEXICO	742	881	1042	1150	.
	PANAMA	602	777	978	1098	1007
	PORTUGAL	650	856	1312	1462	1726

(CONTINUED)

PER CAPITA GNP (1975 $)

		YEAR				
		60	65	70	75	80
CAT	CNAME					
HIGH INC DEV	SINGAPORE	826	951	.	.	.
	SOUTH AFRICA	892	1079	1248	1369	1394
	SYRIA	375	484	524	741	872
	TAIWAN	381	510	700	968	1436
	TRINIDAD & TOBAGO	1561	1749	1961	2112	2818
	URUGUAY	1284	1250	1328	1365	1669
	VENEZUELA	1466	1701	1916	2171	2302
	YUGOSLAVIA	688	870	1143	1482	.
HIGH INC OIL EXP	KUWAIT	.	14125	12820	12090	12511
	LIBYA	1629	4561	7676	4789	5915
	SAUDI ARABIA	.	2173	2906	2993	5751
EASTERN BLOC	CZECHOSLOVAKIA	.	.	1697	2127	.
	GERMAN DEM REP	.	.	.	.	.
	HUNGARY	.	.	.	.	.
	USSR	.	.	.	.	.
INDUSTRIALIZED	AUSTRALIA	4521	4806	5845	6420	7098
	BELGIUM	4134	5098	6334	7413	8410
	CANADA	3998	4798	5567	6684	7234
	DENMARK	4814	5973	7453	8094	.
	FINLAND	3070	3843	4986	5907	6549
	FRANCE	3680	4565	5694	6640	7680
	ITALY	1990	2482	3255	3490	4146
	JAPAN	1771	2739	4629	5533	6962

(CONTINUED)

PER CAPITA GNP (1975 $)

		YEAR				
		60	65	70	75	80
CAT	CNAME					
INDUSTRIALIZED	NETHERLANDS	4381	5178	6343	7047	7826
	NEW ZEALAND	3403	3901	4168	4811	5185
	SPAIN	1389	2004	2574	3200	3356
	SWEDEN	5615	7011	8146	8797	9241
	SWITZERLAND	7489	8819	10271	10435	11299
	UNITED KINGDOM	3193	3592	4006	4362	4748
	UNITED STATES	5140	6001	6616	7136	8158
	W GERMANY	4824	5755	6973	7585	9149

Appendix Table 7

PER CAPITA RGDP (1975 $)

CAT	CNAME	YEAR 60	65	70	75	80
LOW INC DEV	BANGLADESH	358	393	373	373	434
	BURMA	258	331	324	312	361
	CHINA	505	570	711	883	1135
	GHANA	1006	954	1083	952	708
	INDIA	427	422	451	472	497
	KENYA	412	383	469	438	446
	MALAWI	206	223	259	326	336
	PAKISTAN	412	561	567	594	659
	ZAIRE	288	325	430	382	289
	ZAMBIA	792	829	952	791	690
MIDDLE INC DEV	BOLIVIA	677	797	932	1077	1141
	CAMEROON	563	630	811	833	925
	COLOMBIA	1065	1137	1362	1596	1911
	DOMINICAN REP	863	927	1063	1443	1372
	ECUADOR	776	857	984	1300	1629
	EGYPT	550	720	759	929	1177
	HONDURAS	740	814	907	871	1069
	INDONESIA	356	322	370	536	785
	IRAN	848	1021	1382	2664	1909
	IVORY COAST	749	917	1058	1122	1464
	JAMAICA	1210	1386	1894	1763	1404
	JORDAN	739	1037	896	802	1018
	KOREA	633	726	1123	1530	2011

(CONTINUED)

PER CAPITA RGDP (1975 $)

		YEAR				
		60	65	70	75	80
CAT	CNAME					
MIDDLE INC DEV	MOROCCO	584	866	938	1121	1230
	NIGERIA	814	779	841	1179	1536
	PERU	1155	1465	1657	1860	1810
	PHILIPPINES	658	744	790	912	1010
	THAILAND	494	617	802	930	1169
	TUNISIA	734	874	987	1473	1917
	TURKEY	1039	1155	1394	1738	2048
HIGH INC DEV	ALGERIA	992	892	1129	1740	2103
	ARGENTINA	2134	2407	2743	3159	3209
	BARBADOS	1062	1231	1836	2405	2366
	BRAZIL	924	980	1225	1798	2133
	CHILE	1679	1910	2176	1834	2381
	COSTA RICA	1220	1431	1671	1835	2221
	CYPRUS	1285	1713	2349	1811	3114
	GABON	846	1137	1795	4771	4860
	GREECE	1393	1969	2705	3360	3922
	HONG KONG	890	1452	1994	2559	4053
	IRAQ	996	1266	1287	2088	3114
	ISRAEL	2081	2827	3483	4154	4081
	MALAYSIA	1014	1159	1281	1532	2305
	MEXICO	1381	1657	1988	2276	2578
	PANAMA	1129	1479	1894	2026	2149
	PORTUGAL	1171	1498	2158	2397	3047

(CONTINUED)

PER CAPITA RGDP (1975 $)

		YEAR				
		60	65	70	75	80
CAT	CNAME					
HIGH INC DEV	SINGAPORE	1033	1188	1980	2875	3251
	SOUTH AFRICA	1538	1823	2138	2412	2346
	SYRIA	698	920	952	1935	2203
	TAIWAN	732	963	1319	1735	2443
	TRINIDAD & TOBAGO	2214	2393	2397	3173	4218
	URUGUAY	2546	2434	2708	2731	3248
	VENEZUELA	2385	2578	2618	3346	3647
	YUGOSLAVIA	1256	1590	2027	2591	3318
HIGH INC OIL EXP	KUWAIT	.	.	.	.	.
	LIBYA	.	.	.	.	.
	SAUDI ARABIA	.	.	.	.	.
EASTERN BLOC	CZECHOSLOVAKIA	3189	3452	4027	4607	4908
	GERMAN DEM REP	3006	3525	4100	4923	5532
	HUNGARY	2272	2706	3077	3559	3861
	USSR	2084	2507	3142	3636	3943
INDUSTRIALIZED	AUSTRALIA	3854	4465	5455	5919	6188
	BELGIUM	3120	3854	4866	5554	6084
	CANADA	4015	4846	5570	6788	7451
	DENMARK	3741	4748	5646	5969	6336
	FINLAND	2880	3600	4525	5192	5657
	FRANCE	3179	3964	5091	5864	6679
	ITALY	2350	2898	3793	3870	4634
	JAPAN	1711	2630	4355	4905	5735

(CONTINUED)

PER CAPITA RGDP (1975 $)

		YEAR				
		60	65	70	75	80
CAT	CNAME					
INDUSTRIALIZED	NETHERLANDS	3203	3893	4890	5321	5713
	NEW ZEALAND	3656	4294	4322	4769	4543
	SPAIN	1741	2582	3253	4032	4179
	SWEDEN	4207	5190	6032	6749	6779
	SWITZERLAND	4254	5065	5849	6082	6480
	UNITED KINGDOM	3459	3906	4345	4601	5145
	UNITED STATES	5248	6178	6747	7132	7986
	W GERMANY	3664	4386	5369	5758	6876

Appendix Table 8

PER CAPITA GNP, ADJUSTED GDP (1975 $) AND RATIO (%)

		YEAR		
		81		
CAT	CNAME			
LOW INC DEV	BANGLADESH	77	422	547.6
	BURMA	124	373	299.6
	CHINA	.	.	.
	GHANA	284	715	251.3
	INDIA	153	516	338
	KENYA	286	441	154.3
	MALAWI	.	344	.
	PAKISTAN	218	680	312
	ZAIRE	188	269	143.1
	ZAMBIA	360	645	179.2
MIDDLE INC DEV	BOLIVIA	390	1082	277.3
	CAMEROON	515	947	184
	COLOMBIA	778	1907	245
	DOMINICAN REP	658	1406	213.7
	ECUADOR	812	1639	202
	EGYPT	404	1248	309.1
	HONDURAS	404	993	246
	INDONESIA	304	851	279.8
	IRAN	.	1643	.
	IVORY COAST	857	1359	158.6
	JAMAICA	867	1340	154.6
	JORDAN	742	1031	139
	KOREA	1101	2092	190

(CONTINUED)

PER CAPITA GNP, ADJUSTED GDP (1975 $) AND RATIO (%)

		YEAR		
		81		
CAT	CNAME			
MIDDLE INC DEV	MOROCCO	532	1166	219.3
	NIGERIA	505	1488	294.8
	PERU	557	1809	325
	PHILIPPINES	442	1018	230.5
	THAILAND	469	1177	251.2
	TUNISIA	928	1996	215.1
	TURKEY	994	2038	205.1
HIGH INC DEV	ALGERIA	1263	2037	161.3
	ARGENTINA	1569	2839	181
	BARBADOS	1901	2300	121
	BRAZIL	1256	1981	157.8
	CHILE	1480	2512	169.7
	COSTA RICA	1226	1871	152.6
	CYPRUS	2093	2977	142.2
	GABON	2760	4830	175
	GREECE	2981	3779	126.8
	HONG KONG	.	4403	.
	IRAQ	.	1892	.
	ISRAEL	3182	4236	133.1
	MALAYSIA	1152	2274	197.4
	MEXICO	.	2724	.
	PANAMA	1018	2142	210.4
	PORTUGAL	1719	3076	178.9

(CONTINUED)

PER CAPITA GNP, ADJUSTED GDP (1975 $) AND RATIO (%)

CAT	CNAME	YEAR 81		
HIGH INC DEV	SINGAPORE	.	3460	.
	SOUTH AFRICA	1419	2358	166.2
	SYRIA	852	2466	289.6
	TAIWAN	1488	2594	174.3
	TRINIDAD & TOBAGO	2938	4452	151.5
	URUGUAY	1639	3149	192.1
	VENEZUELA	2274	3488	153.4
	YUGOSLAVIA	.	.	.
HIGH INC OIL EXP	KUWAIT	9915	.	.
	LIBYA	4757	.	.
	SAUDI ARABIA	5554	.	.
EASTERN BLOC	CZECHOSLOVAKIA	.	.	.
	GERMAN DEM REP	.	.	.
	HUNGARY	.	.	.
	USSR	.	.	.
INDUSTRIALIZED	AUSTRALIA	7017	6284	89.55
	BELGIUM	8251	5777	70.02
	CANADA	7424	7600	102.4
	DENMARK	.	6241	.
	FINLAND	6608	5750	87.01
	FRANCF	7672	6625	86.36
	ITALY	4124	4506	109.3
	JAPAN	7134	5839	81.85

(CONTINUED)

PEP CAPITA GNP, ADJUSTFD GDP (1975 $) AND RATIO (%)

CAT	CNAME	YEAR 81		
INDUSTRIALIZED	NETHERLANDS	7690	5617	73.05
	NEW ZEALAND	5553	4682	84.31
	SPAIN	3338	4080	122.2
	SWEDEN	9170	6668	72.72
	SWITZERLAND	11314	6583	58.18
	UNITED KINGDOM	4658	5108	109.7
	UNITED STATES	8269	8168	98.77
	W GERMANY	9200	6805	73.97

Appendix Table 9

RETAIL PRICE OF MOTOR GASOLINE (1975$/GALLON)

		YEAR													
		65	70	71	72	73	74	75	76	77	78	79	80	81	82
CAT	CNAME														
LOW INC DEV	BANGLADESH	.	.	.	.	.	.	.	.	.	.	.	.	.	.
	CHINA	.	.	.	.	.	.	.	.	.	.	.	.	.	.
	GHANA	1.22	0.67	0.71	0.54	0.66	0.88	1.02	0.97	0.91	0.78	0.67	1.38	2.15	1.90
	INDIA	1.16	0.75	0.89	0.88	0.87	1.92	1.60	1.35	1.26	1.36	1.46	1.63	1.45	1.42
	KENYA	0.87	0.75	0.77	0.76	0.72	1.04	1.13	1.03	1.11	1.39	1.32	.	1.51	.
	MALAWI	.	.	.	.	.	.	.	.	.	.	.	.	.	.
	PAKISTAN	0.96	0.97	1.16	0.59	0.62	0.88	0.88	0.95	0.96	0.95	.	1.11	1.13	0.94
	ZAIRE	.	.	.	.	.	.	.	.	.	.	.	.	.	.
	ZAMBIA	.	.	.	.	.	.	.	.	.	.	.	.	.	.
MIDDLE INC DEV	BOLIVIA	0.38	0.32	0.31	0.30	0.21	0.19	0.17	0.26	0.24	0.23	0.21	0.50	0.54	0.38
	CAMEROON	.	.	.	.	.	.	.	.	.	.	.	.	.	.
	COLOMBIA	0.24	0.36	0.23	0.19	0.17	0.14	0.11	0.20	0.24	0.26	0.45	0.47	0.48	0.48
	DOMINICAN REP	.	0.51	0.55	0.52	0.57	0.75	0.78	0.74	0.82	0.76	1.28	1.45	1.41	.
	ECUADOR	.	0.31	0.29	0.21	0.22	0.20	.	.	0.13	0.13	0.12	0.12	.	0.25
	EGYPT	.	.	.	.	.	.	.	.	.	.	.	.	.	.
	HONDURAS	.	.	.	.	.	.	.	.	.	.	.	.	.	.
	INDONESIA	.	0.46	0.40	0.39	0.45	0.45	0.52	0.61	0.57	0.53	0.45	0.60	0.53	0.78
	IRAN	0.51	0.42	0.40	0.39	0.37	0.37	0.34	0.30	0.40	0.45	0.40	0.35	0.96	.
	IVORY COAST	.	.	.	.	.	.	.	.	.	.	.	.	.	.
	JAMAICA	0.67	0.49	0.48	0.47	0.46	1.12	1.01	1.01	1.53	1.22	1.30	1.39	1.28	1.18
	KOREA	.	.	.	.	.	.	.	.	.	.	2.14	.	.	.
	MOROCCO	0.96	0.83	0.89	0.96	1.09	1.41	1.39	1.38	1.42	1.49	1.91	2.26	1.54	1.53
	NIGERIA	.	.	.	.	.	.	.	.	.	.	.	.	.	.

(CONTINUED)

RETAIL PRICE OF MOTOR GASOLINE (1975$/GALLON)

CAT	CNAME	65	70	71	72	73	74	75	76	77	78	79	80	81	82
		YEAR													
MIDDLE INC DEV	PERU	0.31	0.29	0.28	0.27	0.26	0.23	0.35	0.73	0.83	0.61	0.58	0.49	0.54	0.56
	PHILIPPINES	0.43	0.25	0.24	0.22	0.22	0.67	0.65	0.67	0.76	0.70	0.79	1.43	1.42	1.25
	THAILAND	0.60	0.49	0.47	0.45	0.48	0.70	0.64	0.73	0.65	0.73	1.02	1.12	1.21	1.04
	TUNISIA	1.20	1.02	0.97	1.05	1.97	1.52	1.47	1.39	1.39	1.35	1.35	.	.	.
	TURKEY	0.70	0.64	0.52	0.54	0.51	0.82	0.72	0.60	0.52	1.08	0.98	1.37	0.92	1.04
HIGH INC DEV	ALGERIA	.	.	.	.	.	.	.	.	.	.	.	.	.	.
	ARGENTINA	0.43	0.53	0.52	0.31	0.73	1.40	1.44	0.52	0.74	0.75	0.85	1.03	0.76	0.61
	BARBADOS	.	.	.	.	.	.	.	.	.	.	.	.	.	.
	BRAZIL	0.51	0.51	0.53	0.44	0.35	0.67	1.11	1.43	1.34	1.25	1.15	2.12	.	1.57
	CHILE	0.38	0.32	0.37	0.31	0.70	0.70	0.84	0.83	0.81	0.68	1.13	1.14	1.13	0.96
	COSTA RICA	.	.	.	.	.	.	.	.	.	.	.	.	.	.
	CYPRUS	.	.	.	.	.	.	.	.	.	.	.	.	.	.
	GABON	.	.	.	.	.	.	.	.	.	.	.	.	.	.
	GREECE	1.10	0.89	1.01	0.98	1.08	1.86	1.66	1.51	1.61	1.64	2.07	1.87	1.25	1.22
	HONG KONG	.	.	.	.	.	.	.	.	.	.	.	.	.	.
	IRAQ	.	.	.	.	.	.	.	.	.	.	.	.	.	.
	ISRAEL	0.41	0.71	0.84	0.70	0.76	1.38	1.45	1.56	1.64	1.12	1.71	1.63	1.19	1.14
	MALAYSIA	.	.	.	.	.	.	.	.	.	.	.	.	.	.
	MEXICO	0.41	0.33	0.32	0.31	0.29	0.46	0.64	0.62	0.41	0.39	0.35	0.30	0.26	0.27
	PANAMA	0.55	0.45	0.43	0.57	0.57	0.88	0.80	0.90	0.89	0.83	1.08	1.30	1.25	1.21
	PORTUGAL	1.20	1.03	1.00	1.02	1.04	1.55	1.63	1.72	1.58	1.59	1.61	2.05	1.63	1.47
	SINGAPORE	.	.	0.76	0.80	1.08	1.06	1.04	0.99	0.95	0.97	0.96	1.12	1.05	0.96
	SOUTH AFRICA	0.72	0.61	0.61	.	0.71	0.86	0.92	0.93	1.08	1.06	1.80	1.62	1.30	1.09

(CONTINUED)

RETAIL PRICE OF MOTOR GASOLINE (1975$/GALLON)

CAT	CNAME	65	70	71	72	73	74	75	76	77	78	79	80	81	82
HIGH INC DEV	SYRIA	.	.	.	.	.	.	.	.	.	.	.	.	.	.
	TAIWAN	.	.	.	.	.	.	.	.	.	.	.	.	.	.
	TRINIDAD & TOBAGO	.	.	.	.	.	.	.	.	.	.	.	.	.	.
	URUGUAY	0.56	0.89	1.01	0.85	1.04	1.41	1.28	1.33	1.40	1.29	.	2.08	1.98	.
	VENEZUELA	0.14	0.11	0.11	0.12	0.11	0.14	0.14	0.13	0.12	0.11	0.10	0.09	0.08	0.14
	YUGOSLAVIA	0.60	0.67	0.60	0.78	0.88	1.32	1.06	0.97	1.24	1.16	1.83	1.72	.	1.63
HIGH INC OIL EXP	KUWAIT	.	.	.	.	.	.	.	.	.	.	.	.	.	.
	LIBYA	.	.	.	.	.	.	.	.	.	.	.	.	.	.
	SAUDI ARABIA	0.29	0.24	0.32	0.25	0.27	0.13	0.11	0.11	0.10	.	0.14	0.15	0.11	0.10
EASTERN BLOC	CZECHOSLOVAKIA	.	.	.	.	.	.	.	.	.	.	.	.	.	.
	GERMAN DEM REP	.	.	.	.	.	.	.	.	.	.	.	.	.	.
	HUNGARY	.	.	.	.	.	.	.	.	.	.	.	.	.	.
	USSR	.	.	.	.	.	.	.	.	.	.	.	.	.	.
INDUSTRIALIZED	AUSTRALIA	0.58	0.63	0.52	0.57	0.65	0.65	0.69	.	0.63	0.77	0.99	0.99	1.05	0.93
	BELGIUM	0.99	0.92	0.93	1.03	1.39	1.57	1.31	1.36	1.48	1.53	1.68	2.08	1.60	1.47
	CANADA	0.58	0.56	0.56	0.52	0.70	0.63	0.60	0.60	0.61	0.55	0.53	0.53	0.69	0.72
	DENMARK	1.01	0.92	0.92	0.97	1.26	1.48	1.35	1.33	1.44	1.57	2.08	2.16	1.69	1.50
	FINLAND	1.13	0.83	0.88	0.89	1.00	1.33	1.23	1.40	1.48	1.42	1.53	1.97	1.64	1.46
	FRANCE	1.23	1.03	1.01	1.06	1.30	1.45	1.56	1.33	1.51	1.81	1.80	1.95	.	1.24
	ITALY	1.15	1.08	1.23	1.28	1.21	1.85	1.67	1.61	1.83	1.78	1.81	2.02	1.61	1.47
	JAPAN	0.87	0.72	0.75	0.89	1.02	1.49	1.36	1.29	1.45	1.71	1.68	1.78	1.51	1.37
	NETHERLANDS	0.89	0.85	0.92	1.00	1.39	1.50	1.41	1.44	1.46	1.51	1.62	1.89	1.47	1.37

(CONTINUED)

RETAIL PRICE OF MOTOR GASOLINE (1975$/GALLON)

		YEAR													
		65	70	71	72	73	74	75	76	77	78	79	80	81	82
CAT	CNAME														
INDUSTRIALIZED	NEW ZEALAND	.	.	.	.	.	.	.	.	.	.	.	.	.	.
	SPAIN	0.98	0.74	0.76	0.78	0.95	1.27	1.14	1.15	1.24	1.26	1.70	1.84	1.50	1.23
	SWEDEN	0.99	0.89	0.97	1.05	1.24	1.29	1.24	.	1.28	1.25	1.46	1.73	1.54	1.31
	SWITZERLAND	0.79	0.72	0.77	0.91	1.10	1.23	1.33	1.42	1.31	1.62	1.93	1.83	1.46	.
	UNITED KINGDOM	0.98	0.88	0.87	0.88	0.95	1.37	1.27	1.19	1.05	0.95	1.60	1.70	1.55	.
	UNITED STATES	0.55	0.50	0.51	0.49	0.49	0.61	0.60	0.57	0.58	0.54	0.67	0.80	0.74	0.70
	W GERMANY	0.92	0.81	0.88	0.97	1.44	1.39	1.25	1.32	1.28	1.39	1.55	1.61	.	1.13

Appendix Table 10

NUMBER OF CARS PER 1000 POPULATION

CAT	CNAME	YEAR 60	65	70	75	80	82
LOW INC DEV	BANGLADESH	0.19	0.24	0.43	0.33	0.48	0.51
	BURMA	0.83	1.02	1.07	1.19	1.23	1.25
	CHINA	0.05	0.04	0.06	0.12	0.23	0.29
	GHANA	3.04	3.53	4.62	5.86	5.57	5.38
	INDIA	0.65	0.87	1.14	1.23	1.34	1.26
	KENYA	5.36	5.14	5.92	7.19	6.93	6.65
	MALAWI	1.87	1.64	2.17	2.08	2.31	2.24
	PAKISTAN	1.27	2.34	2.56	2.90	3.43	3.73
	ZAIRE	2.26	1.89	2.97	3.52	3.25	3.14
	ZAMBIA	10.41	12.17	14.58	18.67	19.68	19.50
MIDDLE INC DEV	BOLIVIA	1.71	2.63	4.48	6.05	9.01	8.90
	CAMEROON	1.73	2.80	4.94	7.08	10.31	10.75
	COLOMBIA	5.69	6.69	11.21	15.77	20.07	23.11
	DOMINICAN REP	3.37	7.84	8.69	13.67	15.13	16.47
	ECUADOR	2.10	3.33	4.53	7.45	8.10	11.27
	EGYPT	2.60	3.32	3.98	5.84	10.30	11.15
	HONDURAS	2.84	4.48	4.77	5.89	10.84	11.25
	INDONESIA	1.11	1.59	2.00	2.83	4.21	4.81
	IRAN	4.26	5.47	9.81	18.23	28.89	31.55
	IVORY COAST	3.48	7.69	10.62	10.77	14.62	18.23
	JAMAICA	20.25	26.14	34.76	25.25	41.10	45.05
	JORDAN	3.73	6.12	6.70	12.30	28.12	34.60
	KOREA	0.52	0.58	1.94	2.43	6.56	7.67

(CONTINUED)

NUMBER OF CARS PER 1000 POPULATION

		YEAR					
		60	65	70	75	80	82
CAT	CNAME						
MIDDLE INC DEV	MOROCCO	10.73	12.42	14.71	18.50	20.94	22.61
	NIGERIA	0.72	1.19	1.44	2.51	6.49	7.89
	PERU	7.81	13.23	17.07	18.42	17.93	19.80
	PHILIPPINES	3.18	4.27	7.43	8.74	9.31	9.05
	THAILAND	1.83	2.20	5.17	6.43	9.13	9.10
	TUNISIA	10.50	11.06	12.94	18.29	20.88	21.01
	TURKEY	1.66	2.81	3.90	9.57	15.68	17.41
HIGH INC DEV	ALGERIA	14.81	7.85	10.73	18.25	26.72	29.66
	ARGENTINA	22.99	41.25	60.64	87.76	110.86	124.17
	BARBADOS	34.78	57.39	80.42	95.42	101.60	101.59
	BRAZIL	7.68	13.82	23.47	46.48	64.99	62.64
	CHILE	7.59	11.43	18.79	25.07	41.94	39.37
	COSTA RICA	12.90	15.34	22.72	30.51	37.69	39.65
	CYPRUS	47.89	57.29	90.16	103.44	140.00	149.85
	GABON	3.19	6.46	11.00	26.92	45.45	52.54
	GREECE	5.19	12.20	25.77	48.46	92.54	105.44
	HONG KONG	10.59	15.20	24.64	27.53	46.59	51.97
	IRAQ	5.85	6.83	7.20	10.49	13.38	12.68
	ISRAEL	12.56	32.46	50.91	82.32	104.96	128.10
	MALAYSIA	13.20	19.44	26.69	39.46	56.43	61.74
	MEXICO	13.10	17.75	24.51	40.54	60.79	64.68
	PANAMA	16.00	23.62	31.16	39.40	51.58	53.76
	PORTUGAL	17.85	34.56	63.85	99.47	123.12	125.24

(CONTINUED)

NUMBER OF CARS PER 1000 POPULATION

		YEAR					
		60	65	70	75	80	82
CAT	CNAME						
HIGH INC DEV	SINGAPORE	40.98	57.66	71.06	66.22	67.70	75.88
	SOUTH AFRICA	51.70	57.45	69.07	83.02	83.88	84.27
	SYRIA	3.62	5.11	4.74	6.83	8.28	8.61
	TAIWAN	0.75	1.20	3.41	9.85	19.66	32.15
	TRINIDAD & TOBAGO	37.14	57.01	72.72	93.80	118.42	166.03
	URUGUAY	38.74	42.38	49.65	52.82	58.56	78.64
	VENEZUELA	35.22	42.06	52.88	75.51	92.42	89.82
	YUGOSLAVIA	2.95	9.66	35.39	72.00	108.41	119.98
HIGH INC OIL EXP	KUWAIT	89.29	122.08	150.94	202.28	284.26	307.49
	LIBYA	12.96	26.11	50.50	102.88	129.62	130.01
	SAUDI ARABIA	5.43	9.83	13.98	18.62	70.40	91.48
EASTERN BLOC	CZECHOSLOVAKIA	20.07	29.18	57.67	101.89	149.42	158.29
	GERMAN DEM REP	17.50	38.87	67.91	111.60	151.34	168.01
	HUNGARY	3.34	9.99	23.25	55.06	94.61	.
	USSR	2.98	4.01	6.80	18.59	31.09	35.67
INDUSTRIALIZED	AUSTRALIA	196.37	254.25	310.64	359.48	410.61	420.85
	BELGIUM	80.34	141.65	213.65	266.71	318.42	325.37
	CANADA	223.38	268.81	308.37	382.44	426.07	428.06
	DENMARK	89.13	156.26	218.80	256.92	274.10	267.98
	FINLAND	41.40	99.76	154.45	211.53	254.34	279.34
	FRANCE	121.41	180.01	242.55	295.11	358.28	378.24
	ITALY	39.72	105.29	190.09	269.76	310.66	342.51
	JAPAN	4.85	22.23	84.66	154.56	203.33	215.70

(CONTINUED)

NUMBER OF CARS PER 1000 POPULATION

		YEAR					
		60	65	70	75	80	82
CAT	CNAME						
INDUSTRIALIZED	NETHERLANDS	45.49	103.57	175.75	248.83	305.40	323.78
	NEW ZEALAND	217.81	272.17	316.03	368.32	397.58	413.03
	SPAIN	9.29	25.30	70.39	135.02	202.15	222.11
	SWEDEN	159.61	232.07	284.70	337.03	349.02	353.73
	SWITZERLAND	95.02	156.84	220.61	280.36	356.07	392.59
	UNITED KINGDOM	105.44	165.65	210.27	248.95	276.22	288.85
	UNITED STATES	340.02	385.50	433.62	496.75	547.49	547.99
	W GERMANY	78.24	152.09	222.63	289.48	381.54	364.50

Appendix Table 11

CAR FUEL EFFICIENCY (KG/CAR)

CAT	CNAME	YEAR 60	65	70	75	80	82
LOW INC DEV	BANGLADESH	0.0	0.0	0.0	2340.6	1456.8	1121.6
	CHINA	65408.1	0.0	69147.3	75412.2	44590.8	36237.3
	GHANA	7236.7	4881.4	4194.0	4334.9	4049.5	3880.7
	INDIA	3065.8	2796.8	2495.9	1717.9	1679.0	2069.8
	KENYA	2836.7	2087.3	2646.9	2705.2	2948.2	2294.2
	MALAWI	0.0	3009.4	2838.8	3337.6	4144.4	3495.3
	PAKISTAN	3701.0	2631.4	2777.2	1304.0	2185.4	1931.4
	ZAIRE	4601.0	4697.6	1983.3	2246.1	2302.8	2160.5
	ZAMBIA	0.0	2375.1	2405.3	2061.4	1638.7	1371.8
MIDDLE INC DEV	BOLIVIA	19147.4	15671.7	12539.1	12688.2	8803.0	9579.0
	CAMEROON	5459.2	2906.9	2810.7	2188.2	3935.6	4579.6
	COLOMBIA	12646.5	12317.5	8676.6	6995.8	6231.8	5460.0
	DOMINICAN REP	7781.8	2090.4	5527.0	4818.7	3435.9	2567.6
	ECUADOR	24621.5	16519.3	14464.8	13932.9	20807.4	15914.4
	EGYPT	4222.8	3953.6	4044.2	6633.5	3278.8	3097.2
	HONDURAS	7392.7	4674.8	6963.5	5173.6	2487.8	2377.8
	INDONESIA	13869.6	7524.6	5137.3	4910.1	4838.8	4859.6
	IRAN	5140.2	3955.0	4303.8	4933.1	3497.9	2716.2
	IVORY COAST	7443.5	4614.4	2864.7	2797.1	2911.5	1532.5
	JAMAICA	2367.0	4791.7	5399.4	5609.7	2437.2	1819.0
	KOREA	11953.9	11093.9	11281.7	6239.5	3303.2	1969.0
	MOROCCO	2338.8	1626.0	1514.8	1213.4	951.7	820.2
	NIGERIA	6958.5	5423.8	5799.1	6669.6	5285.8	4312.9

(CONTINUED)

CAR FUEL EFFICIENCY (KG/CAR)

CAT	CNAME	YEAR 60	65	70	75	80	82
MIDDLE INC DEV	PERU	7519.6	5136.0	5182.8	5770.2	3921.4	3179.4
	PHILIPPINES	10041.2	8660.0	6783.3	5010.8	3496.1	2622.2
	THAILAND	8196.7	8362.9	3736.6	5243.4	4196.4	3895.7
	TUNISIA	1859.8	1337.5	1466.4	1366.2	1240.8	1318.6
	TURKEY	9578.6	5863.0	7531.9	4864.4	2522.6	2562.4
HIGH INC DEV	ALGERIA	2374.1	2560.7	3162.0	2442.2	2614.7	2678.7
	ARGENTINA	4408.8	3879.4	3019.9	1886.0	1942.0	1677.4
	BARBADOS	2140.0	1621.2	2439.4	2850.2	2148.4	2096.0
	BRAZIL	6084.0	4178.5	3384.1	2179.0	1072.1	935.9
	CHILE	10700.0	8951.5	7024.0	3623.9	2525.8	2965.7
	COSTA RICA	2942.5	2545.4	2069.2	2147.2	1657.0	1545.6
	CYPRUS	2430.0	2216.0	1887.1	1260.7	1175.8	1201.0
	GABON	7133.3	5522.6	4474.5	1375.7	1284.0	1854.7
	GREECE	5672.0	3375.2	3065.9	2310.3	1706.5	1620.0
	HONG KONG	2172.9	1297.0	1013.8	969.5	901.6	989.8
	IRAQ	6110.5	5300.9	6064.4	3887.5	7031.4	6836.1
	ISRAEL	8358.1	4056.0	3304.8	2513.0	1935.6	1876.8
	MALAYSIA	0.0	0.0	2041.2	1405.7	1743.3	1698.6
	MEXICO	7683.6	5814.6	5365.6	3715.5	3461.3	3294.6
	PANAMA	5046.0	3780.7	3668.6	3782.2	0.0	0.0
	PORTUGAL	1364.7	986.1	965.1	915.8	622.3	701.4
	SINGAPORE	1185.3	1243.7	1513.0	2003.6	2270.1	2229.2
	SOUTH AFRICA	1892.5	1919.7	1883.7	1869.1	1603.3	1714.6

(CONTINUED)

CAF FUEL EFFICIENCY (KG/CAR)

CAT	CNAME	YEAR 60	65	70	75	80	82
HIGH INC DEV	SYRIA	8365.5	4405.9	7061.3	8504.6	9068.8	7619.5
	TAIWAN	0.0	0.0	0.0	0.0	0.0	0.0
	TRINIDAD & TOBAGO	3635.3	0.0	2542.9	2226.7	0.0	0.0
	URUGUAY	2653.2	2616.7	1864.9	1440.9	1382.9	954.7
	VENEZUELA	5913.5	5944.8	5631.8	4910.9	5303.4	5086.1
	YUGOSLAVIA	0.0	0.0	0.0	0.0	0.0	0.0
HIGH INC OIL EXP	KUWAIT	7062.0	4930.0	2975.9	2358.5	2447.3	2379.3
	LIBYA	3852.0	2124.8	2095.1	1926.0	2267.5	2446.5
	SAUDI ARABIA	7661.2	6583.0	6170.7	9067.3	5495.9	4229.2
EASTERN BLOC	CZECHOSLOVAKIA	0.0	0.0	0.0	0.0	0.0	0.0
	GERMAN DEM REP	770.4	719.7	1635.6	1393.5	1313.8	1156.8
	HUNGARY	5751.7	3535.0	2796.3	2031.5	1479.2	1140.9
	USSR	38499.9	37143.8	28273.9	13639.7	8542.2	7721.5
INDUSTRIALIZED	AUSTRALIA	2201.2	2175.5	2067.3	2094.3	1941.6	1810.6
	BELGIUM	1574.9	1228.9	1129.4	1144.2	996.6	894.2
	CANADA	3155.9	3062.2	3177.8	3122.9	2889.2	2546.6
	DENMARK	2154.7	2198.1	1484.9	1288.9	1279.0	1136.0
	FINLAND	2001.1	1514.8	1591.5	1440.2	1195.8	1158.6
	FRANCE	1128.8	1061.6	1084.4	1092.6	949.9	1001.3
	ITALY	1449.9	1175.3	1091.2	815.5	742.6	661.7
	JAPAN	9844.3	3857.2	1845.6	1312.6	1154.8	1112.6
	NETHERLANDS	2489.6	1640.9	1418.1	1141.8	1269.1	977.6
	NEW ZEALAND	1890.4	1506.8	1688.1	1566.2	1404.1	0.0

(CONTINUED)

CAR FUEL EFFICIENCY (KG/CAR)

CAT	CNAME	YEAR 60	65	70	75	80	82
INDUSTRIALIZED	SPAIN	2117.9	1651.5	1137.6	1009.5	815.3	616.1
	SWEDEN	1433.1	1592.6	1290.6	1256.7	1305.0	1348.4
	SWITZERLAND	1693.3	1658.5	1634.6	1457.4	1310.1	1249.4
	UNITED KINGDOM	1524.5	1301.5	1314.3	1210.8	1285.9	1246.5
	UNITED STATES	2925.1	2831.7	2991.7	2883.6	2541.9	2419.9
	W GERMANY	1365.8	1170.7	1214.5	1195.8	1093.6	1105.2

Appendix Table 12

PERCENT OF POPULATION BETWEEN AGES 15 AND 64 (%)

		YEAR			
		60	70	80	82
CAT	CNAME				
LOW INC DEV	BANGLADESH	52.5	51.0	51.0	55.0
	BURMA	59.0	57.0	55.0	55.0
	CHINA	56.0	.	61.0	63.0
	GHANA	53.0	49.5	49.5	51.0
	INDIA	55.7	54.6	55.0	57.0
	KENYA	51.0	51.6	50.0	47.0
	MALAWI	55.5	52.1	53.0	50.0
	PAKISTAN	51.8	50.5	50.0	51.0
	ZAIRE	52.5	52.8	54.0	52.0
	ZAMBIA	50.5	51.5	50.9	50.0
MIDDLE INC DEV	BOLIVIA	54.0	54.0	54.0	53.0
	CAMEROON	59.2	55.7	54.0	54.0
	COLOMBIA	51.0	50.5	59.0	60.0
	DOMINICAN REP	49.0	49.1	50.0	53.0
	ECUADOR	52.0	50.8	51.2	52.0
	EGYPT	55.0	54.7	56.0	57.0
	HONDURAS	52.0	51.2	50.0	.
	INDONESIA	56.1	53.5	56.0	57.0
	IRAN	51.0	50.0	51.0	52.0
	IVORY COAST	55.0	54.8	52.0	53.0
	JAMAICA	54.0	48.5	50.0	54.0
	KOREA	53.8	55.7	60.0	62.0
	MOROCCO	53.0	48.3	52.6	51.0

(CONTINUED)

PERCENT OF POPULATION BETWEEN AGES 15 AND 64 (%)

		YEAR			
		60	70	80	82
CAT	CNAME				
MIDDLE INC DEV	NIGERIA	54.1	53.0	52.0	50.0
	PERU	52.0	51.9	53.0	54.0
	PHILIPPINES	52.3	53.6	51.0	53.0
	THAILAND	52.6	50.8	52.0	53.6
	TUNISIA	52.5	50.0	53.0	56.0
	TURKEY	55.2	54.0	54.0	59.0
HIGH INC DEV	ALGERIA	52.0	48.8	49.0	49.0
	ARGENTINA	63.7	63.7	63.0	63.0
	BARBADOS	55.3	54.7	58.8	.
	BRAZIL	53.8	54.3	55.1	55.0
	CHILE	57.0	57.2	61.0	62.0
	COSTA RICA	49.3	51.2	56.0	59.0
	CYPRUS	57.4	60.4	63.0	.
	GABON	60.9	66.8	62.0	.
	GREECE	65.1	64.0	64.0	64.0
	HONG KONG	56.4	59.0	65.0	66.0
	IRAQ	51.4	51.0	51.0	51.0
	ISRAEL	59.1	60.2	59.0	58.0
	MALAYSIA	51.3	51.5	54.0	56.0
	MEXICO	51.0	50.0	50.6	52.0
	PANAMA	52.3	52.4	54.0	56.0
	PORTUGAL	63.0	61.8	63.0	63.0
	SINGAPORE	54.7	57.9	65.0	66.0

(CONTINUED)

PERCENT OF POPULATION BETWEEN AGES 15 AND 64 (%)

		YEAR			
		60	70	80	82
CAT	CNAME				
HIGH INC DEV	SOUTH AFRICA	55.0	55.2	55.0	55.0
	SYRIA	52.0	50.1	50.1	49.0
	TAIWAN	52.4	57.4	63.0	.
	TRINIDAD & TOBAGO	53.2	52.8	58.0	63.0
	URUGUAY	64.4	62.6	63.5	63.0
	VENEZUELA	51.3	50.3	53.0	55.0
	YUGOSLAVIA	63.2	64.8	66.0	67.0
HIGH INC OIL EXP	KUWAIT	63.0	55.0	50.0	52.0
	LIBYA	52.8	52.9	52.0	51.0
	SAUDI ARABIA	54.0	53.0	52.3	52.0
EASTERN BLOC	CZECHOSLOVAKIA	64.0	65.6	65.0	64.0
	GERMAN DEM REP	65.2	61.1	62.0	64.0
	HUNGARY	65.6	67.6	67.0	65.0
	USSR	62.6	63.6	66.0	66.0
INDUSTRIALIZED	AUSTRALIA	61.4	62.8	64.0	.
	BELGIUM	64.5	63.0	64.0	66.0
	CANADA	59.0	61.9	66.0	.
	DENMARK	64.2	64.4	65.0	65.0
	FINLAND	62.4	66.2	68.0	.
	FRANCE	62.0	62.3	63.0	64.0
	ITALY	65.8	65.0	65.0	65.0
	JAPAN	64.1	68.9	68.0	.
	NETHERLANDS	61.0	62.5	65.0	67.0

(CONTINUED)

PERCENT OF POPULATION BETWEEN AGES 15 AND 64 (%)

		YEAR			
		60	70	80	82
CAT	CNAME				
INDUSTRIALIZED	NEW ZEALAND	58.5	59.8	62.0	64.0
	SPAIN	64.0	62.5	63.0	63.0
	SWEDEN	66.0	65.5	64.0	64.0
	SWITZERLAND	.	.	.	.
	UNITED KINGDOM	65.1	62.8	63.0	64.0
	UNITED STATES	59.7	61.9	65.0	.
	W GERMANY	67.8	63.7	65.0	67.0

Appendix Table 13

NUMBER OF TRUCKS AND BUSES PER 1000 POPULATION

		YEAR					
		60	65	70	75	80	82
CAT	CNAME						
LOW INC DEV	BANGLADESH	0.15	0.17	0.30	0.19	0.26	0.33
	BURMA	0.83	1.00	1.12	1.27	1.27	1.27
	CHINA	0.26	0.28	0.59	0.80	1.41	1.71
	GHANA	2.60	2.16	2.76	4.60	4.02	3.85
	INDIA	0.56	0.77	0.75	0.93	1.20	1.19
	KENYA	4.33	3.72	4.19	5.05	5.13	5.07
	MALAWI	1.55	1.15	1.71	1.83	2.32	2.24
	PAKISTAN	0.61	1.05	1.05	1.33	1.31	1.42
	ZAIRE	1.69	1.79	2.28	3.14	2.88	2.87
	ZAMBIA	3.44	3.54	8.99	15.34	15.60	16.00
MIDDLE_INC_DEV	BOLIVIA	2.19	4.36	6.71	4.36	5.83	5.51
	CAMEROON	3.52	3.54	5.01	6.15	8.41	8.82
	COLOMBIA	5.26	5.91	3.93	3.71	5.70	6.05
	DOMINICAN REP	1.93	2.52	4.54	6.81	9.24	10.74
	ECUADOR	4.30	4.02	6.11	11.20	18.70	24.60
	EGYPT	0.62	0.88	1.08	1.57	3.10	4.30
	HONDURAS	2.68	3.57	5.98	8.32	6.23	6.75
	INDONESIA	1.01	1.05	1.05	1.71	3.69	4.75
	IRAN	2.05	1.93	2.59	3.78	8.93	9.71
	IVORY COAST	3.39	5.58	7.55	5.47	7.94	9.82
	JAMAICA	5.64	10.97	9.63	7.35	10.96	12.16
	JORDAN	2.72	2.76	2.57	4.44	10.91	14.29
	KOREA	0.75	0.90	2.06	2.87	7.34	8.46

(CONTINUED)

NUMBER OF TRUCKS AND BUSES PER 1000 POPULATION

		YEAR					
		60	65	70	75	80	82
CAT	CNAME						
MIDDLE INC DEV	MOROCCO	4.04	4.92	5.55	7.35	8.87	9.34
	NIGERIA	0.47	0.54	0.92	1.31	4.54	6.07
	PERU	6.42	8.42	8.70	9.60	9.56	10.42
	PHILIPPINES	2.73	4.04	4.77	6.23	7.37	7.14
	THAILAND	1.91	2.47	4.56	5.95	10.40	10.81
	TUNISIA	5.64	6.50	7.25	11.94	20.86	21.96
	TURKEY	2.49	3.25	4.52	5.05	6.28	7.01
HIGH INC DEV	ALGERIA	7.18	6.30	6.13	9.87	13.45	15.34
	ARGENTINA	18.92	25.76	31.79	34.42	45.27	47.78
	BARBADOS	10.43	15.65	16.67	15.83	18.00	20.32
	BRAZIL	8.38	10.17	13.71	14.58	15.41	15.22
	CHILE	9.06	12.39	15.99	16.54	20.39	19.10
	COSTA RICA	7.82	8.18	15.66	20.77	31.99	37.44
	CYPRUS	10.18	18.98	22.46	25.31	36.92	44.65
	GABON	7.02	8.54	12.00	20.77	29.09	31.52
	GREECE	4.44	8.58	13.33	23.37	45.02	55.57
	HONG KONG	3.13	5.28	7.41	10.18	15.06	16.90
	IRAQ	2.92	4.31	4.49	5.21	7.12	7.04
	ISRAEL	11.28	17.46	30.03	29.54	27.85	28.47
	MALAYSIA	4.40	5.69	6.93	13.16	17.47	18.52
	MEXICO	8.66	9.06	11.70	14.99	22.47	23.91
	PANAMA	6.00	8.27	9.93	11.67	17.11	18.35
	PORTUGAL	5.71	6.71	17.01	27.49	42.39	47.34

(CONTINUED)

NUMBER OF TRUCKS AND BUSES PER 1000 POPULATION

CAT	CNAME	YEAR 60	65	70	75	80	82
HIGH INC DEV	SINGAPORE	9.14	12.55	18.12	20.58	34.77	38.37
	SOUTH AFRICA	13.11	16.07	19.15	31.38	34.49	35.36
	SYRIA	2.70	2.69	2.92	4.68	11.13	12.06
	TAIWAN	1.01	1.39	3.41	7.86	12.36	18.10
	TRINIDAD & TOBAGO	10.83	16.49	19.61	23.98	28.95	46.58
	URUGUAY	30.04	30.48	31.21	28.87	30.82	33.56
	VENEZUELA	13.20	16.66	18.52	29.20	37.22	41.92
	YUGOSLAVIA	2.10	3.44	6.49	11.94	15.70	20.22
HIGH INC OIL EXP	KUWAIT	50.00	45.42	49.20	68.02	105.69	109.15
	LIBYA	6.96	12.78	22.91	49.38	60.98	104.63
	SAUDI ARABIA	5.65	7.57	13.08	20.14	65.56	72.31
EASTERN BLOC	CZECHOSLOVAKIA	9.00	10.56	13.87	17.65	22.34	23.35
	GERMAN DEM REP	12.48	18.17	23.23	31.69	36.64	24.50
	HUNGARY	3.00	7.88	15.42	19.47	15.20	.
	USSR	15.61	15.00	18.95	20.10	27.32	30.75
INDUSTRIALIZED	AUSTRALIA	81.28	76.69	77.41	85.52	102.96	111.09
	BELGIUM	19.31	24.68	27.76	29.79	32.12	34.25
	CANADA	58.85	62.71	69.18	95.79	122.78	134.44
	DENMARK	37.07	51.05	52.17	47.27	52.45	49.29
	FINLAND	16.12	19.32	24.08	29.11	34.63	37.31
	FRANCE	35.78	39.18	41.74	45.10	48.09	49.82
	ITALY	13.94	18.58	24.40	28.88	32.92	36.67
	JAPAN	14.69	43.47	83.78	92.49	113.38	124.98

(CONTINUED)

NUMBER OF TRUCKS AND BUSES PER 1000 POPULATION

		YEAR					
		60	65	70	75	80	82
CAT	CNAME						
INDUSTRIALIZED	NETHERLANDS	13.70	19.04	23.10	24.08	24.64	27.13
	NEW ZEALAND	52.83	60.34	64.43	70.23	79.66	83.19
	SPAIN	4.93	12.13	21.94	29.22	36.94	40.02
	SWEDEN	17.39	18.19	19.75	20.84	23.54	24.90
	SWITZERLAND	11.31	15.82	22.46	28.02	28.95	30.44
	UNITED KINGDOM	28.19	31.99	30.82	33.48	34.35	33.35
	UNITED STATES	63.47	73.03	87.75	122.89	153.79	158.11
	W GERMANY	13.14	14.65	16.51	21.69	25.55	59.38

Appendix Table 14

AREA (000 SQ KM)

CAT	CNAME	YEAR 80
LOW INC DEV	BANGLADESH	144
	BURMA	677
	CHINA	9561
	GHANA	239
	INDIA	3288
	KENYA	583
	MALAWI	119
	PAKISTAN	804
	ZAIRE	2345
	ZAMBIA	753
MIDDLE INC DEV	BOLIVIA	1099
	CAMEROON	475
	COLOMBIA	2070
	DOMINICAN REP	49
	ECUADOR	284
	EGYPT	1001
	HONDURAS	112
	INDONESIA	1919
	IRAN	1648
	IVORY COAST	322
	JAMAICA	11
	KOREA	121
	MOROCCO	447

(CONTINUED)

AREA (000 SQ KM)

CAT	CNAME	YEAR 80
MIDDLE INC DEV	NIGERIA	924
	PERU	1285
	PHILIPPINES	300
	THAILAND	514
	TUNISIA	164
	TURKEY	781
HIGH INC DEV	ALGERIA	2382
	ARGENTINA	2767
	BARBADOS	1
	BRAZIL	8512
	CHILE	757
	COSTA RICA	51
	CYPRUS	9
	GABON	268
	GREECE	132
	HONG KONG	1
	IRAQ	435
	ISRAEL	21
	MALAYSIA	330
	MEXICO	1973
	PANAMA	77
	PORTUGAL	92
	SINGAPORE	1

(CONTINUED)

AREA (000 SQ KM)

CAT	CNAME	YEAR 80
HIGH INC DEV	SOUTH AFRICA	1221
	SYRIA	185
	TAIWAN	36
	TRINIDAD & TOBAGO	5
	URUGUAY	176
	VENEZUELA	912
	YUGOSLAVIA	257
HIGH INC OIL EXP	KUWAIT	18
	LIBYA	1760
	SAUDI ARABIA	2150
EASTERN BLOC	CZECHOSLOVAKIA	128
	GERMAN DEM REP	108
	HUNGARY	93
	USSR	22042
INDUSTRIALIZED	AUSTRALIA	7687
	BELGIUM	31
	CANADA	9976
	DENMARK	43
	FINLAND	337
	FRANCE	547
	ITALY	301
	JAPAN	372
	NETHERLANDS	41

(CONTINUED)

AREA (000 SQ KM)

		YEAR
		80
CAT	CNAME	
INDUSTRIALIZED	NEW ZEALAND	269
	SPAIN	505
	SWEDEN	450
	SWITZERLAND	41
	UNITED KINGDOM	245
	UNITED STATES	9363
	W GERMANY	249

Appendix Table 15

POPULATION DENSITY (PEOPLE/SQ KM)

CAT	CNAME	YEAR 80
LOW INC DEV	BANGLADESH	616
	BURMA	52
	CHINA	106
	GHANA	49
	INDIA	211
	KENYA	28
	MALAWI	52
	PAKISTAN	103
	ZAIRE	12
	ZAMBIA	7
MIDDLE INC DEV	BOLIVIA	5
	CAMEROON	18
	COLOMBIA	13
	DOMINICAN REP	121
	ECUADOR	28
	EGYPT	42
	HONDURAS	33
	INDONESIA	79
	IRAN	23
	IVORY COAST	25
	JAMAICA	199
	KOREA	314
	MOROCCO	45

(CONTINUED)

POPULATION DENSITY (PEOPLE/SQ KM)

CAT	CNAME	YEAR 80
MIDDLE INC DEV	NIGERIA	83
	PERU	14
	PHILIPPINES	170
	THAILAND	93
	TUNISIA	39
	TURKEY	58
HIGH INC DEV	ALGERIA	8
	ARGENTINA	10
	BARBADOS	250
	BRAZIL	15
	CHILE	15
	COSTA RICA	43
	CYPRUS	72
	GABON	2
	GREECE	71
	HONG KONG	4840
	IRAQ	30
	ISRAEL	188
	MALAYSIA	41
	MEXICO	35
	PANAMA	25
	PORTUGAL	107
	SINGAPORE	2430

(CONTINUED)

POPULATION DENSITY (PEOPLE/SQ KM)

CAT	CNAME	YEAR 80
HIGH INC DEV	SOUTH AFRICA	24
	SYRIA	47
	TAIWAN	494
	TRINIDAD & TOBAGO	228
	URUGUAY	17
	VENEZUELA	16
	YUGOSLAVIA	87
HIGH INC OIL EXP	KUWAIT	76
	LIBYA	2
	SAUDI ARABIA	4
EASTERN BLOC	CZECHOSLOVAKIA	119
	GERMAN DEM REP	155
	HUNGARY	115
	USSR	12
INDUSTRIALIZED	AUSTRALIA	2
	BELGIUM	320
	CANADA	2
	DENMARK	119
	FINLAND	14
	FRANCE	98
	ITALY	189
	JAPAN	313
	NETHERLANDS	343

(CONTINUED)

POPULATION DENSITY (PEOPLE/SQ KM)

		YEAR
		80
CAT	CNAME	
INDUSTRIALIZED	NEW ZEALAND	12
	SPAIN	74
	SWEDEN	18
	SWITZERLAND	154
	UNITED KINGDOM	228
	UNITED STATES	24
	W GERMANY	245

Appendix Table 16

URBAN POPULATION AS PERCENT OF TOTAL POPULATION (%)

		YEAR		
		60	70	82
CAT	CNAME			
LOW INC DEV	BANGLADESH	5.0	8.0	12.0
	BURMA	9.0	.	28.0
	CHINA	18.0	21.6	21.0
	GHANA	23.0	29.2	37.0
	INDIA	18.0	20.0	24.0
	KENYA	7.0	10.0	15.0
	MALAWI	4.0	.	10.0
	PAKISTAN	22.0	25.0	29.0
	ZAIRE	16.0	.	38.0
	ZAMBIA	23.0	30.0	45.0
MIDDLE INC DEV	BOLIVIA	34.0	.	45.0
	CAMEROON	14.0	20.3	37.0
	COLOMBIA	48.0	60.0	65.0
	DOMINICAN REP	30.0	39.8	53.0
	ECUADOR	34.0	39.0	46.0
	EGYPT	38.0	42.0	45.0
	HONDURAS	23.0	28.7	37.0
	INDONESIA	15.0	17.0	22.0
	IRAN	34.0	41.0	52.0
	IVORY COAST	19.0	28.0	42.0
	JAMAICA	34.0	42.0	48.0
	KOREA	28.0	41.0	61.0
	MOROCCO	29.0	35.0	42.0

(CONTINUED)

URBAN POPULATION AS PERCENT OF TOTAL POPULATION (%)

		YEAR		
		60	70	82
CAT	CNAME			
MIDDLE INC DEV	NIGERIA	13.0	16.0	21.0
	PERU	46.0	57.0	66.0
	PHILIPPINES	30.0	32.0	38.0
	THAILAND	13.0	13.0	17.0
	TUNISIA	36.0	44.0	54.0
	TURKEY	30.0	38.4	44.0
HIGH INC DEV	ALGERIA	30.0	49.0	45.0
	ARGENTINA	74.0	78.0	83.0
	BARBADOS	.	.	.
	BRAZIL	45.0	56.0	69.0
	CHILE	68.0	75.0	82.0
	COSTA RICA	37.0	40.0	43.0
	CYPRUS	35.6	39.0	.
	GABON	17.0	24.4	.
	GREECE	43.0	52.5	64.0
	HONG KONG	89.0	90.0	91.0
	IRAQ	43.0	58.0	70.0
	ISRAEL	77.0	84.0	90.0
	MALAYSIA	25.0	27.0	30.0
	MEXICO	51.0	60.0	68.0
	PANAMA	21.0	.	53.0
	PORTUGAL	23.0	26.2	32.0
	SINGAPORE	100.0	100.0	100.0

(CONTINUED)

URBAN POPULATION AS PERCENT OF TOTAL POPULATION (%)

CAT	CNAME	YEAR 60	70	82
HIGH INC DEV	SOUTH AFRICA	47.0	47.8	50.0
	SYRIA	47.0	43.5	49.0
	TAIWAN	36.0	45.0	.
	TRINIDAD & TOBAGO	22.0	21.0	22.0
	URUGUAY	80.0	82.0	84.0
	VENEZUELA	67.0	76.0	84.0
	YUGOSLAVIA	28.0	34.8	44.0
HIGH INC OIL EXP	KUWAIT	72.0	76.0	91.0
	LIBYA	23.0	33.0	58.0
	SAUDI ARABIA	30.0	49.0	69.0
EASTERN BLOC	CZECHOSLOVAKIA	47.0	55.2	64.0
	GERMAN DEM REP	72.0	73.7	77.0
	HUNGARY	40.0	45.6	55.0
	USSR	49.0	56.7	63.0
INDUSTRIALIZED	AUSTRALIA	81.0	85.2	89.0
	BELGIUM	66.0	70.7	73.0
	CANADA	69.0	75.7	76.0
	DENMARK	74.0	79.7	85.0
	FINLAND	38.0	50.7	64.0
	FRANCE	62.0	71.7	79.0
	ITALY	59.0	64.4	70.0
	JAPAN	63.0	71.3	78.0
	NETHERLANDS	80.0	78.0	76.0

(CONTINUED)

URBAN POPULATION AS PERCENT OF TOTAL POPULATION (%)

		YEAR		
		60	70	82
CAT	CNAME			
INDUSTRIALIZED	NEW ZEALAND	76.0	81.1	85.0
	SPAIN	57.0	66.0	76.0
	SWEDEN	73.0	81.1	88.0
	SWITZERLAND	.	.	.
	UNITED KINGDOM	86.0	88.5	91.0
	UNITED STATES	70.0	69.0	78.0
	W GERMANY	77.0	81.3	85.0

Appendix Table 17

PERCENT OF URBAN POPULATION IN LARGEST CITY (%)

		YEAR	
		60	80
CAT	CNAME		
LOW INC DEV	BANGLADESH	20	30
	BURMA	23	23
	CHINA	6	6
	GHANA	25	35
	INDIA	7	6
	KENYA	40	57
	MALAWI	.	.
	PAKISTAN	20	21
	ZAIRE	14	28
	ZAMBIA	.	35
MIDDLE INC DEV	BOLIVIA	47	44
	CAMEROON	26	21
	COLOMBIA	17	26
	DOMINICAN REP	50	54
	ECUADOR	31	29
	EGYPT	38	39
	HONDURAS	31	33
	INDONESIA	20	23
	IRAN	26	28
	IVORY COAST	27	34
	JAMAICA	77	66
	KOREA	35	41
	MOROCCO	16	26

(CONTINUED)

PERCENT OF URBAN POPULATION IN LARGEST CITY (%)

CAT	CNAME	YEAR 60	YEAR 80
MIDDLE INC DEV	NIGERIA	13	17
	PERU	38	39
	PHILIPPINES	27	30
	THAILAND	65	69
	TUNISIA	40	30
	TURKEY	18	24
HIGH INC DEV	ALGERIA	27	12
	ARGENTINA	46	45
	BARBADOS	.	.
	BRAZIL	14	15
	CHILE	38	44
	COSTA RICA	67	64
	CYPRUS	.	.
	GABON	.	.
	GREECE	51	57
	HONG KONG	100	100
	IRAQ	35	55
	ISRAEL	46	35
	MALAYSIA	19	27
	MEXICO	28	32
	PANAMA	61	66
	PORTUGAL	47	44
	SINGAPORE	100	100

(CONTINUED)

PERCENT OF URBAN POPULATION IN LARGEST CITY (%)

CAT	CNAME	YEAR 60	YEAR 80
HIGH INC DEV	SOUTH AFRICA	16	13
	SYRIA	35	33
	TAIWAN	.	.
	TRINIDAD & TOBAGO	.	.
	URUGUAY	56	52
	VENEZUELA	26	26
	YUGOSLAVIA	11	10
HIGH INC OIL EXP	KUWAIT	75	30
	LIBYA	57	64
	SAUDI ARABIA	15	18
EASTERN BLOC	CZECHOSLOVAKIA	17	12
	GERMAN DEM REP	9	9
	HUNGARY	45	37
	USSR	6	4
INDUSTRIALIZED	AUSTRALIA	26	24
	BELGIUM	17	14
	CANADA	14	18
	DENMARK	40	32
	FINLAND	28	27
	FRANCE	25	23
	ITALY	13	17
	JAPAN	18	22
	NETHERLANDS	9	9

(CONTINUED)

PERCENT OF URBAN POPULATION IN LARGEST CITY (%)

		YEAR	
		60	80
CAT	CNAME		
INDUSTRIALIZED	NEW ZEALAND	25	30
	SPAIN	13	17
	SWEDEN	15	15
	SWITZERLAND	.	.
	UNITED KINGDOM	24	20
	UNITED STATES	13	12
	W GERMANY	20	18